GUATEMALA

A Natural Destination

Richard Mahler

John Muir Publications
Santa Fe, New Mexico

John Muir Publications, P.O. Box 613, Santa Fe, NM 87504

First edition. Second printing April 1994

Library of Congress Cataloging-in-Publication Data
Mahler, Richard.
    Guatemala : a natural destination / Richard Mahler. — 1st ed.
      p. cm.
    Includes bibliographical references and index.
    ISBN 1-56261-075-9
    1. Guatemala—Description and travel—1981- —I. Title.
F1464.2.M27   1993
917.28104'53—dc20   92-33775
                                             CIP

Cover Art: Glen Strock
Designer: Susan Surprise
Typeface: Plantin
Printer: Publishers Press
Typesetting: Copygraphics, Inc.

Distributed to the book trade by
W. W. Norton & Company, Inc.
New York, New York

Contents

Acknowledgments

The author wishes to acknowledge the many people who so generously provided the insight and assistance that made this book possible. Particular thanks go to my new friends in Guatemala who—often on painfully short notice—went out of their way to answer questions, arrange introductions, open personal files, volunteer information, and make important suggestions. They include Jay and Mary Lou Ridinger, Hartmut Zersch, Suzan Williams, Lynn Beahan, Mike Shawcross, Francesca Sanchinelli, Tammy Ridenour, Alfredo Toriello, Miguel and Roxy Ortiz, Daniel Saxon, Lucy Hood, Roger Brenner, Mark Rogers, María Esther Zaldivar, Paul Kronick, Santiago Billy, Andreas Lehnhoff, Federico Fahsen, Antonio Ferrate Felice, Alfredo Nakasuma, Lidia Josefina Chavarría, David Whitacre, María Elena de Ovalle, Dennis and Luise Wheeler, Norman Schwartz, and Conrad Reining. Special assistance was also provided by Linda Jukofsky of the Tropical Conservation Newsbureau in Costa Rica and forester Tony Shebbeare of Vancouver, British Columbia.

Those who were of great help in the United States include Wayne Bray, Nancy Portrero, Pam Smith, Sukey Hughes, Kevin Schafer, Dena Liebman, Ed Cray, Eric Taub, Jerry Stearns, Matt Kelly, Susan Leffler, Isabel Alegría, María Martin, Brad Draper, Mike and Marcy O'Connor, Linda Shockley, Ken Luboff, Frank Ortiz, and Rosa Carlson. For their research facilities, I am indebted to the Santa Fe Public Library, the University of California at Los Angeles, the University of Minnesota, and America On-Line computer information service.

Special thanks go to my talented photographers—Kevin Schafer, Don Usner, and Jim Smith—and equally skilled editors, Jill Mason and Sheila Berg. I also wish to acknowledge the important contributions of Vickie Gabin, Mike Shawcross, Tom Noble, Steele Wotkyns, Conrad Reining, and Deborah Rivel, each of whom read all or part of the manuscript and made valuable suggestions.

At the Guatemala Tourist Commission, special thanks go to Lisa Torun, Sandra Monterroso, María de Mérida, and Gustavo Cabrera. José Orive and María Landis of the Guatemala Embassy in Washington, D.C., also provided much-needed logistical support.

Extra words of appreciation go to Isabel Jennings, for her patience and encouragement as I learned to communicate in Spanish, and to Steele Wotkyns, whose passionate vision, probing questions, and warm friendship helps make books such as this one possible. For unfailing support during the research and writing phase of this project, my heartfelt thanks go to my best friend and favorite traveling companion, Sue Dirksen, and to my parents, Don and Mary Mahler, who have always encouraged my wanderlust and been there when I needed them. Inspiration and research assistance also was provided by the late Donald Boltz, whose love of learning, dry wit, and gentle counsel is deeply missed.

Finally, I express my heartfelt appreciation to the wise, warm, and wonderful *Guatemaltecos*, especially those whose names I have forgotten (or never knew) but who made sure that my days and nights in their beautiful country would never be forgotten.

1

Why Guatemala?

Guatemala has been called—with every justification—the travel bargain of the Americas. It is easily accessible, spectacularly beautiful, friendly, cultured, intriguing, and, yes, very inexpensive.

Yet none of these attributes, taken alone or together, adequately conveys what it is that makes Guatemala a special place. Certainly there are other countries in the world that can fairly be described using the same string of adjectives. Like a delicious salad or lively dinner party, what makes Guatemala unique is no single ingredient or characteristic but the sum of its many parts.

And what parts it has! From the black sand beaches of the Pacific Coast to the icy peaks of thirty-three volcanoes, from cactus-studded deserts to grassy savannas, Guatemala is one of the most ecologically diverse countries in the world. Its name, in fact, is a Mayan word for "land of many trees." Within an area the size of Tennessee, visitors will find tropical jungles, highland pine forests, whitewater rivers, crystalline lakes, coral reefs, and limestone caverns as well as modern skyscrapers, Spanish colonial cathedrals, and ancient Mayan cities.

Guatemala also has other, more mundane, points to recommend it: a pleasant springlike climate, a modern international airport, and a substantial tourism infrastructure of good roads, hotels, restaurants, and services.

Still, a traveler's strongest impressions are derived not from Guatemala's incredible natural beauty, awesome monuments, or considerable creature comforts but rather from the country's nine million warm-hearted people and their indomitable spirit. Whether practicing Spanish verb conjugations with a middle-class family in Antigua or discussing proper *plátano* preparation with a peasant fruit seller in the Huehuetenango market, travelers are almost always treated with the most gracious charm.

About half of the Guatemalan people are full-blooded Native American Indians, descended directly from the wise and proud Maya, whose sophisticated civilization flourished here for more than a thousand years. Millions of Guatemalans dress, speak, work, and worship almost exactly as their ancestors did when the Spanish conquistadors marched down from Mexico some five centuries ago. In today's Guatemala you can witness the living Maya culture, complete with ceremonial sacrifices, elaborate timekeeping rituals, and the cultivation of such sacred crops as corn and cacao. Walking through the colorful, crowded market of Quetzaltenango, a trained observer can instantly determine what village a costumed vendor comes from, what dialect he or she speaks, and even that person's rank in the local social order. A few miles away, in Chichicastenango, one can witness the melding of Mayan and Christian traditions as Catholic priests and Indian *cofrades* walk side by side through clouds of burning copal incense before a sacred image of Jesus or the Virgin Mary.

Guatemala is the most Indian of Central American nations and also the birthplace of Spanish colonialism along the Mesoamerican isthmus. More than a third of its citizens now identify themselves as Ladinos (westernized Indians or those of mixed Indian-European descent), and their heritage is reflected in the remnants of Spain's sixteenth-century conquest: the magnificent churches and ornate public buildings of Antigua, once the New World's most populous capital save Mexico City and Lima. One stumbles upon colonial Guatemala in the country's humid eastern rain forest, too, where the red-brick fort of San Felipe hunkers over the Río Dulce, and on the temperate slopes of Sierra Madre volcanoes, where the elegant mansions of the *patrones* preside over vast coffee and sugarcane plantations. It is the presence of these two vital and often clashing cultures, along with those of the Caribbean coast Garifuna and other ethnic minorities, that enrich and enliven Guatemala and also curse it with poverty, hunger, and civil unrest.

Coming to Guatemala means bearing witness to it all, for it is impossible to travel here without confronting the best and worst that this remarkable country has to offer. They exist side by side for all to see; socioeconomic problems are not neatly shunted aside or covered up as in many countries that might consider themselves more advanced.

Every traveler planning a trip to Guatemala will almost certainly be asked at least once—if not many times—some variation of this: "Aren't you afraid, what with all the political unrest and repression down there?" This is a fair question, given Guatemala's appalling human rights record over the past twenty-five years and its history of horrific repression and violence. The nation's death toll during the 1980s was proportionately equivalent to two million Americans being murdered or "disappeared" and at least twenty-five million others being displaced or injured. Fortunately, the level of political violence has been sharply reduced in recent years; and both the civilian government and the military appear to be moving slowly but steadily toward democracy.

Some potential visitors will choose not to go to Guatemala because the risk of violence, like that of devastating volcanic eruptions and earthquakes, is always going to exist. Others may choose to go elsewhere because they do not wish to spend money in a country whose institutional abuse of its citizens is so notorious. In the end, you will have to weigh the pros and cons before following your own conscience. This book tries to deal with Guatemala's perceived shortcomings as fairly and accurately as with its attractions.

Guatemala: A Natural Destination is designed to help lead you to your own adventures, not by asking you to follow in the author's footsteps but by pointing out some favorite pathways others have explored. The author welcomes comments and suggestions based on the routes you have chosen. Please forward information on any inaccurate, outdated, or misleading entries, as well as your thoughts about special people, places, or services that you feel should be added to future editions of this book.

2

Culture and Context

History

By far the best known of the several pre-Columbian civilizations of Guatemala is that of the Maya, believed to have begun evolving there as an agricultural society around 1500 B.C. Recent discoveries at Nakbe in the Petén jungle of northern Guatemala suggest that the first Mayan city may have been founded at that site about 800 to 600 B.C. The ancestors of these Indians arrived much earlier, however. Stone tools have been found in Guatemala's central mountains dating back to 9000 B.C., and worked chips found in neighboring Belize were made as early as 20,000 B.C., an estimated five thousand years after the first waves of nomadic hunters entered Central America from the north.

No one knows exactly where the predecessors of the earliest Maya came from, although they seem to have shared many fundamental beliefs with some of the early Chinese and East Indian people, and it is possible that ancient Mayans and Asians had a shared cultural history. Both groups, for example, explored human links to nature through divination and shamanism as well as intellectual and moral control. In creating these bridges between heaven and earth, humankind assumed the burden of maintaining specific ceremonies as a kind of ritual theater for observing, celebrating, and retaining the order of the natural universe. The Maya chose to explore the cosmos —and their relation to it—through an obsessive preoccupation with the mathematics of eternal time and the solidarity of the basic elements of our universe. These beliefs are manifested in solstice and

equinox markers, for example, as well as enormous astronomical observatories and the precise projection of their calendar as far as 142 nonillion years into the future. Such underlying cosmic concepts of social order are radically different from those that forged the human-centered European civilizations of the Greeks, Romans, and, later on, the Spanish.

During the height of what archaeologists call the Classic period, roughly A.D. 200 to A.D. 800, the Maya flourished throughout most of Guatemala and Belize, as well as northern Honduras, northwestern El Salvador, and the southern Mexican states of Chiapas, Campeche,

Yucatán, and Quintana Roo. Research suggests that the Mayan world drew its strength from a clearly defined ideological backbone that enabled the few to dominate the many. Not only did this allow a ruling elite of priest-kings to emerge but it made feasible enormous construction projects ranging from complex irrigation schemes to elaborately decorated temples and burial crypts.

The strict hierarchy of the Maya was drawn up along feudal lines, with the royal and privileged classes inhabiting the inner cities, while the poor farmers and laborers lived in simple thatched homes in the surrounding countryside. Throughout the Classic era, the Mayan world was composed of independent and frequently antagonistic city-states, in many respects not unlike those of the early Greek civilization. Although these city-states had many ceremonial and religious elements, they were seldom peaceful, particularly from A.D. 500 to 800. The most powerful members of society, a tiny caste of priestly royalty, apparently spent considerable energy planning attacks on their neighbors or, in turn, defending themselves from the marauding armies of their enemies. Nevertheless, time and resources were found to build large, ornate ceremonial structures such as the pyramids of El Mirador, which until relatively recently were the tallest buildings in the Western Hemisphere.

The Maya were master builders and talented artisans, despite the fact that wheels (other than those used in toys), metal tools, and beasts of burden were unknown to them. Their ceramics, weavings, friezes, and jewelry were carefully and beautifully made. Clever and hardworking farmers, the Maya built elaborate aqueducts, causeways, and reservoirs to capture rain water and irrigate their fields of maize, squash, and other crops. They drained swamps and built terraced gardens fertilized by compost and partially shaded by tall trees. Their jungle discoveries gave us chocolate, beans, avocados, pineapples, and rubber. Shrewd and aggressive traders, they exchanged seeds, tools, and other valuable objects with groups as far away as the Anasazi of the American Southwest, the Aztec of central Mexico, and the Inca of Peru.

No one is certain why the Mayan civilization began rapidly deteriorating around A.D. 850. One theory suggests an angry peasant revolt toppled the governing theocracy. Some experts believe the Maya over-

Close-up view of the image of Pascual Abaj, site of ancient Mayan rituals, near Chichicastenango (Photo by Richard Mahler)

exploited the forests, farms, and finite water supplies that sustained them, perhaps at the behest of greedy emperors fighting each other for ever more wealth and territory. Another possible explanation is that severe drought and famine undermined and fatally weakened the culture's infrastructure. Yet another speculates that non-Maya invaders, such as southern Mexico's Toltecs, invaded the territory and seized power by force.

What *is* known is that only scattered physical remnants of the once mighty Mayan civilization remained when the first Spanish explorers arrived early in the sixteenth century. Indeed, many of the Maya city-states had been abandoned for centuries by the time white men first stumbled upon them. The Mayan people had long since fractionalized into warring tribes, although many common cultural traditions were kept going among them.

Today there are still about eight million Maya occupying much of their original homeland. They are the direct descendants of the indigenous people of Guatemala, and many of them maintain the mythological and chronological order that the Spanish tried for centuries to disrupt, discredit, and replace.

The first European to appear anywhere near Guatemala was Christopher Columbus, who cruised its eastern coastline on his fourth trip to the New World in 1502. Shortly thereafter the first *conquistadores* arrived on orders of the Spanish crown. Under a directive from the ruthless Spaniard Hernán Cortés, conqueror of the Aztecs, Pedro de Alvarado was sent south from Mexico City in 1523 with a band of two hundred soldiers and eight hundred Aztec and Tlaxcalan warriors, allied in their mission of taking Guatemala by force. By deceitfully playing off one Indian ethnic group against another, Alvarado quickly and easily took control of the western highlands, although skirmishes continued for another fifty or sixty years. He immediately established a permanent base at Iximché and in 1524 founded the first Guatemalan capital at Tecpán. A few years later Alvarado was given autocratic command of a new political jurisdiction stretching from Chiapas to Panama called the Kingdom of Guatemala.

Under Alvarado, the traditional Indian way of life was completely disrupted. Farmers who had worked the same land for generations were uprooted from their rural homes and forced to live in new towns and villages laid out in a grid pattern by the Spanish. The conquerors forced the Indians to give up many of their customs, religious ceremonies, even their names, under penalty of incarceration, torture, or execution.

Although the early Spanish colonials were disappointed to find little gold or silver in Guatemala, they soon realized that their Indian subjects could be used as slaves in large-scale production of indigo and cochineal (natural blue and red dyes, respectively) as well as other agricultural exports. A wealthy landed aristocracy joined the Catholic church's local hierarchy in maintaining a firm grip on the country's levers of power and privilege. By the middle 1700s, these groups had established a comfortable, sophisticated enclave for themselves which boasted Central America's first publishing house and first college, now the University of San Carlos.

In 1773, a series of severe earthquakes caused the capital to be moved once again, this time to its present location in the broad valley that has become Guatemala City. Antigua was never abandoned, however, and it remains the spiritual heart of the country's Ladino (Spanish-descended) culture. The city was declared a national cultural monument in 1944 and a world heritage site by the United Nations in 1979.

Guatemala, like most of Latin America, became free of Spain in 1821 but was claimed by Mexico under threat of force until 1823. The department of Chiapas was occupied by the Mexican army and permanently severed from the rest of Guatemala.

After declaring its independence a second time, what remained of the country became part of a loose, semiautonomous federation called the United Provinces of Central America that dissolved in late 1838. Political infighting among the region's would-be leaders kept Guatemala under the rule of a Honduran dictator for another nine years.

Even after its official founding as an independent republic on September 15, 1847, Guatemala continued to suffer political troubles and chaotic government. The small Ladino ruling class immediately split into two opposing factions: conservatives, who defended the concentration of power among wealthy landowners and the Catholic church, versus liberals (mostly merchants and businessmen), who favored a gradual dismantling of the church's enormous material empire and reform of the legal system. Battles between these two groups continued, figuratively and literally, for the next hundred years.

Guatemala's founding president, the staunch conservative Rafael Carrera, remained in office until 1865, after which his aggressively status quo policies were pursued by a handpicked successor, Vicente Cerna. In 1871, liberals usurped the long-ruling conservatives in a coup led by Miguel García Granados, who was replaced in the presidency by activist liberal Justo Rufino Barrios in 1873. Concerned about Guatemala's long period of economic decline under Carrera and Cerna, President Barrios committed himself to modernizing the country. Under the conservatives, Guatemalan businessmen and politicians had failed to respond to changes in world markets and allowed the nation's infrastructure to deteriorate. Guatemala's single significant export at the time—a red pigment made from dried carcasses of the cochineal, an insect that feeds on cacti—was being replaced overseas by cheaper synthetic dyes.

Barrios launched an ambitious reform program that included the establishment of a national bank and public school system, the construction of railroads and power-generating networks, and the improvement of highways. He boldly ordered the confiscation of a great deal of church property and abolished the land tenure tradition that had permitted Indians to farm their own property without holding legal deeds. Barrios also implemented a forced labor system that allowed Ladino plantation owners to exploit Indian workers for a specified period of time each year. This controversial edict remained on the books until 1944, allowing the wealthiest families of Guatemala to build huge empires for themselves in the interim. It also enriched hundreds of new immigrants from Germany who, lured by President Barrios with offers of virtually free land and plant stock, began developing coffee into the country's number one industry, as it remains today. His expansionist policies led to an unsuccessful Guatemalan invasion of El Salvador in 1885, where Barrios was killed in battle.

Manuel Estrada Cabrera took over as president in 1898 and presided over Guatemala's affairs by force until 1920, when he was declared legally insane. During Cabrera's regime the government went completely bankrupt, and social unrest threatened to erupt into open revolt. He kept the opposition at bay through the purchased loyalty of iron-fisted generals and ruthless secret police. It was not until 1931, after a series of short-lived administrations failed to restore order and bolster the wracked economy, that some measure of socioeconomic stability returned to Guatemala under the strong-man rule of Jorge Ubico.

Reform-minded Ubico cancelled the Indian debt of servitude instituted by Barrios but immediately introduced new laws that obliged peasants to work on plantations for insignificant wages. He improved health care but paid for the new services by raising taxes and throwing those who could not pay the increase into jail. United Fruit, meanwhile, was granted an exemption from all property taxes and import duties. Ubico developed a network of spies whose information was used by roving death squads to murder dissenters. He could not control the world economy, however, which plunged into deep depression during his administration, nor the scourge of tropical diseases that devastated Guatemala's banana crop. Mass rioting against Ubico's dictatorship forced him to resign in July 1944, and a progressive schoolteacher named Juan José Arévalo was elected to succeed him the following December in the first (relatively) free and fair balloting in Guatemala's history.

During his six-year term, Arévalo started a national welfare program, built new schools, rewrote the labor code, unharnessed the news media, and redistributed power back to local governments. These policies of ''spiritual socialism'' were intensified in the early 1950s by President Jacobo Arbenz, who, after another generally untainted election, came up with a controversial reform plan that would allow small farmers to take over unused public land and cultivate new private parcels carved out of idle tracts held by large private plantations. Wealthy landowners, notably United Fruit, were violently opposed to any kind of land redistribution and sought help from the U.S. government in toppling Arbenz. The U.S. Central Intelligence Agency actively aided and abetted a successful 1954 coup led by Army Colonel Carlos Castillo Armas, which led to the immediate, forced replacement of Arbenz by yet another ultra-conservative dictator. Since the overthrow of Arbenz, Guatemala has been ruled either directly or indirectly by the military, although a nominally civilian government was reestablished in 1986 after the military was guaranteed amnesty from prosecution for any criminal activity. Repression of political dissent, particularly any that espoused liberal or socialistic reform, became routine after the C.I.A. coup but was never completely unchallenged by the Guatemalan people. Violence involving antigovernment guerrillas, military, and paramilitary forces escalated throughout the 1950s and 1960s, culminating in the August 1968 assassination of U.S. Ambassador John Gordon Mein.

In 1977, Central America became a target of the Carter administration's human rights campaign, and relations between the United States and Guatemala soured. Military aid was sharply reduced, then suspended as Guatemala suffered an almost complete breakdown in social order between 1978 and 1984. The economy, wracked by a worldwide recession, also went into a tailspin. After his fraudulent election in 1978, autocratic General Romero Lucas García was overthrown in 1982 by his rival, General Efrían Ríos Montt, who in turn was ousted by yet another hardline general, Mejía Victores, the following year.

An aggressive, reform-minded guerrilla movement and powerful right-wing death squads plunged Guatemala into open civil war throughout the late 1970s and early 1980s. More than 50,000 people were killed, 38,000 "disappeared," and 100,000 were wounded over the course of the decade in violent confrontations that took place throughout the country.

The Guatemalan military's scorched earth campaign was so violent that some 440 villages were completely destroyed. More than a million Guatemalans (one in eight) were internally displaced, and an estimated 200,000 escaped to Mexico, Belize, the United States, and Canada. Thousands of young Indian boys were kidnapped by the military from public streets and markets as part of a campaign calculated to break the will of the rural people.

In 1985, the national constitution was rewritten, and Guatemala's first free election in more than thirty years was held. Vinicio Cerezo, a moderate Christian Democrat whose party had been a frequent death squad target, was elected president for a five-year term. During his administration Cerezo broadened human rights and reduced the role of the military and other security forces in everyday life. His cautious improvements reduced the level of political violence to about a thousand deaths a year and gave the sagging economy a shot in the arm without seriously jeopardizing the privileges of the wealthy elite. Cerezo's successor was Jorge Serrano, head of the Solidarity Action Movement (MAS), who is scheduled to remain in office until the 1995 national elections. The president made headlines by promising to investigate human rights abuses, root out institutional corruption, and normalize relations with neighboring Belize (claimed by Guatemala since 1859). He also appointed the first civilian in decades to head the National Police and further reduced the role of the military in civilian affairs. By emulating Cerezo's go-slow approach to reform, Serrano managed to curb inflation (which reached 83% in 1990) and to stimulate the economy without overtly antagonizing members of the business community. Violence continues but is now less likely to involve direct confrontation with guerrillas, whose members are estimated to have been reduced in number to about three thousand.

The Serrano administration's relations with many foreign governments remain strained, however, because of Guatemala's continuing poor human rights record and failure to aggressively prosecute military and security officials suspected of involvement in the murders of a number of foreign nationals, including at least four U.S. citizens. The Guatemalan judicial system remains largely ineffective, and Serrano is under constant pressure from a small but powerful cadre of domestic constituents who are happy with a system that makes them the "haves" and millions of others the "have nots."

The consensus among many U.S. government officials, business executives, and human rights activists is that although Guatemala's political situation is slowly improving, the nation is a long way from representative democracy and needs continual pressure if it is to change significantly. Their cause was advanced in October 1992, when the Nobel Peace Prize was awarded to Guatemalan Indian rights activist Rigoberta Menchú. A 1992 review by the United Nations Commission on Human Rights agreed that while progress is being made in Guatemala, "security officials are virtually never held accountable for human rights violations."

Indian woman using back-strap loom in Antigua (Photo by Richard Mahler)

Economy

The Guatemalan export economy historically has been based on agricultural commodities, mainly coffee, sugar, bananas, rubber, soybeans, vegetables, and spices, particularly cardamom. About two-thirds of all exports are still farm related, employing about the same ratio of the Guatemalan work force. Agriculture accounts for 26 percent of the $11 billion gross domestic product.

Today tourism is variously listed as Guatemala's largest or second-largest industry, with about 400,000 foreign visitors counted in 1991, an increase of 10 percent from the previous year. It is not known how many of these might be characterized as "true" tourists, however, since authorities do not distinguish among vacationers, visiting business executives, students, and missionaries. Overall, tourism is said to bring Guatemala at least $180 million a year.

In third place among industries is the "nontraditional" sector, including vegetables, flowers, handmade textiles, ceramics, jewelry, and furniture. With the largest industrial base in Central America, Guatemala is also an important manufacturer of pharmaceuticals, chemicals, clothing, wood, and food products. Thanks to lenient tax laws, a number of overseas-financed factories and assembly plants, known as *maquiladoras*, have opened during recent years in Guatemala City and Antigua. The country is a modest producer of petroleum, beef, and fish.

Guatemala's economy, which officially grew by 4.5 percent in 1991, would be in much worse shape if not for the large amount of cash flowing into the country from illegal drug production and transshipment. There is no official estimate of the amount of revenue involved, but U.S. officials have confirmed that Guatemala emerged in the early 1990s as an important transfer point for cocaine and heroin being shipped from Mexico, Asia, and South America to the United States and Europe. Marijuana and opium poppies are also grown in remote areas of the country (the climate is not suited for cocaine-producing coca plants). The drug trafficking situation has apparently developed because of the large number of remote airstrips in Guatemala and the susceptibility of many influential individuals, including government and military officials, to bribery and corruption.

Guatemala's major import categories include manufactured goods, machinery, vehicles, oil, food, and chemical products. About a third of all export trade is with the United States, followed by El Salvador, Germany, Costa Rica, and Italy. Asian countries, particularly Taiwan, Hong Kong, Japan, and South Korea, are rapidly increasing their trade and investment in Guatemala. In recent years there has been a move to privatize the nation's 32 government monopolies.

Religion

Freedom of religion has been guaranteed by Guatemala's national constitution since the late nineteenth century, and there is a wide range of religious expression. In many parts of the country the Catholicism introduced by Spanish missionaries nearly five hundred years ago has melded with indigenous beliefs and practices dating back to the ancient Maya. This so-called folk Catholicism manifests itself in many ways. For example, when the early Spanish priests ordered Indians to stop worshiping their traditional gods of the natural world—representing corn, rain, the sun, and so on—the Mayan response was to give them the names of Christian saints and continue with their prayers. Similarly, Indians often transferred their ceremonial rituals, such as incense burning, animal sacrifices, and street celebrations, to activities sanctioned by the church. In short, they often changed the form of their religious expression but not its substance.

Some Catholic officials have been more receptive to this than others. In Chichicastenango, Santiago Atitlán, Cobán, Zunil, Momostenango, and San Pedro Carchá, Indian languages and rituals have become an integral part of Catholic ceremonies with the blessing and encouragement of local priests. In the Petén, for example, the local bishop takes part in a ceremony in which Indians dance around a sacred stone monument inside a circle of pine needles. And on the venerated steps of the Church of Santo Tomás in Chichicastenango, visitors can see Quiché Indians cross themselves while standing before the doorway, then burn rum and copal incense before speaking aloud to their ancient gods. Inside the church, sand and feather designs are laid out in front of a Christian altar to honor departed relatives in the customary Mayan way. In Ladino-dominated areas, such as Guatemala City, more conservative and traditional forms of Catholic worship are the norm.

Since the 1960s, other Christian denominations have made considerable inroads in Guatemala, and an estimated 35 percent of the population now identifies itself as evangelical or pentecostal Protestant. These groups became especially aggressive in proselytizing after the 1976 earthquake, when they helped organize rural relief efforts throughout the western and central highlands. Missionaries also got a boost in 1982, when the right-wing evangelical General Efrían Ríos Montt took control of the government, at a time when the liberation theology of the Catholic church was under severe attack by the military and roving death squads.

Over the last twenty years many Guatemalan towns and villages have converted, seemingly in their entirety, to the very conservative forms of Protestantism that are being promoted throughout Central America by churches based primarily in the southern United States. In most instances the indigenous folk religions are completely abandoned after conversion. The evangelicals vehemently preach against any use of alcohol, which has been intimately involved in Indian fiestas and religious rituals for thousands of years. The missionaries also decry the practices of *curanderos*, or folk healers, and the ritual brotherhoods known as *cofradías*, which manage Indian governments and organize the elaborate festivals that are a major form of public worship. The evangelicals, like Catholics before them, have been translating the Bible and other religious writings into Mam, Quiché, Kekchí, and Cakchiquel, the four main languages of the contemporary Maya. Baptist missionaries in Lívingston have even translated the New Testament into Garifuna, the largely oral tongue of the region's 25,000 Black Caribs. Evangelicals also now control much of the electronic media in Guatemala, broadcasting religious messages on radio and television twenty-four hours a day throughout the country.

Topography, Natural Resources, and Biodiversity

Guatemala is located at subtropic latitudes and stretches across the isthmus of Central America from the Pacific Ocean to the Caribbean Sea. Guatemala's longest land border (598 miles) is with Mexico, followed by Belize (165 miles), Honduras (159 miles), and El Salvador (126 miles).

Because much of its 42,042 square miles is mountainous, following a chain of thirty-three volcanoes and the nonvolcanic Cuchumatanes range, the country's climate and ecology are astonishingly varied. Fourteen distinct life zones are found at elevations ranging from sea level to over 13,000 feet, each with its own flora and fauna. Nearly 10,000 varieties of plants have been identified in Guatemala, including more than 600 types of orchids, of which nearly 200 are unique to the region. There are 738 known bird species, 251 species of mammals, 214 species of reptiles, 112 species of amphibians, and 220 species of freshwater fish. The number of individual insect species runs into the thousands.

As of 1991, an estimated 39 percent of Guatemala was covered by forests, 13 percent by seasonal farmland, 12 percent by meadows and pastures, 4 percent by permanent crops, and 32 percent by cities, deserts, and other features. Amazingly, large sections of Guatemala remain unexplored and uninventoried by naturalists and ecologists. Among biologists it is not unheard of for an expert working in a remote area to find a plant or animal species that is completely unknown to modern science.

Guatemala is a land of natural extremes. It is home to Central America's deepest lake (1,019-foot Lake Atitlán), highest mountain (13,846-foot Tajumulco), and largest expanse of pristine forest (the Petén wilderness). This is one of the few places in the world where a single day's drive can take you from a steamy coastal banana plantation, past a coffee *finca*, through an apple orchard and highland wheat field, to a windswept sheep pasture overshadowed by an icy alpine peak. You can snorkel in the aquamarine Caribbean in the morning, hike through dank caves and misty cloud forests in the afternoon, and relax in one of nature's medicinal hot springs on a cool mountainside that night.

Population Patterns and Modernization

As of January 1, 1993, the estimated population of Guatemala was 9.7 million. This is a dramatic increase from the roughly three million counted in 1950 and the four million of 1964. At its current annual rate of 2.5 percent a year, Guatemala is one of the fastest-growing nations on earth, which has put a severe strain on the nation's ability to provide its citizens with adequate housing, food, water, electricity, health care, education, transportation, employment, and other basic services.

About half of today's Guatemalans belong to one of twenty-three Mayan Indian ethnolinguistic groups, and nearly all of the others are

The nests of the oropendula, a tropical bird found in the Guatemala jungles, hang like sacks from this tall tree. (Photo by Richard Mahler)

of mixed Indian and European descent, referred to in Guatemala as Ladinos (as are "Westernized" Indians). A small number of Guatemalans are of African, Asian, European, or East Indian heritage, and there are several thousand Garifuna people on the Caribbean coast.

3

Planning the Journey

Travel Advisories

Check with your travel agent about foreign government advisories that may be in force regarding Guatemala. The United States and several other countries, including Italy, the Netherlands, Germany, France, Great Britain, and Japan, have urged their citizens to take certain precautions when traveling in Guatemala, particularly in the northwest highlands of Quiché, San Marcos, and Huehuetenango departments, as well as remote parts of Alta Verapaz and the Petén. The U.S. State Department memorandum for Guatemala warns about violent crime, bus robberies, and roadblocks set up by bandits or guerrillas. A small number of tourists have been robbed or assaulted in recent years, and a few have been raped, kidnapped, and even murdered.

Government advisories change frequently; therefore, you or your travel agent should seek out the most current information before your trip. Contact the State Department's Citizens' Emergency Center before heading to the region. The most up-to-date information is available by calling the State Department "hot line" at (202) 647-5225. In Guatemala City, you may contact the information officer at the U.S. Embassy at 311-541. You can also subscribe to World Status Map, a bimonthly summary of worldwide travel advisories, by calling (800) 322-4685 and asking for a free sample and subscription rates.

Entry and Exit Requirements

All foreign citizens must have a valid passport and tourist card to enter Guatemala. A visa is required for some nationalities, including some British commonwealth countries. Visas and tourist cards are good for 30 days and can be renewed for two consecutive periods totaling no more than 180 days.

Information and materials can be obtained from any of Guatemala's embassies as well as its consulates in Miami, Chicago, New York, Houston, New Orleans, San Francisco, and Los Angeles in the United States and Bonn, Paris, Madrid, Brussels, London, and Rome in Europe (see Appendix for addresses). Visas can be obtained by mail upon inclusion of a passport, 2x2 photograph, application form, and self-addressed, stamped envelope, plus $10. Visas are usually (but not always) available at land borders. Tourist cards are issued by all airlines serving the country. They are also distributed at border crossings and the airport immigration office in Guatemala City. Visas can be renewed for an additional fee of $10. If you wish to stay longer than 90 days, you must either exit and reenter Guatemala (after a minimum of 72 hours) or have a Guatemalan citizen vouch for your financial integrity. It is illegal for tourists to engage in money-making activities in the country without prior governmental permission.

Visa and tourist card extensions may be obtained at the Immigration Office in Guatemala City at 41 Calle 17-36, Zona 8, telephone 714-670 or 714-682.

Exit permits cost about $2.50, but those holding tourist cards or staying less than 30 days are exempt. There is an exit tax of $10 on all airline departures, however.

Corruption is a serious problem at land borders in Guatemala. Some officials overcharge for tourist cards and visas, as well as entry and exit taxes. Others may ask for bribes or demand documents that are unnecessary. Officials may neglect to properly stamp documents, knowing that the visitor will later have to pay a fine or bribe to legally exit the country. The government is trying to eliminate these abuses and encourages tourists not to give in to such practices. Resistance is not always practical—or even feasible—but you should always try to obtain payment receipts and have your papers properly stamped.

Minors traveling without both parents are required to have written authorization from the absent parent (if parents have joint custody) or both (if traveling alone), in triplicate, duly notarized, and stamped by the nearest Guatemalan consulate.

Pets may be brought into Guatemala only with proof of specific required vaccinations. Check with the nearest consulate for details.

Each tourist is allowed to enter the country with up to two bottles of liquor; two cartons of cigarettes; one still, movie, or video camera; one pair of field glasses; and six rolls of film. The regulation on film does not appear to be rigorously enforced, however.

Immunizations and Health Precautions

No vaccinations are required to visit Guatemala, but it is advised that visitors be up to date on immunizations for polio, tetanus, and typhoid. Local public health agencies usually have an up-to-date list of recommendations.

If you are spending more than a week in the jungle, coastal lowlands, or Tikal National Park, antimalarial drugs such as chloroquine or mefloquine are a reasonable precaution. Begin taking them one week before visiting a malaria-infested region and continue for a month after. For information and advice, call the 24-hour Malaria Hotline run by the Center for Disease Control in Atlanta at (404) 332-4555. If left untreated, malaria can be lethal. Dengue fever is also a problem in low-lying areas.

As protection against hepatitis A, many experienced travelers also obtain a gamma-globulin shot, which bolsters the body's immune system for about two months. Some doctors doubt the efficacy of this procedure, however. You will need a yellow fever certificate to enter Guatemala if you have been to a country where the disease has been present within the previous six months.

Cholera, transmitted through contaminated water, sewage, and such raw food dishes as ceviche, is a serious health problem in Guatemala, and caution should always be exercised in eating and sanitation habits. In 1991-92, the incidence of cholera in the country increased dramatically, particularly in rural areas. Preventive inoculations are available, in a two-step procedure, but these provide only marginal protection.

If you feel ill on your return, make sure your doctor is aware of your trip. Many physicians in industrialized countries are unfamiliar with the characteristics and treatments of tropical diseases and can misinterpret their symptoms as influenza or other illnesses.

Iodine tablets, Halazone, or laundry bleach (administered at the rate of 2 drops per liter) can be used to purify tap water, which is chemically treated only in Guatemala City and Antigua. Bottled water is available in the capital and other large cities. Some of the larger hotels have their own water purification systems, and many supply bottled water free of charge. Boiling water for 20 minutes is also effective. Bottled beer and soft drinks are safe; but do not add or accept ice unless you know it is purified. Milk and cheese products are unlikely to be pasteurized except in the best hotels and restaurants. Some travelers carry portable water-filtering systems that eliminate water-borne parasites and other hazards. Others carry enough bleach or iodine to enable them to soak fruits and vegetables they buy at public markets, which may be tainted with germs or pesticides.

Produce market in Chichicastenango (Photo by J. W. Smith)

Carelessness in the consumption of untreated water or milk, as well as uncooked vegetables, peeled fruits, and lightly cooked meat, can easily lead to diarrhea, intestinal parasites, or amoebic dysentery, which is endemic throughout Guatemala. If symptoms of disorders do not diminish or disappear within a few days, see a pharmacist, nurse, or physician. Nearly every community of any size in Guatemala has a clinic and public health practitioner. Diarrhea and dysentery can quickly lead to severe dehydration, which may be fatal if untreated.

The sun is very intense at Guatemalan latitudes; a wide-brimmed hat, sunglasses, and sunscreen (No. 15 SPF or stronger) are advised for northerners, especially those with fair complexions.

Mosquitoes, flies, and biting insects are a problem in lowland areas, jungles, and to some degree the highlands, especially during rainy periods. Bring along strong insect repellents (look for those containing DEET, an acronym for diethylmetaoluamide) and lightweight, natural-fiber clothing that will cover your arms and legs. Some people carry musk oil, citronella, or Avon Skin-So-Soft lotion as an added deterrent against no-see-ums, sand fleas, and other pesky insects. Portable thin-mesh mosquito nets and nontoxic mosquito coils are helpful for those spending extended periods in malaria-infested areas. Certain species of biting flies carry parasites and diseases, some of them dangerous.

Recommended hospitals in Guatemala City are the Bella Aurora (10a. Calle 2-31, Zona 14, tel. 681-951), Centro Médico (6a. Avenida 6-47, Zona 10, tel. 323-335), and Herrera Llerandi (6a. Avenida 8-71, Zona 10, tel. 366-771). Fees for examinations and treatment are nominal, but drugs in hospitals can be expensive. The Red Cross has 24-hour medical service in Guatemala City at 3a. Calle 8-40, Zona 1. In an emergency, dial 125. Red Cross (Cruz Roja) hospital care is also available in Quetzaltenango (tel. 612-746) and Cobán (tel. 511-459).

If you are planning to hike in the high country, try to acclimate yourself first and avoid heavy exertion, overeating, or consumption of alcohol. Those coming from lower altitudes may feel tired, short of breath, and lightheaded for the first couple of days. Freezing temperatures and high winds may be encountered on volcanoes.

You may wish to check with your health insurance carrier before you leave to find out what coverage you have for Guatemala in the event of a medical emergency.

Entry by Air, Land, and Sea

Air

Guatemala is served by a number of direct flights from the United States, Mexico, and Central America. Carriers from Europe generally transfer passengers in Miami or the Caribbean. The privately owned national airline is Aviateca.

Guatemala City's La Aurora International Airport is the arrival and departure point for most foreigners traveling by air. The only other international airport is at Santa Elena, near Flores, which has scheduled flights to Belize and Mexico (see chapter 13 for a complete list of destinations, carriers, addresses, and phone numbers). There are no other commercial air routes within Guatemala, although domestic charters can be arranged.

From the United States, Guatemala is served by Miami (via Taca, United, Lacsa, Iberia, and American), Houston (via Taca, Sahsa, and Continental), New Orleans (via Taca and Aviateca), Los Angeles (via Taca, Lacsa, United, Aviateca, and Mexicana), San Francisco (via Taca and United), and New York (via Lacsa and American).

From Europe, the airlines originating direct flights to Guatemala are KLM (from Amsterdam with stops in Lisbon and Curaçao) and Iberia (starting in Madrid and continuing via Miami, Santo Domingo, or Panama City).

Many carriers serve Guatemala from Latin America and the Caribbean, including Mexicana, Lacsa, Taca, Sahsa, Aviateca, Aerovías, SAM, United, and Copa. Connecting airports include Mexico City, Cancún, Belize City, San Salvador, Tegucigalpa, Kingston, San Pedro Sula, Managua, San Andrés, San José, and Panama City. The easiest connections to or from South America are through Lacsa (via San José, Costa Rica) and Copa or Iberia (both via Panama City).

Those entering Guatemala by private plane must write aeronautic authorities well in advance with anticipated date and time of arrival, place of origin, destination, and routing, names of crew members, type of aircraft, and airplane registration number. Contact: Dirección General de Aeronautica Civil, Aeropuerto La Aurora, Zona 13, Guatemala City, tel. 65-843. That office can also provide a list of airports in Guatemala.

Land

Guatemala is a minimum 4-day drive (approximately 2,000 miles) from the southeast Texas border via the Pan American Highway (Route CA-1), which runs for several hundred miles through Guatemala, entering the country from Mexico at La Mesilla and from El Salvador at San Cristóbal. Up-to-date vehicle registration and title documents are required. Valid driver's licenses and International Operator's Permits (issued by the American Automobile Association with an explanatory page in Spanish) are both honored while driving in Guatemala, but auto insurance policies issued in the United States or Mexico are not.

Other main points of entry by land include Tecún Umán on the Mexican frontier via the Coastal Highway (Route CA-2), which exits El Salvador at Ciudad Pedro de Alvarado. Valle Nuevo, on Route CA-8, and Montecristo, on Route CA-12, are the other main Salvadoran frontiers. The two principal border crossings into Honduras are at El Florido, near that country's Copán ruins, and Agua Caliente farther south, near Esquipulas. The only road crossing into Belize is at Melchor de Mencos on Route CA-13, which continues as Belize's Western Highway all the way to the Caribbean.

If you are crossing the border by bus or taxi, be sure to have your passport and, if possible, a Guatemalan tourist card, which is not always available at each land crossing. Visas, if required for your nationality, should also be obtained in advance.

Sea

The only regularly scheduled public transportation to Guatemala by sea is the twice-weekly ferry between Punta Gorda, Belize, and Puerto Barrios, on the Caribbean coast of Guatemala.

An inland waterway, the Río San Pedro, has daily service between El Naranjo in the Petén to villages along the river in Mexico and, ultimately, the town of La Palma. There are daily buses connecting La Palma with Emiliano Zapata, Palenque, and San Cristóbal de las Casas. El Naranjo has bus connections to Flores and, from there, Guatemala City and Belize.

Small private boats also make charter trips between Puerto Barrios and various towns in Honduras and Belize. Similarly, you can hire boats in communities along the Pacific Coast to transport you between port towns in Mexico and Guatemala. Be sure to check with border officials on both sides of the frontier before departing.

Several cruise ships and passenger-carrying freighters dock occasionally on Guatemala's Pacific and Caribbean coasts. See chapter 13 for details.

If arriving by private boat, you must advise the Captain of the Port of where and when you plan to dock. A list in triplicate of persons aboard and documents of ownership must be submitted to port authorities, and each person on board must have travel papers in order. No visa or tourist card is required for those who do not disembark. If possible, all documents should be stamped by the nearest consulate before departure.

Maritime customs offices are located in Puerto Barrios and Santo Tomás on the Caribbean coast, in Champerico and Puerto Quetzal on the Pacific.

Rail

Passenger entry by rail is limited to Tecún Umán, on the Mexican border. Passenger service to El Salvador via Montecristo has been discontinued. There is also a train from Guatemala City to the Caribbean port city of Puerto Barrios, with boat connections to Belize (by ferry via Lívingston to Punta Gorda) and Honduras (by private launch). Rail service in Guatemala is notoriously poor and should be avoided.

Climate

Many first-time visitors are pleasantly surprised by Guatemala's year-round springlike weather. They often come expecting hot, humid, subtropical conditions, when in fact much of the country is temperate. This Land of Eternal Spring, as many Guatemalans refer to their country, enjoys an annual mean temperature of 75 degrees Fahrenheit.

Cool nights and warm days are the norm in Guatemala's highlands, with lows generally in the 40s and 50s and highs in the 70s and 80s.

Extremes are greatest during the dry season, December through April, when the very highest elevations can be cold enough to snow at night and lower levels can be sweltering during late afternoon. Pack a jacket or sweater if visiting from December through February. Quetzaltenango is the coolest major city, with overnight lows consistently in the 40s. Temperatures are slightly warmer in Guatemala City, Antigua, and Panajachel—each around 5,000 feet in elevation—occasionally rising to 90 degrees in March or April but invariably dropping to the 50s or 60s at night. Even during the wet season, rain in the highlands usually falls only for brief periods in the late afternoon, although 20-day monsoons sometimes occur.

Along the Pacific and Caribbean coasts and in the Petén, the climate is much wetter and warmer. Expect lows in the 60s and 70s, highs in the 80s and 90s—or more—at any time of the year. Rains can be steady and torrential from May through November, with periodic thunderstorms during other times.

The low mountains and river valleys of southeast Guatemala are always warm but considerably drier than the coasts and jungle. This part of the country has been heavily deforested, which has contributed to development of an arid, desertlike climate. Parts of the central highlands, particularly along the Motagua River valley, are also hot, bare, and dry.

What to Bring

A good money belt that can be concealed underneath clothing is essential for travel in Guatemala, as in most parts of the world. Some travelers prefer packs or belts that are worn externally, but these have the disadvantage of being both visible and accessible to criminals. Whichever you choose, be sure to carry a photocopy of your passport, tourist card (or visa), and other important papers in a separate place in case the money belt or pack is lost or stolen. Under a strictly enforced Guatemalan law, foreigners are required to carry passport, tourist card, and/or visa at all times.

Many people insist on carrying traveler's checks whenever they go abroad. In the smaller towns and villages of Guatemala, however, changing traveler's checks may be impossible, and if they are stolen it may be extremely difficult to replace them or obtain a refund. You may be better off carrying cash that is strategically and discreetly hidden in various pockets.

A small knapsack or fanny pack is also useful for carrying cameras, lenses, and film. Earplugs are handy for light sleepers and those not used to the constant din of Guatemalan roosters, radios, buses, and traffic jams. You may wish to bring a Walkman-style tape player for the same reason.

Clothing requirements vary dramatically in Guatemala, depending on when and where you are going. In the department of the Petén, for example, the temperature averages 77 degrees Fahrenheit with tropical humidity year-round. The Pacific and Caribbean coasts are just as warm and damp, if not more so. The major cities of Guatemala City, Antigua, and Quetzaltenango are high enough in elevation to be cool at night, especially during the winter. Communities at even higher altitudes, including many of the mountain villages, are downright cold when the sun goes down and may reach only 50 or 60 degrees during the day in wintertime. A wool sweater or jacket, long pants, and hat are recommended here during December and January.

Throughout the country, the warmest daytime temperatures are experienced in March and April, and the rainiest months are June through October, although rain can fall any day of the year. Packing an umbrella, rain parka, or poncho is prudent. March and April are the driest months in all parts of Guatemala.

Trousers are acceptable for women, but shorts, halter tops, and scanty attire are discouraged for both sexes except at beaches, resort areas, and in the Petén. Guatemala is a country where religious feelings run deep, and revealing dress is considered offensive.

It is against the law to import or wear military-style clothing (e.g., camouflage patterns) or military equipment, and such items are subject to confiscation.

Major brands of toiletries, contact lens materials, tampons, and cosmetics are widely available in Guatemalan cities at reasonable prices. It is not necessary to bring extra supplies of these items unless you will be spending most of your time in the hinterlands. You also do not need to carry candles, towels, sheets, toilet paper, or purified water except in remote areas or if you will be staying in the most budget-priced hotels.

It is the author's observation that most travelers take far too much on a trip rather than too little. People you meet on a trip are unlikely to remember what you wore, and two or three changes of compatible natural fiber clothing should be sufficient, plus personal toiletries, cosmetics, notebooks, medicines, and documents. Keep in mind that white clothing is difficult to keep clean on the road and linen wrinkles almost immediately. Cotton, silk, and rayon garments are the quickest to dry, an important consideration when time is precious and schedules tight.

Books and shoes are especially bulky and heavy; careful thought should be given to each such item. If you start off with more than 30 pounds of luggage for a 2-week trip—or more than two carryon bags— you are almost certainly carrying more than you will need in Guatemala. If you have indeed forgotten a piece of clothing or toilet article, these things can always be obtained in any good-sized town. It is always a good idea to make a list of everything in your luggage (including serial numbers) so that if it is lost or stolen you will know exactly what is missing.

Reservations

Advance reservations are recommended during Guatemala's high season, December through Easter, and are increasingly advisable during the rest of the year. Beach and lake resorts, for example, are often busy with domestic visitors on weekends and holidays, especially during March and April. The two weeks before Easter are a summer holiday for public school students, and the week immediately prior to Easter, Semana Santa (Holy Week), is a vacation time for everyone. Reservations should be made in advance for such popular Semana Santa destinations as Antigua, where choice hotel rooms are secured as much as a year ahead.

Bookings should also be considered for lodging at national parks and nature reserves, such as Tikal, where space is at a premium. Remember that you are more likely to find discounts on room rates,

Pension Bonifaz, an elegant old hotel in Quetzaltenango (Photo by Sue Dirksen)

particularly for extended stays, during the low season. The months with fewest foreign visitors are May and September.

Phone numbers and addresses for hotels, nature reserves, and tour companies can be found in chapter 13 or the portion of the text relating to that particular geographic area. A comprehensive directory of hotels that includes addresses, phone numbers, and prices can also be obtained directly from the Guatemala Tourist Commission, INGUAT, or through the nearest consulate.

Dialing Guatemala direct is very easy from overseas telephones, and most hotels are happy to take reservations by fax or phone.

Maps and Tourist Information

Good background materials, including a detailed "tourist map" and brochures, are available from the various Guatemalan consulates in the United States and other countries. You may also try the Guatemala Tourist Commission in Miami (tel. 305 442-0651) and other cities (see Appendix for list). The tourist commission, known by the Spanish acronym INGUAT, has its main office at 7a. Avenida 1-17, Centro Civico, Zone 4, Guatemala City, where there is a multilingual information desk on the ground floor that is open daily from 9:00 a.m. to 5:00 p.m. Allow at least two weeks for a reply by mail.

INGUAT also has offices in Antigua, Quetzaltenango, Panajachel, Santa Elena, the Guatemala City airport, and at major border crossings. Information and services vary from one office to another, but there is usually at least one knowledgeable person on duty who speaks English. Basic tourist information about Guatemala is also available from any of the tour operators listed in chapter 13.

Maps of Guatemala are available in the United States and Europe from well-stocked bookstores, plus the Rand McNally chain of travel stores and the American Automobile Association. The National Geographic Society has produced many good maps of the region, including "Spain in the Americas" (1992), "West Indies and Central America" (1981), and, especially recommended, "Land of the Maya" (1989).

By far the most detailed maps of Guatemala are produced by the government's Instituto Geográfico Militar (Avenida de las Américas 5-76, Zone 13, Guatemala City) and are sold at the institute's headquarters (photocopies only) and a few specialty shops. These cover the country in 259 sections, using a large-scale (1:50,000) format with accurate contours. The series was in the process of being updated and reissued in 1992.

4

Welcome to Guatemala

Guatemala is the northernmost country in Central America, straddling the land bridge as it narrows between Mexico on the north and El Salvador and Honduras to the south. Belize and the Caribbean Sea form Guatemala's eastern border, and the Pacific Ocean its southwestern boundary. Guatemala is about the same size as Louisiana.

Practicalities

For the convenience of the reader, all prices in this book are listed in U.S. dollars. Based on 1992 research, they are subject to obvious fluctuation and should be used only as a general guideline.

Guatemala is on Mayan Standard Time, equivalent to the Mountain Time Zone of the United States (an hour ahead of Los Angeles, two hours behind New York). There is no "daylight savings" time, since at this subtropical latitude, there are roughly twelve hours of daylight throughout the year.

Almost all electrical outlets are 110 volts, alternating current (AC). Standard American plugs and appliances can be used everywhere except in a few remote areas where higher voltages are required or power supplies are erratic. If you have any doubts about the electrical system in use, ask the building's owner or manager before plugging in.

Language

Spanish is the official language of Guatemala, and the more fluency you have in it, the easier you will get along here. If nothing else, it will facilitate marketplace bargaining.

The majority of Guatemalans—including a surprising number who work in the tourist industry—speak little or no English. About half of the population is of Indian descent, and an estimated 85 percent of these people speak one of twenty-three mutually unintelligible languages (and virtually no Spanish). Despite these linguistic barriers, important information always seems to get communicated through gestures, facial expressions, and commonly understood words.

The type of Spanish spoken in Guatemala is typified by its formality, with an emphasis on politeness, honor, and respect. Those familiar with more modern forms of the language at times may find it rather archaic. For example, Guatemalans sometimes use the old pronoun *vos* instead of *tu* as the familiar form of the singular "you." Except for "tu" when addressing children, foreigners should not use these pronouns. Guatemalan speech is usually slowly and carefully enunciated, rarely slurred as in neighboring Mexico or the Caribbean island countries. Guatemalan Spanish contains some words of Indian origin, particularly place-names, that incorporate the Mayan *x* (pronounced *zsh*) and *j* (which is vocalized as in English instead of remaining silent as in standard Spanish). See the Appendix for a glossary of distinctively Guatemalan words and phrases.

When visiting the many parts of Guatemala with a Mayan majority, be aware that the Spanish you will hear is not always grammatically correct. In fact, your Spanish may be considerably better than that of the people with whom you are trying to communicate.

In Antigua and other communities frequented by a large number of beginning Spanish students, residents tend to be eager to help. With prompting, they will patiently correct your mistakes, something most other Guatemalans are much too polite to do.

Carrying a small Spanish dictionary or phrase book is advisable for travelers who are less than fluent. Especially recommended are the pocket-size *Collins Gem English-Spanish Dictionary* by Mike Gonzalez (London: Collins, 1989) and *Latin American Spanish Phrasebook* (Berkeley: Lonely Planet, 1991).

At the Airport

The point of entry for most visitors is Guatemala City's modern La Aurora International Airport, located a few miles south of downtown in Zona 13. As you exit your plane and are funneled through *migración* (immigration), an office of the Guatemalan government's tourism commission will be on the right. This is an excellent place to buy a tourist card, obtain information about popular destinations, and have your travel questions answered. INGUAT also helps book hotels and arrange transportation for visitors. Staff members are friendly and helpful, and most speak excellent English as well as other major languages.

Immigration and *aduana* (customs) formalities are handled quickly and efficiently. There is no health check or entry tax. You can immediately change money at a Banco de Guatemala counter near the baggage claim area. Official rates are virtually the same at all of the country's banks, and it is advisable to obtain at least some local currency here.

The glass doors beyond the customs counters open directly onto the busy road that passes in front of the terminal, where you can easily find a taxi or hotel shuttle bus. Some car rental agencies are across the street, and most others are nearby on Avenida de la Reforma.

Taxis have no meters, so be sure to establish a fare before getting in. A registered taxi can always be identified by the letter *A* at the beginning of its license plate number. In mid-1992, it cost no more than $8 for a ride to Zones 1 and 4, less than that to Zones 9 and 10 (one person, two bags). Beware of freelance porters who may try to grab your luggage and steer you toward a particular cab. They will expect a tip in return for their help, whether or not it has been requested.

Public buses, which are invariably crowded but cost only a few cents, stop just outside the airport terminal parking lot during the day and next to the taxi stand at night. Bus schedules and routes change often in Guatemala City, so be sure to double-check locally before proceeding on any bus route.

La Aurora airport can be a confusing place when you are leaving the country. Check-in stations are on the upper level, departure lounges and immigration counters in the basement. The airport's few rest rooms are dirty and well hidden. Yet there is a well-staffed information desk, plus restaurants, souvenir shops, duty-free stores, and even a pharmacy. Banks and newsstands may be closed on Sundays and holidays, so make sure you come with pocket money and something to read. There is a $10 mandatory exit tax, payable only in U.S. dollars or Guatemalan *quetzales*. Be sure to check in at least 2 hours before any departing international flight. Some flights require reconfirmation of ticketed reservations at least 72 hours before departure.

A growing number of international flights serve the Santa Elena–Flores airport in the Petén. Formalities are equally simple there, and all essential services are available, including a bank and an INGUAT office. See chapters 11 and 13 for further details.

At the Border

Land border entry into Guatemala is less efficient than at either of the international airports. Theoretically, tourist cards and visas can be obtained at any crossing, but do not count on it, especially at La Mesilla, where the Pan American Highway enters from Mexico. Sloppy paperwork and bribery are serious problems, so make sure you have all necessary documents and that they are properly stamped before proceeding. Some officials illegally demand excessive fees or "tips" and may stall processing if these are not paid. If you are crossing the border by bus or in a tour group, this is apt to be less of a problem because the tour operator will handle payment. If you are driving a vehicle, be sure that its 30-day entry permit is properly stamped and noted in your passport.

The main crossings from Mexico are at La Mesilla and the Pacific Highway at Tecún Umán. A third crossing is at El Carmen. From

Belize, the sole crossing is at Melchor de Mencos, and the primary entry points from El Salvador are at San Cristóbal Frontera, on the Pan American Highway, and at Valle Nuevo. Other Salvadoran entry points are at Anguiatú and Pedro de Alvarado. Honduran crossings are at El Florido, near Copán; Agua Caliente, near Esquipulas; and La Ermita, near Chiquimula.

There are customs and immigration officials to process entry by boat at El Naranjo, via the Río San Pedro, and Puerto Barrios, vía the Punta Gorda ferry. There is a Mexican immigration office at Frontera Corozal, on the west side of the Usumacinta River, and a Guatemalan equivalent on the opposite bank was expected to open in 1993 at Betél.

Getting Around

One of the beauties of Guatemala for the traveler is its small size. Within hours, you can drive or be driven to almost any part of the country. Exceptions are the Petén and remote parts of the highlands, all of which can still be reached within a day or two. Many travelers opt for public transportation—bus or airplane—although cars can be rented in the main cities, and guides with autos are widely available at a daily rate. Many taxi drivers will also negotiate an hourly or half-day rate for travelers who want to base themselves in larger towns and take excursions into the countryside. Another option is to sign on with a tour group; in some cases, this is pretty much the *only* way to see the more remote villages, nature reserves, and archaeological sites.

Each mode of transport has its pros and cons. A private car, for example, allows you to go when and where you please, but road conditions are poor in isolated areas, gas can be scarce (and costly), and security, especially at night, is a major consideration. A journey by public bus is inexpensive but may be terribly uncomfortable and time-consuming. Airplanes and even helicopters can be chartered; however, the expense is significant. Unless you are a diehard train buff, rail travel in Guatemala cannot be recommended under any circumstances. Consider all your options carefully, and inquire locally before making a decision.

An Indian girl selling hand-woven bracelets and belts (Photo by Sue Dirksen)

Money Matters

Guatemala's monetary unit, the quetzal, has historically been one of the most stable currencies in Central America. In late 1992, with the annual inflation rate running at about 10 percent, the quetzal was being exchanged at slightly fewer than five to the U.S. dollar, or about 20 cents each. Because the rate of exchange is in constant fluctuation, all prices in this book are quoted in dollars, not quetzales. There are 100 *centavos* to a quetzal, which is symbolized by the letter *Q*. Named for Guatemala's elusive national bird, the quetzal comes in notes of 1 to 100 in several denominations. The two largest bills, 50 and 100, can be very difficult to change in markets, small shops, and outlying communities. Coins are issued in one, five, ten, and twenty-five centavo pieces. The green and invariably grimy 1-quetzal note, sometimes called a *billete*, is the most common currency in circulation and is particularly handy on buses and in public markets.

The government-owned Banco de Guatemala will exchange most international currencies. Other banks are more likely to change dollars and major European currencies only. You are better off changing money in large cities, because many parts of the country have no facilities whatsoever for exchanging currency.

Banking hours are generally 8:30 a.m. to 3:00 p.m., Monday through Friday, with an extra half hour on Friday afternoons. In bigger towns some banks are also open on Saturday mornings. All are closed on holidays, including Wednesday through Friday of Holy Week.

Most banks, with the notable exception of those in the Guatemala City airport and Antigua, are so bureaucratic that changing money is a laborious process involving much paperwork. Be sure that you are standing in the correct line (this is usually unmarked, so you will need to ask someone) and that, as always, you have your passport and tourist card with you.

Traveler's checks are accepted in urban Guatemala but are given a slightly lower exchange rate by banks. Cashing a traveler's check in a bank usually requires one or more signatures from a bank officer, which can make the process even lengthier than changing foreign currency. There are Thomas Cook and American Express offices in Guatemala City if you need to replace stolen checks. Be sure to carry your checks and a list of serial numbers separately.

Credit cards are accepted by major hotels and tour companies, plus a growing number of restaurants. The most widely accepted are MasterCard and Visa. A processing fee of about 3 percent is usually added when credit cards are used, even when drawing currency on a Guatemalan bank.

Personal checks drawn on foreign banks are rarely accepted in Guatemala, although there are a few branch offices of some international banks where you can cash a check, including Lloyds and Barclay's.

There is a 7 percent value-added (sales) tax, referred to by the acronym IVA, on all goods and services in Guatemala. Some exemptions are taxi and bus tickets and merchandise bought in public markets. There is a separate tax on hotel rooms.

American Express and many other companies can arrange currency wire transfers from the United States, and there are Western Union offices in many Guatemalan towns.

Mail, Telephone, and Media

If you are calling Guatemala from the United States, first dial 011 for an international circuit, then Guatemala's country code, 502. If you are calling Guatemala City, the next number will always be the city code, which is 2. For anyplace else, the city code is 9. Most local numbers have six digits, but older phones, particularly in the capital, may have only five. When calling from within Guatemala, use 02 before Guatemala City numbers and 0 before the numbers of other cities.

The government's domestic telephone monopoly is called Guatel. Local calls are inexpensive, but outside of the capital there are very few coin-operated public phones. If you cannot find a pay phone, all sizable towns have a Guatel office where local and long-distance calls can be made between 7:00 a.m. and 10:00 p.m. The procedure involves standing in line and giving an operator the number you wish to ring, then waiting for your name to be called. You will be directed to a booth when your party has been reached. Collect calls can be made on long-distance and some international connections, including the United States. Some hotels have direct-dial telephones, but they are the exceptions to the rule and rather expensive. There are also direct-dial public phones with international operators at the

Guatemala City airport. Making calls within the country is often more difficult than calling Guatemala from abroad because local switching equipment is inadequate. If you receive a busy signal—or nothing at all—keep trying; you should eventually get through.

Phone directories in Guatemala can be very misleading: the waiting list for installation of new telephone numbers is so long that many residents assume an existing number under someone else's account. Therefore, it is not unusual for a listing to be in the name of a defunct business or a person who has since moved or even died.

All post offices (*correos*) are open from 8:00 a.m. to 4:00 p.m., with the exception of the main branch in Guatemala City, which closes at 7:00 p.m. The office in Tikal maintains irregular hours.

Postage rates are one of the many great bargains in Guatemala, and, thankfully, the postal system is fairly efficient in its handling of postcards and letters. Packages are another story. There are complicated regulations concerning how parcels may be wrapped, and anything sent overseas must be inspected by postal officials *before* it is sealed. For faster service, try UPS, DHL, or Federal Express, or a local shipping specialist such as Get Guated Out in Panajachel or the Pink Box in Antigua.

First-class airmail between Guatemala and the United States or Europe typically takes about 10 days to reach its destination. Postcards are delivered within 3 to 6 weeks.

Despite Guatemala's history of repressive government, the country's media are surprisingly outspoken, although direct criticism of the military is virtually unheard of and attacks on politicians are muted. There is no censorship board and no press licensing. One 1988 international media survey gave Guatemala top ranking in eight categories.

Nevertheless, newsrooms are periodically ransacked, burglarized, or firebombed, and many journalists in Guatemala have been killed, kidnapped, "disappeared," injured, or exiled over the past twenty years in the pursuit of truth. This has had an understandable chilling effect on reportage.

The most popular daily newspapers are *Prensa Libre*, *Siglo XXI*, *La Hora*, and *El Gráfico*, published in the capital and available in most parts of the nation. There are several weekly periodicals, the most widely read of which is a glossy news magazine called *Crónica*. Local English-language papers appear from time to time in Guatemala City and Antigua. The best of the lot in recent years has been *This Week in Central America*, an irreverent and opinionated regional report on business and politics based in Guatemala City, and *Antigua Times*, a bimonthly catering to expatriates. The *International Miami Herald* is available at larger hotels, as are *Time*, *Newsweek*, and *U.S. News & World Report*.

There are over one hundred radio stations in Guatemala and about two dozen TV stations. Most of these concentrate almost exclusively on entertainment or religion, with mediocre news coverage. Some of the news programs on TV and radio are actually owned and produced by staffs separate from the broadcast station on which they appear. The government also produces a newscast for the TV station it operates. Satellite and cable channels from the United States, including CNN and HBO, are available in Guatemala City and in more expensive hotels throughout the country. Complete program listings are published daily in *Prensa Libre* and other newspapers.

Taxes and Tipping

Moderate tips of about 10 percent are customary in Guatemala when paying for restaurant meals. Tipping is also expected for hotel porters, maids, doormen, tour guides, and others who provide personal services. Tipping taxi drivers is not a Guatemala tradition, but the practice is becoming more common with the influx of foreign visitors.

As mentioned above, there is an automatic value-added tax of 7 percent on restaurant food and beverages and a hefty 17 percent on lodging.

In major hotels, tips average $2 per person to bellboys for check-in and check-out assistance. Hotel maids are generally tipped 50 cents per person per night and doormen $1 for hailing taxis.

Business Hours

Most businesses are open from 8:00 or 9:00 a.m. to 6:00 or 7:00 p.m., Monday through Friday, with a siesta break from noon to 2:00 p.m. Retail stores and some other businesses are open Saturday mornings. Shopping centers are usually open from 9:00 a.m. to 8:00 p.m., Monday through Saturday. Government and professional offices are generally open continuously from 9:00 a.m. to 5:00 p.m., Monday through Friday. Banks are usually open from 8:30 or 9:00 a.m. to 2:30 or 3:00 p.m. Museums and art galleries generally are open from 9:00 to noon and 2:00 to 6:00 p.m., closing Monday or Wednesday. Archaeological sites are open every day except principal holidays from 8:00 a.m. to 5:00 p.m.

Most businesses are closed on the following public holidays: January 1, Semana Santa, May 1, June 30, August 15 (Guatemala City only), September 15, October 20, November 1, December 24-25, and December 31.

In addition, each town and village has its own saint's day and fiesta day(s), when virtually everything shuts down for dances, parades, fireworks displays, and other forms of public celebration.

Hazards and Safety Issues

Violent crime and civil unrest have been an unfortunate fact of life in Guatemala for many years, and the 1990s have proven to be no exception. On the positive side, military repression has eased somewhat since 1986, and recent civilian governments have managed to curb the more blatant abuses of human rights. Guerrilla and paramilitary activity continues to inflict casualties, however, and it is important to check on conditions locally before entering a questionable area, including certain neighborhoods in Antigua and Guatemala City. The northwestern highlands and remote parts of the Petén and Alta Verapaz have also seen a high degree of civil unrest.

Most of the recent crime that affects tourists is economic rather than political in its motivation. Muggings and street robberies are committed by thugs and delinquents who apparently feel they have little to lose, particularly since law enforcement tends to be lax and subject to corruption. Civilian police departments have long been notoriously weak and ineffective, since much of their job has been long usurped by the military, which has rightly pulled back from that role in recent years.

Pickpockets are a problem in large cities and around public markets. Carry only small amounts of cash in your pockets and secure other valuables in a hidden money belt or a hotel safe. Avoid flashing large amounts of money or jewelry in public view and bring your camera only when you will be using it. If you must carry a purse, keep the strap over your shoulder and a firm grip on the purse itself. Park vehicles in a protected place, especially at night. A good rule of thumb is to exercise the same commonsense precautions you would use in any big city or unfamiliar environment.

Native Food and Drink

Guatemala is not known as a gastronomical paradise—for good reason. The native food, differing only slightly from Indian to Ladino to Caribbean regions, is usually simple and bland. The emphasis is on corn tortillas, white rice, black beans, plátanos (fried bananas), squash, and the occasional piece of fried, roasted, or stewed chicken. Although onions, pepper, chili, garlic, and *achiote* spice are added to Guatemalan dishes with some regularity, there is nothing incendiary on the typical menu. Traditional meat dishes, such as *pepián* and *pulique*, are often served with a red or dark sauce, but these tend to be mildly flavored. Guacamole (avocado salsa) and *chirmol* (a red pepper sauce) are sometimes served as side dishes. They are a welcome complement to the tamales (cornmeal-wrapped meat pies) and stuffed peppers that are part of native Guatemalan cuisine.

One thing is certain: you will not go hungry during your visit. Food and drink (except wine and most spirits) are readily available and inexpensive throughout the areas of Guatemala usually visited by foreigners. Local beer is moderately priced, and rum is downright

The Carrot Chic Restaurant and video bar in Panajachel (Photo by Richard Mahler)

cheap. Locally produced alcoholic beverages include *caldo*, a fruit punch, and *rompopo*, a concoction made with rum, eggs, and sugar. *Horchata*, the milky rice drink popular in southern Mexico, is also available here, as is *aguardiente*, a high-octane sugarcane brew popular at fiesta time. In lowland areas you may also be offered homebrew cashew wine.

As in most of Latin America, lunch (*almuerzo*) is frequently the biggest meal of the day. Many businesses and offices shut down between noon and 2:00 p.m. to accommodate this custom. Dinner (*cena*) begins around 7:00 or 8:00 p.m. and may continue as late as midnight. Breakfast (*desayuno*) is typically light fare, such as toast, coffee, eggs, and/or fruit. Guatemalans have a sweet tooth, and bakeries and candy vendors can be found throughout the country. Despite its status as one of the world's premier coffee exporters, do not expect to find a good cup of coffee in Guatemala. Almost all of the best beans are exported, and restaurant patrons are often served a lukewarm liquid flavored by dehydrated coffee crystals or powdered Nescafé.

Fresh fruit and salad are available in most restaurants, but caution should be exercised whenever you are uncertain about cleanliness in storage and preparation. Hepatitis, cholera, and other infectious diseases are easily transmitted through careless handling and washing of these foods. The same applies to ceviche, the marinated raw fish salad popular here and in other parts of Latin America. A good rule of thumb is not to eat fish, meat, fruits, or vegetables that are not thoroughly cooked, unless you have great confidence in the restaurant or can peel the fruits and vegetables yourself.

In Guatemala City and Antigua, and to a lesser extent Panajachel and Quetzaltenango, there are many restaurants serving international cuisines, from Chinese to German to Brazilian, as well as fast-food outlets, including McDonald's, Pizza Hut, Taco Bell, and Burger King. The Guatemalans are very fond of fried chicken, and local chain stores such as Pollo Campero do a brisk business.

Holidays, Fiestas, and Festivals

Legal national holidays are January 1, Holy Week (dates vary), May 1 (Labor Day), June 30 (Army Day), September 15 (Independence Day), October 20 (Revolution Day), November 1 (All Saints' Day), December 24, December 25, and December 31.

Virtually every city, town, and village in Guatemala, from the largest to the smallest, devotes at least one day each year to some sort of communitywide celebration. Often these commemorate the Catholic saint who has been adopted as the patron of that locale, although pre-Columbian beliefs and rituals are frequently woven into the festivities. The fiesta may be held only on the specific saint's day, or it may be held over a week-long period that reaches a climax on the saint's birthday. What all fiestas have in common is an often chaotic mishmash of dancing, drinking, eating, music making, and igniting of fireworks. Processions and parades are also usually part of the scheduled events. Some include very specialized elements, such as the flying of huge kites at Santiago Sacatepéquez and racing of horses at Todos Santos. On any day of the year at least one festival is probably happening somewhere in Guatemala, but the most likely times to encounter one are during the week preceding Easter, the Christmas and Lenten seasons, and All Saints' Eve or Day (October 31 and November 1).

INGUAT publishes an invaluable fifty-page directory of fiestas that is available from any of its offices, as well as from Guatemalan embassies and consulates. The booklet is cross-referenced by region and date, with a brief description of annual events and their origins as scheduled in each city, town, and village. Ask for the *Directorio de Fiestas*.

Crafts, Markets, and Shopping

Guatemala has a long, colorful native handicraft tradition that continues to be an extremely important part of the economy. This is particularly true in the Indian highland villages, where there is localized specialization in designs and art forms from one community to the next. These crafts are popularly known by the collective terms *artesanía* or *típica*.

Handwoven textiles are probably the most popular craft purchase in Guatemala. These items display brilliant colors and intricate designs that relate to their specific place or tribe of origin. The weavings can be purchased in the form of raw cloth or finished garments, including everything from trousers (*pantalones*) to skirts (*faldas*) to hats (sombreros). Most popular is the ubiquitous blouse worn by indigenous women, called *huipil* (pronounced wee-PEEL), which may be worn over skirts or pants, stretched on a frame, or displayed on a wall. These weavings—in untailored lengths called *corte*—usually contain cotton fiber, with wool or silk threads sometimes mixed in. Acrylic fibers are becoming more common. Quality, availability, and prices vary considerably for these and other handmade items, depending on where you are.

While textiles are by far the most common artesanía purchase, bargains can also be found on high-quality wood carvings, leather goods, straw hats, ceramics, baskets, mats, furniture, and jewelry. Many of the oldest and most valuable items have already found their way into museum and gallery collections, however. Inexpensive souvenir items include wrist and hair bands, slingshots made in the shape of animals, and embroidered coin purses (see chapter 12 for more details).

As a rule, prices are much lower in public markets than they are in shops. Lower prices are also more likely the farther you get from the main tourist towns—Antigua, Panajachel, and Chichicastenango—and the closer you get to the article's place of manufacture. Your best bet is almost always to buy an item from the person who made it in his or her home village.

Buying in public markets gives a visitor access to the very heart of Guatemala's indigenous culture, since the buying and selling of artesanía predates the arrival of the Spanish and is still often carried out in hushed tones, although the younger generations are becoming increasingly aggressive. Bargaining is a vital part of this tradition, and foreigners are expected to participate. In fact, sellers may feel puzzled or even offended if you do not engage in this friendly ritualistic game. Experienced bargainers usually start by offering about half of the first price that is quoted, then working their way toward a middle-ground compromise that will likely be about two-thirds or three-fourths of the original price. Remember to look around and compare prices before starting any serious negotiating. And do not start bargaining unless you intend to purchase the item. Bargaining is not allowed in most "fixed price" shops or where price tags have been attached to merchandise. Check local English-language tourist publications such as *Aquí en Guatemala* and the *Antigua Times* for up-to-date information about retail stores selling artesanía. Beware of locals who promise to go to the market and buy típica for you. Once you have given them your cash, there is a good chance you will never see them (or your money) again.

Here are some weekly market days in communities most frequented by tourists:

Chimaltenango–Monday, Thursday
Sacapulas, Nebaj, Chichicastenango–Thursday, Sunday
Santiago Atitlán, San Francisco El Alto–Friday
Todos Santos, Senahú–Saturday
Esquipulas, Rabinal, Tactic, Salamá–Sunday
Palin–Wednesday, Friday
Sololá–Tuesday, Friday
Zunil, Tucurú–Monday
Momostenango–Wednesday, Sunday
Totonicapán, Santa Cruz del Quiché–Thursday, Saturday
Antigua–Monday, Thursday, Saturday
Guatemala City, Huehuetenango, Cobán, Quetzaltenango,
    Panajachel, Lívingston–every day

5

Conservation and Responsible Tourism in Guatemala

The quetzal, a brilliantly colored bird with a long swooping tail, is a fitting symbol for the ongoing campaign to protect Guatemala's rich and unusual natural environment. It is a rare creature, independent in spirit and resplendent in form. Quetzals have been prized and revered since ancient times, when the Maya collected and traded their bright feathers like money. Despite repeated attempts, modern zoologists have been unable to keep the quetzal alive in captivity, and human destruction of its mountain habitat seriously threatens the bird's survival in the wild. Its cloud forest range in Guatemala, once over 20,000 square miles, is now reduced to 3 percent of that original territory. In contrast to the hundreds of thousands of quetzals that probably flitted among the Maya during ancient times, today there are only an estimated 45,000 Guatemalan birds, mostly in the rugged Sierra de las Minas and Cuchumatanes Mountains.

In the paradoxical case of the quetzal, people profess one set of values but act out another. Guatemalans clearly love their national bird, but nonetheless they (with the support of multinational corporations) continue to cut down the dense foliage that provides its nesting sites and sustenance.

So it is with the conservation movement of Guatemala. The words from political leaders, industrialists, and bureaucrats sound good—professing a firm commitment to protection of the environment—yet much destructive activity is occurring each day, often in direct violation of laws and policies already on the books.

One example is the cutting of timber along riverbanks. Guatemala has wisely forbidden tree removal within a specified distance of any waterway because it greatly increases topsoil erosion and contributes to sedimentation, which in turn jeopardizes aquatic life and raises the likelihood of flooding. The practice also destroys critical wildlife habitat, especially for monkeys, raccoons, waterfowl, and other creatures that prefer a riparian environment. Yet a visit to any sizable river in Guatemala confirms that the law is being ignored, as peasant farmers and wealthy plantation owners are allowed to cultivate their ubiquitous corn, coffee, squash, and beans right down to the water line.

Historical Context

Ironically, the consequences of such ecological abuses in Guatemala may have already been written about in history books. Anthropologists suspect that one primary reason for the Mayan civilization's decline was widespread degradation of the environment in the latter years of the empire. This apparently occurred through overharvesting, nutrient depletion, deforestation, and misappropriation of limited water resources. For many centuries previously, the Maya *had* lived in balance and harmony with their surroundings, managing their natural resources creatively and wisely. Farmland was composted and fertilized, allowed to lie fallow, and cultivated with diverse crops that complemented one another. Swamps were drained, and terraced gardens were watered with ingenious irrigation systems. But by the late eighth century, the Mayan population apparently had grown to the point that it was consuming much more than nature could replace. As a result, nearly all that physically remains of a complex and impressive society has been reclaimed by a forest whose balances, processes, and rhythms were violated or ignored.

The people of Guatemala are again at a crossroads. The population of their country could double by the year 2020. As a direct result of this unchecked growth, forests, wetlands, and other vital ecosystems are being destroyed at an alarming rate. Pollution of the nation's air, land, and water is almost completely unregulated. As one foreign aid official put it, "Trying to solve environmental problems here without addressing population growth is like trying to mop up a flooded kitchen without first turning off the faucet." Fortunately, there are hopeful signs that Guatemala's alarming rates of ecological destruction and exploitation are at last being checked. During the 1980s, a strong environmental movement emerged among Guatemalan students, educators, and professionals, and its ideas have become more and more popular among all classes, ages, and ethnic groups. During the Cerezo administration (1985–1990), the National Commission for the Environment (CONAMA) was created, which immediately began working to slow deforestation and to set up large and biologically significant nature reserves. Following in this effort under President Jorge Serrano were several nongovernmental organizations dedicated to conservation and environmental education. Foremost among the latter is Defenders of Nature, a private nonprofit group that has been working closely with Conservation International, the Nature Conservancy, and other U.S. and European environmental groups. The U.S. government, through its Agency for International Development, has provided much support for projects that promote wise use of the country's natural resources.

More and more decision makers in the Guatemalan government and industry seem to be paying attention to what the country's environmental activists are saying and doing. One indication is the growing commitment by the Guatemala Tourist Commission to *ecoturismo*—tourism that promotes a respectful appreciation of nature, indigenous cultures, and archaeological sites. By actively supporting such efforts, today's tourist can actually be a part of the solution to the problem of environmental and cultural degradation.

Plant and Timber Extraction

The rain forests and highlands of Guatemala may have been the first places in the world where corn, avocados, guava, yucca, runner beans, and chocolate were domesticated as food plants. Tomatoes, squash, and other plants also appear to have been brought here from other parts of the Americas for cultivation. Around many archaeo-

Deforestation by Kekchí Maya in Sierra Chamá of Alta Verapaz (Photo by Richard Mahler)

logical sites, the descendants of fruit and nut trees planted centuries ago by the Indians are still productive sources of nutritious food for local residents as well as animals and birds. But twentieth-century Guatemala is not like the ancient Mayan world.

The modern world's seemingly insatiable appetite for tropical lumber, for example, has had a terrible impact on Guatemala's lush, beautiful forests. No one knows exactly how much timber is being harvested in the Petén, the nation's northern wilderness, but estimates hover at around 80,000 acres a year. Experts predict that if the present rate of destruction continues, there will be virtually no forest left in this Ohio-size ecosystem by the year 2020. An estimated 40 percent of the Petén's forest cover has been lost since 1940 to the ceaseless slashing of chainsaws and machetes.

The nation, it seems, is stymied by a web of conflicting interests and traditions. The centuries-old practice of slash-and-burn *milpa* agriculture demands that forest be cut down and burned for such favored subsistence crops as corn, squash, and beans, which exhaust the thin topsoil within three or four years. After the earth lies fallow for another seven years, a new crop is traditionally planted. Farmers sometimes choose to grow plantation crops using obsolete techniques that are often not well suited for the specialized growing conditions of the Petén.

Government encouragement of the migration and resettlement of landless Guatemalan peasants in the Petén is a policy that relieves pressure for land reform in other parts of the nation but puts increased demand on the fragile ecosystem. As long as officials consider agrarian reform in the south and west to be subversive, this trend is likely to continue. For now, the powerful independent executive in charge of the development and colonization agency for the Petén (INTA) has the power to sell government land to whomever he wishes, a prospect that is apparently too good for landless peasants to pass up. In 1992, officials estimated 300 Guatemalans a week were taking advantage of the ongoing land grab.

The new push toward cattle production as a source of export income is another important factor in changing Guatemala's land-use priorities. More than 60 percent of the country's beef is shipped overseas, primarily to fast-food chains in the United States. Typically, cattle ranchers move in when farmers move out, after nutrient exhaustion, ground compaction, and weed growth have made cultivating those lands difficult.

Despite its requirements for management plans and quotas, the government's granting of logging concessions, often to active or retired military officers, results in the overharvesting of such valuable trees as mahogany and cedar (worth up to $10,000 each) and the illegal cutting and shipment of such timber to Mexico and Belize. As many as 10 or 20 trees may be destroyed for every one that is shipped. The Petén's 200 unarmed forestry police are powerless to stop trucks whose drivers pull pistols at roadblocks and pay hundreds of dollars in bribes to ship a full load to a sawmill. The army shows little interest in stopping such shipments, possibly because its own members are allegedly involved in the activity.

Even areas that have been granted some degree of official environmental protection, such as the Maya Biosphere Reserve, are suffering from unauthorized agriculture and cash extraction businesses. The capture and export of wild parrots, monkeys, and other exotic wildlife is a huge business in Guatemala, for example, with many more animals captured than nature can replace. While a limited number of economic activities are legal in the buffer zones surrounding Guatemala's parks, there is insufficient law enforcement, and bribery is endemic.

The construction of roads by loggers, game poachers, and oil explorers through freshly cut swaths of jungle inevitably brings a new wave of settlers, many of them poorly educated peasants whose hunting and farming practices are environmentally wasteful and scientifically unsound. Some of these homesteaders become chainsaw-toting "pirates," who cut and sell illegally harvested trees to unscrupulous timber companies.

Guatemala's northern border with Mexico is becoming painfully permeable. A now-famous satellite photo published in the October 1989 "La Ruta Maya" issue of *National Geographic* (updated in the November 1992 issue) showed the dramatic contrast between Mexico's stripped landscape on the northern side of the frontier and Guatemala's relatively intact subtropical forest on the opposite side of the boundary. Many roads now make incursions across the unpatrolled border, bringing illegally harvested game (deer, peccaries, cats, birds, crocodiles) and timber (mahogany, cedar, ceiba) out of the Petén and hundreds of homesteading Mexican milpa farmers in.

Seeds of Change

Despite the rapid pace of deforestation, there is ample cause for optimism in Guatemala. More and more logging companies seem to be complying with permit restrictions that limit the number and species of trees that can be removed from a specific area over a given period of time. These firms are also becoming more involved in reforestation, having made the happy discovery that certain commercially valuable softwoods can be grown quicker and more easily in the fragile jungle soil. Timber is a multimillion-dollar business in this part of Guatemala, and logging companies are eager to find new sources of profits. It should be noted that a shift to plantation-style forestry may make sense in areas that have already been cut, but the approach does not replicate the diverse ecosystem that was there originally.

More rural residents are turning toward sustainable harvesting of indigenous forest products, including chicle, rubber, allspice, *xate* (an ornamental palm used by florists), wild nuts, and wild fruits. Timber cutters are also more willing to select faster-growing "secondary" trees like rosewood, rather than such prized but slow-growing hardwoods as mahogany. Conservation International and other groups are following a model pioneered by the nonprofit organization Cultural Survival in Brazil, where rain forest products are being used in natural oils, sponges, bowls, and foodstuffs sold both domestically and overseas. They are also designing ways to increase local wages and manage selective timber harvesting.

Guatemaltecos have also become aware that the tourist trade is at stake. Tens of thousands of nature lovers come to the jungle each year to see exotic birds and animals, marvel at orchids, float rivers, and explore Mayan ruins—spending much-needed dollars and creating many jobs in the process (more than the timber industry, in fact). Nobody comes to this part of the world to see a desert, as Guatemalans in the dry wastelands of Jalapa and El Progreso are well aware. Guatemalans do not want their country to look like El Salvador, where virtually all of the forest cover has been removed, much of the land has become almost totally unproductive, and ecotourism is nonexistent.

Sustainable Use of Natural Resources

For *Peteneros* like Adrián Velásquez, the jungle is both home and work place. Every few months, he and his neighbors set off through the forest in search of the bright green leaves of the xate palm, a low-growing species recognizable by its many long fronds. Velásquez and his fellow *xateros* (xate cutters) hack off a few of the fronds and carry them back to their village in a plastic bucket or burlap sack. Their proper cutting does not injure the xate.

The harvested fronds are sent to San Benito, near Flores, where they are sorted and packaged for export to florists throughout Europe and the United States. The palm leaves are prized for their long-lasting color and are used in formal flower arrangements with lilies, tulips, roses, and other blossoms.

Xate collecting is part of a trend toward "sustainable development" of Guatemala's forests, whereby industries that thrive on non-threatening use of jungle resources are encouraged. Men like Velásquez earn twice as much money collecting xate as they would growing corn. Taken as a whole, their efforts annually contribute $6 million or more in foreign exchange to the Guatemalan economy.

More than 3,100 square miles of the northern Petén have been designated an "extractive reserve" by the Guatemalan government, where Velásquez's and some seven thousand other families are allowed to make their living from nondestructive exploitation of the Maya Biosphere's natural treasures. It is hoped that the forest gatherers will eventually organize themselves into cooperatives that can train and license members, cracking down on individuals who overcut xate palms, overtap chicle, or chop down allspice trees to get at a few choice berries in the uppermost branches.

"People who live in the forest will use it one way or another," explained ecologist Jim Nations of Conservation International in a 1990 interview with *Buzzworm* magazine. "If they are forced to use it in a bad way because of policies that encourage its destruction, then that's exactly what they'll do. But if they are encouraged to use it in a way that lets the forest survive, then that's good for them and the forest. The Berlin Wall approach doesn't work in the middle of nowhere."

Sustainable harvests of wild jungle products in Guatemala include allspice, peppercorn, rattan, hearts of palm, xate palm, rubber, and chicle. The latter is tapped from the *chicozapote* tree (also called sapodilla) for use as a chewing-gum base. The market for chicle declined with the introduction of synthetics in the 1940s but has been revived in the 1990s as gum manufacturers in Japan and other countries have reverted to natural formulas. Other valuable extractives that can be cultivated and harvested without damaging the ecosystem include vanilla, sarsaparilla, camphor, cinnamon, bamboo, cacao, honey, and quinine (an antimalarial compound from the *chinchona* tree).

Environmental Education

The change in ecological awareness is not limited to Guatemala's Petén. José Carlos Solares is a farmer in San José del Rinconcito, located in a heavily cultivated area 50 miles southwest of Guatemala City. A small river runs through his village, providing residents with year-round water for drinking, bathing, washing clothes, irrigating crops, and raising livestock. "But the water is being contaminated by the coffee industry," Solares points out, "so we must fight to save the river." He is one of nearly a thousand community leaders handpicked by the local conservation organization Amigos del Bosque (Friends of the Forest) to attend week-long classes on grass roots management of natural resources.

"The quality of life for many Guatemalans has deteriorated in past years from misuse of the environment," says Josefina Chavarría, executive director of Amigos. "Our project focuses on rural communities because they are the ones most affected by the country's politics and violence, and they have suffered most from economic and social neglect."

Students in the Amigos del Bosque classes are encouraged to share their communities' environmental problems and to discuss possible solutions based on what is easily available to them. Erosion and water contamination on coffee plantations, for example, can be stemmed by the planting of shade trees that bear harvestable fruits and nuts. One valuable lesson of such discussions, organizers say, is that participants learn the potential of regional involvement. "Many speak different languages and never travel outside their own communities," explains Chavarría. "But when they have this opportunity to study together, they discover that they have a great deal in common."

Chavarría believes that among rural Guatemalans, "new ideas work best when they are demonstrated by someone people know and trust"; therefore, it is most effective to train respected community leaders who will pass on their knowledge to others. Students are given basic information about soil, water, air, plants, and animals. They are told, for example, how killing the delicious-tasting agouti for food affects the health of the forest, since this rabbit-sized rodent

This sign urges Guatemalan farmers to use reforestation techniques in managing their land. It is part of a national campaign to reduce the destruction of wildlife, soils, and water supplies. (Photo by Richard Mahler)

is a critical agent in the dispersal of large seeds. Attendees are taught how to prevent soil erosion, purify water, build latrines, and start plant nurseries. When they return to their villages, graduates of the course are given colorful posters that illustrate what they have learned. "Illiteracy in these areas is as high as 85 percent," says Chavarría. "Posters are a fun and effective way to get our message across."

Magdalena Ubico Mota, a 21-year-old schoolteacher from Joyabaj, northwest of Guatemala City, turned a neighbor's home into an informal classroom to pass on what she learned in the Amigos course. Mota works with children in the mornings, then holds classes for adults in the evenings. "I can teach them about deforestation, how to plant in terraces to prevent erosion, and how to use pesticides safely," she explains.

Such success stories reinforce a concept that has become a guiding principle in natural resource protection: wherever local people are involved from the beginning in planning and carrying out conservation programs, both the environment and people prosper.

Under Guatemala's Protected Areas Law, enacted in 1989, more than forty parks and preserves around the country now enjoy federally enforced legal protection. The government's National Council of Protected Areas (known by its Spanish acronym CONAP) is working with Conservation International, the Nature Conservancy, World Wildlife Fund, Compañeros de las Américas, the Peregrine Fund, and other environmental organizations to make ecological assessments of these areas, train forest rangers and caretakers, and develop strategies for sustainable development of selected portions of forests, savannas, and wetlands. Regrettably, salaries for many of those hired to help protect the parks and reserves are so low that they must spend much of their time tending gardens, hunting, and fishing to survive. This is further exacerbated by lack of high-level government support. The U.S. government's Agency for International Development has been providing financial assistance to try to remedy such problems.

Social and Economic Issues

There are many examples of creative and cooperative approaches to helping Guatemala conserve and manage its natural resources, but the country's biggest problem in this context is undoubtedly the most difficult to solve. In 1950, the country's population was just under 3 million. By 1993, it had grown to an estimated 9.7 million, two-thirds of this number living in extreme poverty. At the current rate of increase, there will be more than 19 million Guatemalans by the year 2020, most engaged in a constant search for new milpa plots and firewood sources (an estimated 12% of the country's forest cutting is for domestic fuel use). In the final analysis, resolving the environmental dilemmas facing Guatemala cannot happen until issues involving basic social, political, economic, land tenure, and human rights questions are addressed as well.

Guatemalan policymakers have many problems in common with developing nations throughout the world, but there are several factors that make their country's current situation unique from an environmentalist's point of view:

• About one-third of all land cover is already eroded or seriously degraded, some of it irretrievably. This is especially significant because much of the soil is composed of unconsolidated volcanic ash that is highly susceptible to erosion when exposed to the elements. Erosion—often from slash-and-burn agriculture, timber harvesting, and mining—leads to rapid silting of rivers and lakes, contaminating water supplies, killing fish, disrupting the ecosystem, increasing the likelihood of flooding, and threatening irrigation systems.

• Private property rights are considered sacrosanct in Guatemala, and many landowners resent any attempt to dictate what they can or cannot do with their holdings. In 1991, however, two lawsuits filed by landowners eager to cut timber in a federally protected area (the Sierra de las Minas Biosphere Reserve) were dismissed by Guatemala's Court of Constitutionality. The legal standing of all parks and reserves was strengthened by the decisions of this court, the highest in the country for constitutional issues.

• Oil exploration and drilling threaten the Petén, coastal lowlands, and several wilderness areas, as do proposed hydroelectric projects that would flood agricultural areas, displace residents (and wildlife), and increase evaporative water loss.

• Road building related to army maneuvers and military-related timber extraction, as well as dam building and oil exploration, destroys forest habitat and encourages migration of homesteaders into what were once wilderness areas.

• With the encouragement, cooperation, and partial funding of the U.S. Drug Enforcement Agency and U.S. State Department, many rural areas in Guatemala have been sprayed with Round-Up, malathion, paraquat, and other powerful herbicides designed to defoliate plantations of marijuana and opium poppies. Too often the long-term result is contaminated land, non-drug-related crop losses, and illness among humans, poultry, livestock, and other animals.

• The continued use of powerful agricultural fertilizers and pesticides in Guatemala has done untold damage over the years, polluting ground water, fouling streams, and jeopardizing plant and animal life. When fruits and vegetables produced in Guatemala exceed pesticide levels set by the United States and Europe, they are usually distributed on the local market. The cumulative result, according to one

Enjoying one of the many soothing waterfalls of the Alta Verapaz region (Photo by Richard Mahler)

estimate, is that Guatemalans have more DDT in their body fat than any other people in the world.

• The uncontrolled growth of Guatemala City—from less than 300,000 residents only four decades ago to over 2 million today—has created an environmental catastrophe. The capital is running out of clean water, clean air, and cheap energy. Its streets reach gridlock during morning and evening commute times. Factories and garbage dumps disperse tons of toxic material into the sky around the clock. Diesel fumes choke the downtown area, and dense smog settles in the valleys on calm days and overnight, escalating the risk of heart disease, asthma, lead poisoning, and cancer for all residents. Without a liquid waste treatment system, Guatemala City's sewers have turned one of the country's largest waterways, the Motagua, into a dead river full of solvents, heavy metals, and human excrement. Here, as in the rest of Guatemala, thousands of residents have no sanitary facilities whatsoever.

Another issue government leaders are grappling with is how to respond to proposals for shipment of toxic wastes and other garbage to Guatemala from industrialized countries, such as the United States and Germany. Some Guatemalan businessmen think they can make big profits importing, reprocessing, and disposing of thousands of tons of waste, including solvents, radioactive soil, plastics, and sludge. Others believe the incineration of imported garbage can provide badly needed electricity. As industrial nations find it more difficult to dispose of their dangerous wastes at home, more companies are turning to developing nations as a possible dumping ground. According to Greenpeace, Central America is already the preferred destination for the toxic incinerator ash of many U.S. cities.

Several of the many wild rivers of Guatemala are in danger of being dammed for generation of hydroelectric power, flood control, drinking water, and agricultural irrigation. About 15 percent of the country's electricity is now generated by a massive hydroelectric generator on the Río Chixoy, high in the Sierra de Chamá of Alta Verapaz. Poor construction, a lack of spare parts, and fluctuating water levels have forced this plant to operate far below its planned capacity, and engineers are once again eyeing the Río Cahabón farther east as the possible site of a new project, despite the presence of earthquake faults in the area. Below the Chixoy dam, meanwhile, siltation has fouled much of that river's large and important watershed.

Along Guatemala's northwestern border with Mexico, the scenic Usumacinta River has long been seen by the Mexican government as a hoped-for source of electricity. In spring 1992 there were indications that Mexico might be abandoning the idea after being advised by its own scientists that it would be an ecological disaster of immense proportions, putting a large part of the Petén wilderness under water and destroying many thousands of acres of forest and wetland habitat, not to mention priceless ancient Mayan artifacts.

The challenging and competing demands of a rapidly growing population, lackluster economy, and threatened environment have put Guatemala's policymakers in an unenviable position. The difficult decisions they are being forced to make are unlikely to satisfy any single constituency, including environmentalists.

"We and the U.S. want to save [our] forests," Environment Minister Jorge Cabrera told *U.S. News & World Report* in 1990, "but for us it is not just an ethical problem. We are not talking about quality of life for our people. . . .We are talking about our survival."

6

Guatemala City, Antigua, and the Central Highlands

The central highlands are the most industrialized and heavily populated part of Guatemala, responsible for more than half of the country's manufacturing and home to one-third of its citizens. This mountainous area also contains many intriguing historical monuments, several important Mayan ruins, and some of the best scenery in the country. The climate is pleasing, and the people are friendly. There are hotels, restaurants, attractions, and services suited to the needs and budget of every kind of traveler. For these reasons and more, the central highlands are highly recommended for at least part of any visit to Guatemala.

This region encompasses the south-central part of the Sierra Madre mountain range, which is bisected by deep ravines and valleys. The central highlands include Guatemala City and Antigua, current and past capitals of the nation. Lakes, pine forests, hot springs, volcanoes, archaeological sites, and traditional Indian villages are among the area's rural attractions.

Guatemala City

Guatemala City is a paradox. It is the first glimpse of Guatemala for hundreds of thousands of incoming visitors each year, yet it is everything the rest of the country is not. Variously referred to as Guate or El Capital by locals, Guatemala City is ugly, crowded, noisy, and pol-

The neo-Gothic Yuritta Chapel in Guatemala City (Photo by INGUAT)

luted. Its two million-plus residents inhabit a high plateau—about 4,500 feet above sea level—that drops off into plunging canyons on its outskirts. Little planning has gone into the development of Guatemala City, and it now faces serious shortages of electricity, water, public transportation, police protection, housing, parks, and jobs.

Like Mexico City to the north, the Guatemalan capital is home to a large number of peasants who have been displaced by civil unrest or migrated from the countryside in the hope that a better life awaits them. Tragically, this is almost never the case, and many poor people end up homesteading in tiny shacks made of plywood, cardboard, and plastic without benefit of clean running water or sanitary facilities. From time to time, security forces oust them from their makeshift camps, but they soon return.

An urban sore thumb in a country noted for its spectacular natural beauty and simple traditions, Guatemala City is understandably given short shrift by many visitors. Most leave as quickly as possible for the western highlands, Tikal, Antigua, Panajachel, or other popular destinations.

Despite its drawbacks, Guatemala City does have worthwhile attractions and hidden charms. With its broad avenues, high-rise buildings, and cosmopolitan restaurants, the capital can be a pleasant place to get acclimated, take care of errands, and learn about the country's history, culture, and natural resources. A visit to the fine archaeology museum in Aurora Park, for example, is a helpful prerequisite for a trip to Tikal, since it is where many of that ancient city's finest artifacts have wound up. One can see a scale-model replica of Tikal at its height, along with stelae, friezes, and carvings from this and other major Mayan ruins.

Guatemala City is a bustling place, full of street vendors selling everything from cheap ballpoint pens to knock-off Rolex watches. Homeless children walk the streets, begging and prostituting. Soldiers with machine guns are an everyday sight. There are modern shopping centers, too, and some of the biggest and best public markets in the country. The capital is where you will find government offices, embassies, and corporate headquarters, along with tour operators, national museums, cathedrals, libraries, and galleries. If you need to extend your visa, set up an excursion, mail a package, or buy some last minute típica, this is the right place. Guatemala City is also home to several symphonies and theater companies and is the only community in the country with any significant nightlife, unless your definition is limited to bars and disco lounges.

History

Hemmed into the broad Valley of the Hermitage, surrounded by lush green hills and smoldering volcanoes, Nueva Guatemala de Asunción was founded on the first day of 1776, after the original Spanish colonial capital at Antigua (officially named La Antigua Guatemala) was leveled in a series of terrible earthquakes. The valley was mostly empty at the time, home to a few farmers and the ancient ruins of Kaminal Juyú, which are now surrounded by apartment buildings. Guatemala City was laid out in the classic Spanish colonial grid pattern around a central plaza. The capital grew slowly at first but soon became the largest city in Central America.

The new site has not been immune to earthquakes of its own: Guatemala City has been devastated by major temblors in 1917, 1918, and 1976. The last one killed more than 25,000 people throughout the country and destroyed most of the few colonial buildings that had not been knocked down fifty-eight years earlier.

Thanks to generous international contributions and characteristic Guatemalan resolve, the city has been almost completely rebuilt. Modern hotels, restaurants, apartment houses, office towers, and shopping centers seem to be everywhere. Unfortunately, they are mostly stucco, concrete, steel, and glass monstrosities of uninspired design. Unlike Antigua and Quetzaltenango, where a deliberate effort has been made to rebuild in conformity with traditional styles, Guatemala City's architecture has precious little visual appeal.

The contrast of rich and poor is dramatic here. Wealthier Ladino residents have withdrawn to the shady suburbs, where they are hidden behind high walls and barbed wire fences, leaving vast stretches of the noisy inner city to the modest boxlike homes of the middle class and the shanties of the largely Indian peasantry. Things are improving visually, however, as the city's parks department continues to plant about 50,000 new trees each year.

Like nearly all Guatemalan cities, the capital is divided into geographic zones, comparable to American zip codes. The oldest part of the city, surrounding the Parque Central, is Zone 1, an intriguing collection of historic buildings and busy markets. But the hub of commerce has moved south to Zone 4's high-tech civic center and financial headquarters and to the wide avenues of Zones 9 and 10. Around the perimeter are the factories, warehouses, and manufacturing centers that employ many Guatemala City residents, whose own modest neighborhoods are spread flat and low across the smoggy horizon.

What to Wear

Like the rest of the country, Guatemala City has distinct wet seasons (May through November) and dry seasons (December through April). Rain can occur at any time of the year, however, often in short, intense late afternoon or early evening cloudbursts called *aguaceros*.

Because of its altitude, year-round temperatures in the capital are mild, rising to the 70s or 80s most days, dipping into the 50s or 60s at night. Appropriate clothing is comfortable and informal, such as cotton casual wear. Women are accepted in pants almost everywhere, and the coat-and-tie rule for men is invoked only in the most conservative offices and poshest restaurants. Guatemalans are rather reserved and traditional people, however, and as mentioned previously, the wearing of shorts or skin-revealing clothing away from lakes, beaches, or steamy jungles is frowned upon.

Orientation

Guatemala City has nineteen separate geographic zones (*zonas*), each with its own numbered grid pattern. Numbered avenues (*avenidas*) run from north to south and numbered streets (*calles*) from east to west. Thus an address of 6a. Avenida 8-22, Zona 1, is on Sixth Avenue, between Eighth and Ninth streets at building number 22, in Zone 1. The lowercase *a* appearing immediately after the number of a street or avenue is merely the Spanish abbreviation for the street's proper name. For instance, 7a. Avenida is the proper contraction for Séptima Avenida (Seventh Avenue).

It is important to remember that the exact same address often exists in several different zones, therefore, it is essential to know the zone number. The situation is aggravated by the fact that many intersections are marked poorly, if at all; and some roads in the older parts of town are also still identified by their original colonial names, since replaced on most maps by the numbers-only system. Many thor-

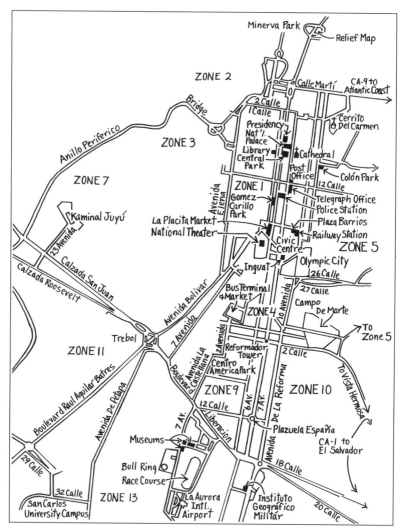

Guatemala City

oughfares have one-way traffic or are divided by wide traffic medians.

A first-time visitor's confusion may be intensified by the fact that two parallel streets or avenues sometimes have the same number. In these instances the second street or avenue, which is usually narrow or shorter, is identified by a capital letter *A*. For example, 13a. Calle A is a small street that runs parallel between 13a. Calle and 14a. Calle.

Only four sections of Guatemala City—Zones 1 and 4 downtown, plus 9, 10, and 13 in the upscale business district—are of much interest to foreign visitors, since they contain the majority of hotels, restaurants, offices, museums, and other tourist attractions. The broad, tree-lined Avenida de la Reforma bisects Zones 9 and 10, connecting the urban center with La Aurora International Airport. An extension of Avenida de la Reforma, 7a. Avenida, is one of the main thoroughfares of Zones 1 and 4.

The official Guatemala Tourist Map (*Mapa Turístico*), available from any INGUAT office, includes an excellent detailed map of the capital as well as Antigua and other cities. You would do well to carry a copy of this map with you while memorizing landmarks and getting oriented. After a day or two, Guatemala City's pragmatic layout will begin to make sense.

Pedestrians need to be extremely wary in the capital. There are virtually no crosswalks, and traffic does not yield to those on foot. Be careful and look both ways when crossing any intersection: speeding and flaunting traffic laws are common pastimes in this macho, seatbelt-free culture.

Unfortunately, Guatemala City has no single central bus station. Instead, it has several public terminals, plus a number of private stations operated by individual bus companies exclusively for their own passengers. Most of these are spread around Zone 1, in the older and northernmost part of the city, although one large public bus terminal is located in the adjacent Zone 4. Because arrival and departure points (and schedules) for the various bus lines change frequently, you will need to check locally when planning trips in or out of Guatemala City. Most coastal, Salvadoran, and eastern destinations are served by the frenzied Zone 4 terminal at 1a. Avenida and 7a. Calle; most highland towns are reached by buses leaving from the terminal at 1a. Calle and 3a. Avenida in Zone 1.

The local bus system is inexpensive and extensive, serving virtually all of the capital. The buses are invariably crowded, however, and the sheer number of routes and schedules can be intimidating at first. Also, the final destination of a bus, identified by a placard in the front window, is sometimes reached by such a long and painfully slow route that you are better off taking a taxi or even walking.

Weavers in San Antonio Aguas Calientes display their wares (Photo by Don Usner)

Buses shuttle up and down Avenida de la Reforma between Zones 1, 2, 4, 9, and 10 along the most touristed routes. Since schedules quickly become outdated, you will do best to make local inquiries before using the municipal bus lines. Few of the drivers speak English, but most hotel personnel and cab drivers have a good working knowledge of the system.

Guatemala City taxis are plentiful and relatively cheap, although they become noticeably scarcer and more expensive at night. A registered taxi always bears a license plate that begins with the capital letter A. Those meeting the standards of the tourist commission will bear the INGUAT emblem. Always settle on the amount you are going to pay *before* setting out, and always be prepared to bargain.

There are several major car rental agencies operating in Guatemala City, offering everything from four-wheel-drive Land Rovers to luxury limousines. You will find agency offices at the airport, in major hotels, and along Avenida de la Reforma. Renting a car in Guatemala is comparatively expensive, however, with rates similar to what you would pay in the United States or Europe. Make sure you understand your insurance coverage before signing any contracts, as liability varies dramatically from one rental company to the next. Some companies, for example, do not provide insurance coverage covering accident damage or towing. You can obtain the names of several reputable agencies that sell comprehensive insurance policies for drivers in Guatemala and Central America from Hertz, Avis, Dollar, and other major car rental chains that have good reputations in the region (see Appendix for a complete list).

Drive defensively in Guatemala City: the locals are aggressive behind the wheel and frequently ignore signs, signals, and even sirens. Stoplights are often turned off at night, and avenida traffic is then given the right of way over calles. Fill your tank before heading out of Guatemala City; gas stations are rare in the countryside. Park your car in a garage or guarded lot (*parqueo* or *estacionamiento*) and remove your valuables, especially at night. Young boys will invariably offer to look after your car when you park in a public place, and refusing their services may be an invitation to vandalism or theft. The prudent course is to appoint one youth to remain on guard and reward him with a modest tip.

Tourist Information

INGUAT has its main office in Zone 4 at the corner of 7a. Avenida and Calle de la Ciudad de Olimpia, near the Civic Center. Telephone 311-333 or 311-347. INGUAT distributes free maps and brochures from 8:30 a.m. to 5:00 p.m. Monday through Friday, 8:00 a.m. to noon Saturday. Questions are answered in Spanish or English (and sometimes other languages) at the information booth on the ground floor.

The Military Geographic Institute (Instituto Geográfico Militar) at Avenida las Américas 5-76 in Zone 13 sells good road maps as well as provincial and topographic maps. Most of the more detailed maps are not for sale but can be inspected at the institute's offices. Photocopies of some are also sold in a few bookstores around the country, notably Casa Andinista in Antigua.

A number of hotel newsstands and large bookstores cater to foreign visitors interested in material on Guatemala. Try the Hotel Camino Real (Avenida de la Reforma and 14a. Calle, Zone 10), Hotel Conquistador Sheraton (Via 5, No. 468, Zone 4), Arnel (9a. Calle and 7a. Avenida, Zone 1), or El Establo (Avenida de la Reforma 14-34, Zone 10). Another good bet is the Libro Club, across from the Hotel Camino Real.

The English-language weekly newspaper *Guatemala News* is published every Friday. The tourist-oriented monthly *Viva Guatemala* and the bimonthly *Enjoying Guatemala*, both in English, are distributed free through hotels and restaurants.

Fiestas and Holidays

The more colorful festivals are held outside the capital, but Guatemala City celebrates the days leading up to Christmas and Easter with much pageantry and celebration. Because Easter falls during the height of the Guatemalan summer, many outdoor fairs are held in the public parks at this time of year. In the weeks leading up to Easter you may also see young men covered from head to foot in green shrouds and wearing black gloves: they are students and political activists who hand out literature and collect donations from drivers during traffic jams.

The capital's annual feast days honoring the Virgen de la Asunción occur August 14-16, with most events scheduled in the city's churches, Hipódromo del Norte, and Jocotenango neighborhood. As one would expect, there are parades, fireworks, and speeches on the various anniversaries of national independence and revolution (see chapter 4).

Banking

Some of the more efficient full-service banks in the capital are the Banco de Guatemala (Centro Cívico, 7a. Avenida, Zone 4), Lloyds Bank (8a. Avenida 10-67, Zone 1), Banco Industrial (7a. Avenida 11-20, Zone 1), and the Banco de Guatemala airport branch, which is usually open on Sundays and holidays. Hours for other banks are generally from 8:00 a.m. to 2:30 p.m., although some offices are open later on weekdays and Saturday mornings. Because Zone 4 is Guatemala City's financial center, banks along its main thoroughfares are fairly efficient in changing foreign currency and similar transactions.

Major credit cards, traveler's checks, and small-denomination U.S. currency are widely accepted in Guatemala City. A fee is often charged for converting traveler's checks or processing of credit cards. There is an American Express office and mail center at the Banco del Café, Avenida de la Reforma 9-00, Zone 9, tel. 311-311. You can draw cash against a credit card there or at Credomatic, 7a. Avenida 6-22 (4th floor) in Zone 9, tel. 317-436.

Telephones and Post Offices

Public telephones are hard to find in Guatemala City, as in the rest of the country. They accept 10- and 25-centavo coins. For long-distance and international calls, try the office of the national phone monopoly, Guatel, where there are more than a dozen phones for walk-in use. Musicians sometimes give impromptu concerts for those standing in line, which can make it hard to hear and be heard. Guatel is at 7a. Avenida and 12a. Calle in Zone 1. International telegrams can be sent from the same location. Collect calls can be made overseas from public phones in the lobbies of the Camino Real, El Dorado, and Conquistador hotels as well as at the airport.

By law, stamps are sold only at post offices. The main one is at 7a. Avenida and 12a. Calle in Zone 1. Domestic telegrams are also sent from there. Hours are 8:00 a.m. to 7:00 p.m. weekdays, 8:00 a.m. to 3:00 p.m. Saturdays. This is the most efficient post office in the country when it comes to sending and receiving overseas packages; look for the English-language parcel post sign in the back on the ground floor. Remember that packages sent to foreign countries must be inspected *before* they are sealed. Stamp collectors can buy packets of Guatemalan stamps at the Filatelica window in the Central Post Office.

Outgoing mail may be sent from a few public postal boxes (look for the *buzón correo*) and most hotel reception desks. There are several private shipping services in Guatemala City that will ship packages overseas; Federal Express, UPS, and DHL are among them.

Camping and Youth Hostels

Camping is not very popular among Guatemalans, and you will find few campgrounds in and around the capital. (In fact, formal campgrounds are pretty much limited to Tikal and a few lakes and beaches.) Try Las Hamacas, a family-oriented place on the outskirts of Guatemala City at Kilometer 32 on the highway to Amatitlán. The moderately priced facility allows a maximum of two children per couple. There is no charge for kids up to 2 years of age, and there is a 25 percent discount for those 12 and under.

If you have a recreational vehicle or travel trailer, some of the larger hotels will allow you to "camp" in their parking lots or at least store your vehicle if you stay in one of their rooms. Trailer parks in the Amatitlán area south of Guatemala City include Auto Mariscos and Le Red, both at Kilometer 33 on the main highway.

Youth hostels do not exist in Guatemala, probably because hotel prices are already so low that nobody sees any advantage in starting one.

What to See and Do
Zone 1
This is the oldest, busiest, and loudest neighborhood in the capital. It is also the most crowded: its cramped streets and narrow sidewalks are jammed with vehicles and pedestrians, particularly during weekday rush hours and weekend nights. The two main, parallel, shopping streets, 6a. and 7a. Avenidas, are lined with stores of every description, although most upscale businesses have relocated to the relative calm of Zone 9 or 10.

A good orientation point is the main plaza, Parque Central, boxed in by 5a. and 6a. Avenidas and 6a. and 8a. Calles. Once the site of a huge public market, the plaza is now a wide and pleasant expanse of grass and monuments above an underground parking lot. The northern side is dominated by the National Palace, an imposing gray-green neoclassic building faced with imitation stone, completed in 1943 to house the offices of the president and executive branch of government. The upper-floor reception halls and a small, unimpressive archaeological museum in the basement are open to the public, as are several inner courtyards and patios. The interior stained-glass and painted murals that tell the story of Guatemalan history are especially impressive. Security at the National Palace is tight, as one would expect, but tourists are welcome. Hours are 8:00 a.m. to 4:30 p.m. Monday through Friday and until noon on Saturday.

On the eastern boundary of the park is Guatemala City's main cathedral (Catedral Metropolitana), one of the few colonial structures in the city not destroyed by earthquakes and well worth a visit. Built between 1782 and 1868, the cathedral blends baroque and neoclassical elements in its regal facade. The interior of the church contains many old paintings and elaborate gold-covered altars, some brought from Antigua when the capital was moved here. Next door is another colonial-era structure, the Archbishop's Palace, noted for its enormous wooden doors. On the opposite side of the plaza from the cathedral is the National Library, a modern structure housing many important documents relating to the history of Guatemala and Central America. Visitors are welcome to use these national archives.

Immediately behind the Cathedral on 8a. Calle (between 7a. and 9a. Avenidas) is the Central Market, moved into a new concrete structure after the 1976 quake. The block-square building has three levels: the top is a parking lot, the middle section a handicraft market, and the basement a food, flower, and general merchandise pavilion. Prices are reasonable, especially for shrewd bargainers. You can buy fine textiles and crafts from all over Guatemala without much competition from other tourists, since they routinely overlook this festive place. There are a number of inexpensive restaurants on the bottom floor.

Northeast of the market are two of the most impressive churches in Guatemala City. La Merced (11a. Avenida and 5a. Calle) is of baroque design and was completed in 1813. It houses a beautiful collection of religious artifacts retrieved from the ruins of colonial Antigua. At the top of a small hill on 11a. Avenida, near 1a. Calle, five blocks east and north of Parque Central, is La Ermita del Carmen, a church and hermitage rebuilt to conform to its seventeenth-century design after the devastating 1917 earthquake. This landmark, perched atop El Cerrito del Carmen, was originally built in 1620—the first church in the valley—and is known for its classic architecture, ornate gold and mahogany altar, lovely gardens, and sweeping view of the city, especially appealing at sunset.

South of Parque Central, in the heart of the claustrophobic 6a. Avenida shopping district at the corner of 13a. Calle, is the glass-domed Church of San Francisco. Parts of this building have survived intact since 1780, and the interior is known for its large wood carving of the Sacred Heart. This, along with some paintings and statues, was salvaged from the 1773 earthquakes in Antigua. One block south of La Iglesia de San Francisco is the police headquarters, located in a bizarre medieval-looking castle decorated with fake battlements.

There are several museums in Zone 1. The National History Museum (9a. Calle 9-70) houses a small collection of colonial furniture, firearms, paintings, and other artifacts. Nearby, at 10a. Avenida 10-72, is the National Museum of Popular Arts and Crafts, with a surprisingly limited collection of traditional Indian textiles and clothing, along with some pottery, jewelry, paintings, and other artwork. If forced to make a choice, you are much better off visiting the private Ixchel Museum in Zone 10 for a more comprehensive overview of Guatemala's handmade textiles. The national museums are open from 9:00 a.m. to noon and 2:00 to 4:00 p.m. daily except Monday for a token admission fee.

Near the boundary with Zone 4 is the Civic Center, a high-rise complex of government ministries and banks dominated by City Hall, known for its famous interior mural entitled *The Mestizo Race of Guatemala*, painted by Carlos Mérida. This a large, bold portrayal of the Ladino history of the country by one of its finest artists.

The Church of La Merced, in the colonial capital of Antigua (Photo by Richard Mahler)

Overlooking the Centro Cívico is the Fortress of San José, an old Spanish battlement containing a small military museum. The fort has been converted into a park, dominated by the strikingly modernistic blue-and-white National Theatre building. Guatemala's National Symphony, Chamber Orchestra, and two ballet companies (one classic, the other folkloric/contemporary) perform here occasionally in one of three auditoriums. A small hill on the theater grounds offers a good view of the city. Unfortunately, this park is locked much of the time, apparently for security reasons.

Hotels and Restaurants: More expensive accommodations in the downtown area include the Hotel Pan American (9a. Calle 5-63, tel. 26-807), located a block west of the Parque Central. This is an elegant, 58-room, older hotel with an excellent restaurant that is open to the public and where you will be served by waiters in Quiché Maya costumes. Regrettably, noise in this busy commercial neighborhood can be a real problem for light sleepers. Another option is the 202-room Ritz Continental (6a. Avenida A 10-13, tel. 81-674, or in the U.S. 402-498-4300), a modern facility with pool, TV, and air conditioning. There are also two restaurants on the premises.

Moderately priced hotels include La Posada Belén, whose helpful owner, Francesca Sanchinelli, speaks fluent English and some French (13a. Calle A 10-30, tel. 513-478). The 10-room hotel is located in an old colonial home on a quiet side street. Meals are available to guests in a dining room lined with antiques and artifacts. This establishment is highly recommended. In the same price range and not far away is the comfortable 42-room Colonial (7a. Avenida 14-19, tel. 22-955), which offers breakfast and some rooms with private baths. The Colonial is also recommended, though located near a busy intersection.

Inexpensive places to stay in Zone 1 include the Chalet Suizo (14a. Calle 6-82, tel. 86-371), a longtime favorite among budget travelers. The rooms—of variable quality—overlook a pleasant interior courtyard. Popular with young foreigners is Hotel Spring (8a. Avenida 12-65, tel. 26-637), a large, older place, where you have a choice of shared or private bath. A third option is the Centenario (6a. Calle 5-33, tel. 80-381), with a dining hall and 42 rather basic rooms.

Besides the hotel restaurants, which are generally very good, there are several other recommended eateries in Zone 1. These include Altuna (5a. Avenida 12-31), specializing in Spanish cuisine; Canton (6a. Avenida 14-20), for reliable Chinese food; Los Cebollines (6a. Avenida 9-75), serving delicious local variants of popular Mexican dishes; and Ranchón Antigüeño (13a. Calle 3-50), with typical Guatemalan food. The best night spot is El Mesón de Don Quijote (11a. Calle 5-22), run by a smiling Spanish expatriate who makes everyone feel welcome. The drinks are cheap, food mediocre, and live music so appallingly bad that it is great fun to listen to. The Gallito, on 9a. Calle between Avenidas 8 and 9, is another longtime favorite, with a huge marimba band and giant dance floor.

Zone 2

A small, older neighborhood that is rather sedate and overlooked, Zone 2 has little to offer the casual visitor except shady Minerva Park, located on the edge of a deep ravine that marks the northern boundary of the capital. Here you can see an enormous three-dimensional relief map of Guatemala, complete with topographically exaggerated mountain ranges, volcanoes, and real water designating the nation's lakes and rivers. If you are the sort of person who gets oriented by looking at maps, it may be helpful to visit at the beginning of your Guatemalan trip. Completed in 1905, this unusual attraction covers nearly 8,000 square feet. Fairs are also held periodically in Minerva Park, which has two public swimming pools and is at the end of Avenida Simeón Cañas.

Zone 4

Acting as a bridge between Guatemala City's "old" and "new," Zone 4 is a mostly commercial area with lots of office buildings, high-rise hotels, modern shopping centers, and only a couple of worthwhile attractions. Foremost among these is La Capilla Yurrita (Ruta 6 at 1a. Calle), a small chapel that looks more like a miniature Russian Orthodox cathedral than the Roman Catholic church that it is. A rich eccentric built this ornate rust-red structure as his private place of worship in 1928, and it was later opened to the public, although hours have always been irregular. The exterior is a mass of fancy grillwork, soaring turrets, and twisting pillars. The inside is like something out of Eastern Europe, with lots of carved woodwork, stained glass, and gilded altars. Sitting inside this neo-Gothic chapel, you would never guess you were in Central America.

Just down the street from La Yurrita (also called Nuestra Señora de las Angustias) Ruta 6 runs into 7a. Avenida, one of Guatemala City's busiest north-south thoroughfares. There are several skyscrapers along this road, notably Edificio El Triángulo (home of Clark Tours) and the Conquistador Sheraton Hotel. A few blocks north is the headquarters of INGUAT, at 7a. Avenida 1-17. Adjacent to the tourist commission is the Olympic City recreation center, where you can sometimes take in a lively soccer match. Most of these sports facilities are closed to nonmembers, however.

A few blocks in the opposite direction, at the corner of 4a. Avenida and 9a. Calle, is one of Guatemala City's largest bus terminals and the adjacent Terminal Market. Both are pretty disorganized, and you will likely have to ask for help to find what you want. Fortunately, most buses to destinations of touristic interest leave from other locations. The market, however, offers some real bargains for those who can put up with the chaotic atmosphere. Sadly, you may also see parrots, turtles, monkeys, and other exotic wildlife being sold illegally, as is the case in large markets throughout Guatemala.

Hotels and Restaurants: At the top of the scale is the Conquistador Sheraton (Via 5 4-68, tel. 364-691 or 312-222, in the U.S. 800-325-3535). This two-tower modern structure offers first-class rooms with private baths, TV, air conditioning, balconies, and, in some cases, complete kitchens. The ground floor is a huge atrium with several restaurants, bars, disco, and gift shop. Several stores, the Kim'Arrin travel agency, and the Edificio Maya office building are also on the Sheraton's bottom level.

More moderate rates are offered two blocks away at the Plaza (Via 7, 6-17, tel. 316-337), a modern but low-key hotel with a full range of services. There are 60 guest rooms, a pool, and meeting facilities.

There are many excellent restaurants to choose from in Zone 4. One of the best is Alicante (7a. Avenida 7-16), specializing in typical dishes of Spain and Guatemala. Prices are low, and there is a pleasant upstairs balcony. Highly recommended.

Franco's, an Italian restaurant (7a. Avenida 4-40) near Alicante, is worth trying, as is the continental, high-priced Las Espadas in the Conquistador Sheraton atrium. The fancy multistory shopping centers along bustling 6a. and 7a. Avenidas, usually overlooked by foreigners, are also a surprising source of good meals. Zone 4 has more than its share of fast-food outlets, too, including the ubiquitous McDonald's, Taco Bell, Burger King, Pizza Hut, and Pollo Campero.

Zone 9

If Zone 4 is the place where wealthy Guatemalans work and run their errands, Zone 9 is where they shop and socialize. The boundary between the two is marked by the Tower of the Reformer, at 7a. Avenida and 2a. Calle. Erected by strong-man President Justo Rufino Barrios to commemorate the liberal coup of 1871 (and his subsequent, activist dictatorship), this imitation Eiffel Tower is capped by a large bell, rung every June 30 to mark the revolution's anniversary. At the southern end of Zone 9 is a monument to Guatemalan independence called El Obelisco, rising high above the intersection of Boulevard Independencia and Avenida de la Reforma.

Of the capital's several main thoroughfares, Reforma is the most scenic. Running parallel and one block east of 7a. Avenida, it is a wide, tree-lined avenue flanked by embassies, luxury apartment buildings, plush restaurants, and deluxe hotels. For strollers, this is the most pleasant boulevard in Guatemala City.

On the top floor of one of the modern office buildings lining Avenida de la Reforma (at 8-16) is the Popol Vuh Museum, which contains a large collection of exquisite pre-Columbian jewelry and artifacts as well as fine colonial art and antiques. A private collector obtained most of these items and was persuaded by the government to set up this museum, operated in association with Francisco Marroquín University. The impressive and nicely displayed holdings include Mayan jade masks and carved stelae, colonial ceramics and religious paintings, figurines, and other priceless treasures. There is also a small but well-stocked gift shop and a library on the premises. None of the displays is marked, so you will need to buy an inexpensive guidebook in addition to paying the small admission fee. Open from 9:00 a.m.

to 5:00 p.m. every day except Sunday. Look for the museum's sign on the ground level facing Avenida de la Reforma. A few blocks farther south, between 10a. and 15a. Calle on either side of Reforma, is an area called La Zona Viva, "the lively zone." The most fashionable stores, restaurants, discos, and nightclubs in Guatemala City are here, under the shadow of the tall Camino Real Hotel, the capital's most deluxe hostelry. It is here that you are most likely to encounter members of the Guatemalan and expatriate elite. Some of the more popular of their hangouts are El Establo, Las Sillas, Mostachon, and Lum's. There are several fine stores selling artesanía in Zone 9; Sombol at Avenida de la Reforma 14-14 is particularly recommended.

Hotels and Restaurants: Expect to pay premium prices for most accommodations in Zone 9. Five-star choices include the El Dorado (7a. Avenida 15-45, tel. 317-777), a big high-rise Americana chain hotel whose rooms offer TV, air conditioning, and other amenities. There is a pool and bar, shopping arcade, and complete fitness center, as well as several restaurants. Somewhat less pricey is the Cortija Reforma (Avenida de la Reforma 2-18, tel. 366-712), a modern sixteen-story hotel with well-appointed three-room suites, each with TV, refrigerator, and balcony. Downstairs there are shops and a lounge but no pool.

The closest thing to moderately priced rooms in Zone 9 are found at the Hotel Villa Española (2a. Calle 7-51, tel. 365-611), a Mediterranean-style structure with courtyard, restaurant, and bar; and the Residencial Carrillón (5a. Avenida 11-25, tel. 324-257), a modern yet small hotel some distance from the Zona Viva. For long-term stays there is Apart-Hotel Alamo (10a. Calle 5-60, tel. 319-817), with rates by the day, week, and month for rooms with kitchens.

Visitors will find a full range of restaurants in Zone 9, ranging from cheap American fast food and Guatemalan cuisine to tony French restaurants and wood-paneled steakhouses. Popular choices include La Miga de Yaacov (7a. Avenida 14-46), a New York-style take-out deli; El Establo (La Reforma 14-36), a book-lined soup and sandwich café; Palacio Royal (7a. Avenida and 11a. Calle), for Chinese fare; seafood specialist Puerto Barrios (across the street from the Palacio); and El Tamal (6a. Avenida 14-49), part of a chain offering low-cost domestic dishes. More expensive choices include Martin's (13a. Calle 7-65), with a varied continental menu; and Pea de los Charangos (6a. Avenida 13-60), known for its large steaks.

Zone 10
Avenida de la Reforma serves as the boundary between Zones 9 and 10, with the latter extending into the fashionable neighborhoods on the east side of this broad, shady thoroughfare.

The Botanical Garden (Avenida de la Reforma at 1a. Calle) is an island of calm in the city's hustle and bustle. It is also an excellent place to see hundreds of the trees, shrubs, and flowers native to Guatemala. Try to stop by before you head for Tikal. The collection is by no means exhaustive, but it provides a good overview of the nation's amazingly diverse flora. Specimens are identified by their Spanish and Latin names only. Open Monday through Friday from 8:00 a.m. to 4:00 p.m., closed December 1 to January 15. Enter on Reforma. The well-landscaped grounds include a small Natural History Museum operated by the University of San Carlos, open weekdays from 8:00 a.m. to noon and 2:00 to 6:00 p.m. It contains some dusty old stuffed birds and other animals indigenous to Guatemala. Admission to both the museum and the garden is free.

Another museum in Zone 10 worth visiting is Museo Ixchel (4a. Avenida 16-27), featuring an excellent collection of thousands of samples of handmade textiles and *traje* (clothing) from throughout Guatemala, including a number of unusual and fascinating ceremonial costumes. Some fine paintings of Indians in their native dress and several nice pieces of jewelry are on display. The history and techniques involved in Guatemala's weaving traditions are explained in illustrations captioned in English and Spanish. There is a small fee to enter this privately owned facility, open from 8:30 a.m. to 5:30 p.m. weekdays, 9:00 a.m. to 1:00 p.m. Saturdays. The group that runs Museo Ixchel funds research on indigenous Guatemalan culture and maintains a small library on the subject. This museum, arguably the best in the entire country, is highly recommended. Books and weavings are also on sale.

For those interested in Mayan archaeology, slide lectures are sometimes given in English by visiting scholars at the larger hotels along Avenida de la Reforma, notably the Camino Real at the intersection of 14a. Calle. As you travel along Reforma you may notice a compound that looks like a poor man's version of a European castle. This is the officers' training school for the Guatemalan military. A few blocks south, also heavily fortified, is the United States Embassy.

Hotels and Restaurants: As in Zone 9, most of the hotels in this area are upmarket. The most popular is El Camino Real (Avenida de la Reforma at 14a. Calle, tel. 681-271, in the U.S. 800-228-3000). A deluxe unit of the Biltmore chain, the Camino Real boasts twin towers with 418 rooms, a number of excellent restaurants, three bars, two pools, several tennis courts, and a gift shop. There is also a disco, a health club, and a conference center. You can make reservations here for luxurious Biltmore-owned hotels on the Caribbean coast and near Tikal.

A smaller high-rise with a less sterling reputation is the Guatemala Fiesta (1a. Avenida 13-22, tel. 322-555 or 322-888). It is quieter than the Camino Real and costs about the same. Besides the usual bar, pool, and disco, the 125-room Fiesta has a large conference center.

More moderately priced are the Moorish-looking Residencial Reforma/La Casa Grande (Avenida de la Reforma 7-67, tel. 310-907 or 365-723), a converted mansion near the U.S. Embassy that offers good food and elegant quarters; and the Alameda Guest House (4a. Avenida 14-10, tel. 680-152), another remodeled home, with 7 charming rooms that share baths.

Among the better Guatemalan handicraft stores in this district are Bizarro (1a. Avenida 13-68) and Colección 21 (13a. Calle 2-75).

Dining options in Zone 10 are too numerous to mention. It is hard to go wrong in this part of town, although the prices are often comparable to those found in the United States and Europe. Popular and recommended are Estro Armónico (15a. Calle 1-11) and Le Rendezvous (13a. Calle 2-55) for French food; Hacienda de los Sánchez (12a. Calle 2-10) for steaks; Los Antojitos (Avenida de la Reforma 15-02) for Guatemalan dishes; and Samba (1a. Avenida and 13a. Calle) for

Brazilian cuisine. The restaurants in the area's hotels, as in Zone 9, are of consistently high quality.

Zone 13

This zone incorporates the airport neighborhood of Guatemala City, immediately south of Zones 9 and 10. The constant takeoffs and landings of jet aircraft make this an extremely noisy area but one worth visiting to take in the several national museums located in Aurora Park, just across 11a. Avenida from the international terminal.

The Museum of Archaeology and Ethnology has a very good collection of Mayan artifacts, including a scale model of Tikal and a vast collection of stelae and incense burners collected from various ruins around the country. A visit to this museum is highly recommended before you head for Guatemala's various archaeological sites. There is also an interesting display of Indian culture that includes many traditional masks and costumes. Unfortunately, as in most Guatemalan museums, the exhibits are not well marked and what little information is presented is mostly in Spanish. If you can read only English, you may get more out of a visit by going with a knowledgeable tour guide, available in the museum lobby, through a local travel agency, or larger hotels. There is a small admission fee for the museum, open Tuesday through Friday from 9:00 a.m. to 4:30 p.m., Saturdays and Sundays from 9:00 a.m. to noon and 2:00 to 4:30 p.m.

Directly across the street from the archaeology museum is the Museum of Modern Art. Despite its name, the collection includes paintings and other artwork produced by Guatemalans over the past two centuries. Except for some large murals, there is not much here that is particularly memorable. The art collection has the same hours as the Museum of Archaeology and Ethnology, with an equally minuscule admission charge.

The third state institution in the Aurora Park complex is the Natural History Museum, offering a surprisingly limited assortment of preserved birds and animals as well as some crystals and other stones. The hours and admission fee are as listed above.

Also in Aurora Park, at the intersection of Boulevard Aeropuerto and 6a. Calle, is the Artisans' Market (Mercado de Artesanías), which displays and sells folk art and craftwork from all areas of the coun-

A ceramic artist makes vases in his Totonicapán studio (Photo by INGUAT)

try. You can get a good overview of what is available in the rest of Guatemala, although prices tend to be higher than at other public markets and the merchandise tends to be touristy. There is a cafeteria here, and marimba concerts are held daily. Hours are 9:00 a.m. to 6:00 p.m. Monday through Saturday, 9:00 to noon on Sunday.

At the far end of the park is the pleasant and worthwhile Guatemala Zoological Garden, recently refurbished and expanded. Unlike those in many zoos, the birds and animals here seem well cared for, and their cages are fairly large. There are lots of shade trees and snack vendors, plus rides for the kids. On weekends the zoo and the rest of Aurora Park is often crowded with families taking in the sights, having picnics, and generally enjoying each other's company. Admission is less than a dollar.

Kaminal Juyú

Overlooked by most visitors to Guatemala City is one of the oldest archaeological sites in Central America. Located on a broad plain in Zone 7, a few miles west of downtown, Kaminal Juyú was inhabited about 2,300 years ago by an ancient and little-known people called the Miraflores, who, like the Maya, were apparently ruled by a powerful religious royalty. The Miraflores tribe was conquered by the pre-

Classic era Teotihuacán of central Mexico, who themselves became dominated by the highland Maya. The city was abandoned, rebuilt, destroyed, and again abandoned about A.D. 900. It was first excavated in 1899. Since then some two hundred mounds have been found, containing temple pyramids, altars, stelae, and various other structures. An estimated 3,000 to 5,000 people lived here during the Miraflores period, many of them probably supported by the trading of cacao beans collected nearby.

Excavation work continues here intermittently, and the site (reached by bus, car, or taxi) may now be toured only with prior permission from the Instituto de Antropología e Historia (Institute of Anthropology and History). Their office is in Zone 1 at 12a. Avenida 11-65 (tel. 531-570). Officials will ask why you wish to visit Kaminal Juyú, and it is usually sufficient to explain that you are a foreign visitor with an interest in the region's archaeology. After issuing a permit, the institute will arrange to have the gates to the site unlocked and may provide an escort.

Kaminal Juyú is unlike the Mayan ruins most visitors are accustomed to. The aboveground site looks like unconsolidated heaps of clay and limestone rubble, covered with large expanses of galvanized steel designed to ward off the elements. Only some statuary and a few stelae are recognizable as ancient artifacts. Underneath the site, however, one finds a maze of passageways leading into dark burial tombs and temple chambers adorned with hieroglyphics and sacrificial altars. (Be sure to bring candles or a flashlight.) The skeletal remains of an adult and a child can still be seen in one subterranean location, although the jade jewelry, sculpture, and ceramic artifacts for which Kaminal Juyú is best known have been removed by archaeologists to far-flung museums or crushed by construction equipment. Looters have absconded with much of the rest.

Experts believe that the city was built during a peaceful time because of its relatively indefensible position on a broad platform of land (this despite Kaminal Juyú's name, which translates as Hill of the Dead). Researchers have concluded that most of the Guatemalan highlands people were in a state of nearly constant warfare after A.D. 1000, by which time Kaminal Juyú had been long abandoned.

Although Kaminal Juyú is now under the protection of the Guatemalan government, its temple and burial mounds are threatened by encroaching development. In fact, most of this ancient ceremonial center has been destroyed during the past thirty years to make way for apartment buildings and commercial structures. The ruins are just west of the intersection of Diagonal 24 and 24a. Avenida in the northwest quadrant of the city. The 16-BC/Kaminal Juyú bus goes directly past the site. You can board a bus at 6a. Avenida and 6a. Calle for the 20-minute trip.

Day Trips from Guatemala City

Lake Amatitlán
Not to be confused with the much larger Lake Atitlán in the western highlands, this beautiful body of water is nestled in the mountains directly north of the Pacaya volcano, about 20 miles (40 minutes) south of the capital on the highway to the Pacific, Route CA-9. The narrow, irregularly shaped lake is about 8 miles long and 3 miles wide, with the small sugar- and coffee-processing town of Amatitlán at its western tip. This is a largely Cakchiquel-speaking community that produced red cochineal dye during the colonial era. Lining the lake's shoreline are a number of vacation homes and cabins used by Guatemalan families who come here on holidays and weekends.

From a distance, Lake Amatitlán looks like a real gem. There are often sailboats and waterskiers skimming along its sparkling surface, and the cottages along its banks are embraced by lush vegetation. A close look reveals that the lake has become woefully polluted. A large power plant chugs away on its shoreline, and litter is scattered around much of its perimeter. An unsightly railroad bridge crosses the lake's midsection.

Despite these blemishes, Lake Amatitlán makes a pleasant day trip. After a scenic drive around the lake, you can take an aerial tramway from Las Ninfas National Park on the southern shore up the steep mountainside to United Nations Park, where there are fine hiking trails and panoramic views. Horses and mules can be rented for

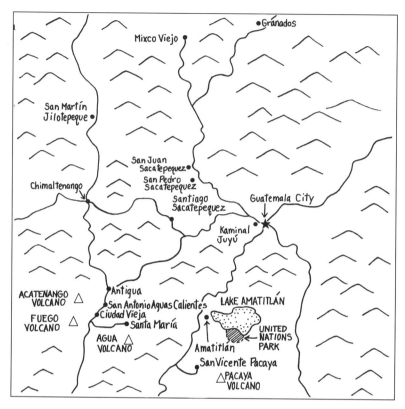

Antigua and Guatemala City

rides through the countryside. The nearly vertical slope above the lake is ideal for hang gliding, and competitions are held here from time to time. The tramway is open from 10:00 a.m. to 1:00 p.m. on weekends.

There are only a few beaches on the lake itself where the water *may* be clean enough for swimming, although the pollution seems to be getting worse. Try the public beach near the town of Amatitlán, where you can also rent a rowboat or take a guided water tour. There are several privately owned pools and bathhouses (*balnearios*) at various geothermal hot springs in the area. A small Mayan ruin lies about 2 miles east of Amatitlán. The ancient Indians considered this a sacred place, and pots and urns that contained their ceremonial offerings are still being retrieved from the bottom of the lake by divers.

The town's feast days are May 3 and June 29, when visitors flock to the sixteenth-century church housing Niño de Atocha, a sacred statue said to possess miraculous powers.

About 10 miles southwest of the lake, off the main road to Escuintla, is the San Pedro Mártir cave complex, noted for its underground river and waterfall. Because of the chamber's unusual twisted shape, the subterranean stream appears to be flowing backward.

There are a number of restaurants around Lake Amatitlán, but you are advised not to eat any fish caught here because of the polluted water. Overnight visitors can find basic rooms at the Blanquita Hotel, Pensión Karla, or Hospedaje Kati. There are several campgrounds and trailer parks on the main road between Lake Amatitlán and Guatemala City. Others are found along the highway to Escuintla and the access road to United Nations Park.

Buses leave Guatemala City for Lake Amatitlán about every half hour from the terminal at 20a. Calle and 3a. Avenida, Zone 1.

Pacaya Volcano

On a clear day, steamy Pacaya volcano is clearly visible from Guatemala City. Rising to an altitude of 8,420 feet, this is one of three Guatemala volcanoes currently considered active. Pacaya has two cones, and the newer one occasionally spews ash, steam, and lava. This is an awesome sight, especially at night.

It is possible to travel by car via the town of San Vicente Pacaya to San Francisco, the village closest to Pacaya, then climb the peak and return to Guatemala City all in the same day. Unless you wish to start out early in the morning, however, it may be easier to spend the preceding night at one of the campgrounds or small hotels near Lake Amatitlán or to camp on the volcano itself.

There are three main trails to the higher peak of Pacaya, each route a fairly easy climb of about an hour and 45 minutes. Return time is about an hour.

As of late 1992, hikers were being urged to use extreme caution on Pacaya. A handful of foreigners have been robbed, beaten, and even murdered along the trail in recent years, and security remains a serious problem. The services of a knowledgeable guide are advised: check with a local travel agency specializing in adventure trips for a recommendation.

Those who decide to make the trek should be in good shape; a few climbers have suffered heart attacks. Check with authorities before starting out, to learn about possible eruptions if nothing else. (Pacaya has been continuously active since the mid-1960s.) For more details and suggestions about climbing this and other volcanoes, see chapters 12 and 13.

Santiago, San Juan, and San Pedro Sacatepéquez

These three small towns, located between 14 and 20 miles northwest of the capital, have the largest Indian populations in the department of Guatemala, the jurisdiction that includes the capital. The Sacatepéquez trio lies in a rich agricultural region interspersed with thick pine forests. When the Spanish arrived, this area was occupied by the Sacatepéquez Indians. Hence the name. Most residents still speak the Cakchiquel language of their ancestors.

San Pedro, the smallest of the communities, is the first you will enter en route from Guatemala City. The huipiles and other textiles woven here are particularly well made and colorful. Friday's market is the best time to find them. Fiesta day is June 29.

Surrounding San Juan, 4 miles past San Pedro, are terraced gardens of produce, sold in the capital, and greenhouses of flowers (mostly carnations), exported overseas by air. The purple and yellow huipiles of the community are very beautiful; some bear representations of two-headed eagles and horses. They can be purchased at the Friday and Sunday markets. June 24 is the annual feast day. A dirt road continues across the barren mountains north of San Juan Sacatepéquez to the ruins of Mixco Viejo.

About 6 miles southwest of San Pedro, north of the Pan American Highway and along the branch road to Antigua, is Santiago Sacatepéquez. This town is noted for its unique All Saints' Day celebration on November 1. Besides the traditional candles and gifts of food left in the community cemetery, the men of Santiago fly huge multicolored circular kites (*barriletes*) made of reed or bamboo sticks and painted paper. Each 9-foot kite is of intricate design and may take months to construct. If the kite begins falling apart after a few crashes, the paper is burned off so that the frame can be covered with a new sheet that will be decorated for the following year. The barriletes are flown as a way of sending messages of comfort, devotion, and affection to the spirits of the dead.

All of these towns can be reached by public buses that leave several times a day from the Zone 4 terminal in Guatemala City.

Mixco Viejo Ruins

Located about 40 miles northwest of Guatemala City near the Motagua River, these excavated ruins squat in an arid, moonlike landscape across a series of barren hilltops. The Mixco Viejo archaeological site is a 1-hour drive beyond San Juan Sacatepéquez at the bottom of the river valley.

The dusty ruins date from about A.D. 1300 and have been badly damaged over the intervening years by Spanish conquistadors, vandals, erosion, and earthquakes. Partial restoration has been carried out by France's Museum of Man and other academic institutions. Entering the ancient city by a single-file causeway, you can still see a number of temples, ball courts, altars, and observation platforms. One unusual aspect of the site is the absence of burial tombs, which suggests that bodies were cremated, an unheard of practice among the highland Maya.

Mixco Viejo, with its twelve pyramid groupings, was the capital of the Pokomán, one of the many warring Maya tribes of pre-Columbian Guatemala. Surrounded by steep ravines, the city is believed to have been home to about 9,000 Indians when Pedro de Alvarado laid siege to Mixco Viejo for three months in 1525. The Spaniards used trickery, stealth, and starvation to finally storm the fortress, massacre its defenders, and relocate survivors to the new town of Mixco, now a suburb of the capital, where a few people still speak the Pokomán dialect.

You can drive to the site from Guatemala City or Antigua in about 2 hours or take a long bus ride to Pachalum on Route 2 which will pass by the entrance to the ruins. Ask the driver or ticket agent to make sure your bus passes the *ruinas*, as some Pachalum buses do not. Several Guatemala City tour operators offer day trips to Mixco Viejo at reasonable rates (see chapter 13).

Camping is allowed at any of the thatched shelters of Mixco Viejo, but you will need to bring your own food and water. Drinks and snacks are sometimes sold here during the day. There is very little traffic to these remote ruins, and you are likely to have them to yourself much, if not all, of the time.

Antigua

History

Originally called Santiago de los Caballeros de Guatemala (Saint James of the Noblemen of Guatemala), Antigua served as Guatemala's capital for more than two centuries after its founding in 1543. The first seat of government had been established by the Spanish conquerer Pedro de Alvarado in 1524 near the Cakchiquel capital of Iximché but was moved after an Indian revolt in 1527 to the lush Almolonga Valley. The site of Ciudad Vieja was the unstable lower slope of the Agua volcano, a few miles south of present-day Antigua. In 1541, only a few days after word arrived from Mexico of Pedro de Alvarado's death there, the new capital was wiped out by a giant mudslide after a volcanic eruption loosened a natural dam below Agua's summit. The facade of Ciudad Vieja's seventeenth-century cathedral is the only structure remaining from the colonial period. Across the plaza stands a gnarled old tree beneath which the first Guatemalan mass was recited in about 1530.

The third capital was rebuilt in a flatter and presumably safer location in the center of the Almolonga Valley, still beneath the shadow of Agua and its taller volcanic neighbors: Acatenango and Fuego. Despite occasional droughts, epidemics, temblors, and eruptions, the new Antigua grew and prospered. By the mid-eighteenth century the city was home to about 70,000 people—almost triple its 1992 population—and was envied throughout the Americas for its gracious living, talented artisans, elegant estates, fine university, walled convents, stone monasteries, and ornate churches. The construction of the streets and avenues of Antigua began at the Plaza Real (now Parque Central) and moved out to the four cardinal directions. The symmetrical design of the city resembles a chessboard, and it is considered one of the better planned cities of Spanish America.

Domes of the Espíritu Santo Cathedral in Quetzaltenango (Photo by INGUAT)

Excellent examples of centuries-old colonial architecture still exist in Antigua, typified by arabesques and stucco latticework, along with wrought iron balconies and window framing. Many structures were reduced to hollow shells by a series of devastating earthquakes that occurred between 1558 and 1773 and, by decree and popular sentiment, never rebuilt. The destruction wrought by the 1773 catastrophe was so complete that a decision was made to move the capital once again, to the tiny farming village that has become Guatemala City.

Ignoring many official orders, hundreds of families refused to abandon the ruins of Antigua, and the city was eventually revived and granted special status by the federal government as a national cultural monument, despite continuing damage inflicted by major earthquakes as recently as 1976.

During the past century, Antigua has been fragrantly enclosed by lush plantations of coffee, macadamia nuts, peppers, oranges, and roses. The city is also a food and furniture manufacturing center and hosts as many as a thousand Spanish students each month in more than sixty language schools. Many of Guatemala's finest artists, writers, and craftspeople make Antigua their home.

Antigua enchants visitors with its narrow cobblestone streets, tree-shaded parks, imposing religious monuments, and old colonial buildings. Many of the latter are false fronts, protected from deliberate destruction by the same strict architectural laws that forbid overhanging signs, garish advertising, and high-rise buildings. A number of structures have been lovingly restored to their original beauty, while others have been taken over by shopkeepers and homesteaders. Some have been modified for use as public buildings or open-air markets. Earthquakes still rumble, and the nearby volcanoes sometimes spew steam, ash, and lava from their peaks, but the *Antigüeños* have learned to take it all in stride.

Today there are about 28,000 permanent residents, including a growing number who commute daily to jobs in Guatemala City, less than an hour away. A number of American and European retirees and expatriates have settled here, giving the town a cosmopolitan feel.

Antigua is a tranquil, laid-back place, ideal for recharging one's batteries after hectic bus rides through the highlands or hot pilgrimages to Tikal and Copán. It is clean and quiet compared to most Guatemalan cities, with some of the best restaurants and hotels in the country. Because of its small size and orderly layout, Antigua is best seen on foot or by bicycle. Horses can also be rented. Wandering among its impeccably restored colonial mansions, churches, and public buildings is like being transported in a time machine back to the days when this was the affluent cultural, religious, economic, and political capital of a powerful empire that stretched from Chiapas to Panama.

Its congenial atmosphere, central location, and fine services make Antigua an excellent base for excursions to Quetzaltenango, Chichicastenango, Lake Atitlán, Iximché, and other recommended destinations in the western highlands. Some travelers start feeling a bit claustrophobic here after a while, though, and it does not take long to see the danger of Antigua becoming perhaps too quaint and precious for its own good. If nothing else, the presence of so many foreigners has succeeded in driving rents and real estate prices up to American standards. Still, this is one of the best places in all of Central America to stroll, study, and shop, particularly for fine textiles, ceramics, and jewelry. Antigua can best be viewed from the summit of La Candelaria Hill, at the north end of the city via Calle de la

Nobleza, but inquire locally before heading here because street crime is sometimes a problem.

Orientation

Antigua is a quick drive or bus ride from Guatemala City, a distance of about 45 miles. Take the Pan American Highway west of the capital to the Antigua turnoff and then along a paved two-lane road that winds through steep canyons and thick forests. (Coming from the opposite direction on the Pan American Highway, watch for the sign in Chimaltenango directing you southeast into the Almolonga Valley.) At 5,000 feet, Antigua is slightly higher than Guatemala City and a bit cooler. After spending any length of time in the energetic capital, first-time visitors will find Antigua positively provincial and serene. It is a conservative town in both temperament and politics, and the commitment to tradition is much more than a ploy for tourist dollars.

Antigua was laid out by the Spanish in a classic grid pattern around a main plaza, the Parque Central, with calles running east-west and avenidas extending north-south. The zone system was never adopted here, but the town is small enough that finding your way around is not much of a problem. As in Guatemala City's Zone 1, streets here are identified by both their original colonial names and a modern numbering sequence. Some streets (and most maps) have signs with one designation or the other but seldom both. Unfortunately, a healthy percentage of intersections have no signs at all, and many buildings have no visible numbers.

Walking-tour maps are available from the INGUAT office (5a. Calle, tel. 320-763) on the ground floor of the Palace of the Captains-General on the south side of the main plaza. The countrywide tourist map has a detail of Antigua's streets. A stop at the INGUAT office at the start of your visit is highly recommended: the efficient, informed, English-speaking staff will help you find a hotel or a private room with a family, dispense restaurant and touring suggestions and information on language schools, and answer any other questions you might have. INGUAT is open daily from 8:00 a.m. to noon and 2:00 to 6:00 p.m. Excellent tourist information is also dispensed in English and other languages at Guatemalan Adventures next door to

Restaurante Doña Luisa at 4a. Calle Oriente 12A.

If you are going to be in Antigua for a while, it is helpful to have one of the more detailed guidebooks to the city. A good summary is found in the widely distributed brochure *Guide to Antigua* by Lynn Durán, but a more thorough treatment, with extensive maps and history, is found in *Antigua Guatemala*, by Elizabeth Bell and Trevor Long. *Antigua For You*, by longtime Guatemala resident Barbara Balchin de Koose, is the most thorough and up-to-date city guide. It was published in 1992 and is widely sold in Antigua and Guatemala City. If you can find a copy, the out-of-print *Antigua Guatemala: City and Area Guide* by local author Mike Shawcross is also excellent. An alternative to reading about the city is hiring a knowledgeable local guide through INGUAT, a travel agency, or a hotel.

What to See and Do in Antigua

As its Spanish founders intended, the Parque Central (Central Park) remains the heart of daily life in Antigua. Until the early 1900s this rectangle of land was an empty expanse of dirt—the site of a daily market as well as public fairs, proclamations, hangings, floggings, and even bullfights. The Fountain of the Mermaids at the center of the park was built in 1793 by Diego de Porres. The market was eventually moved out, however, and trees were planted and permanent walkways laid down. Today the Parque Central is a lovely place to sit and read, practice Spanish with a friend, or simply watch street performers and the passing parade of humanity. It is also a perfect place to begin a walking tour of Antigua.

The layout of buildings around the park reflects strict conformity with colonial traditions: the various institutions of secular and religious power face off against each other on their own "turf" along each side of the Parque.

Looming over the eastern boundary of 4a. Avenida (Calle de Obispo Marroquín) are the ruins of Antigua's original cathedral (built in 1545) and the restored Church of San José, formed by merging the two chapels left standing after the 1773 earthquakes. The impressive interior of San José (also called Metropolitan) features seventeenth-century ornaments and a magnificent carved figure of Christ by Quirio Cataño, the celebrated artist who also sculpted the renowned Black Christ of Esquipulas. Although the reference is not technically correct, this modified church is now popularly called La Catedral. Somewhere beneath the adjacent ruins are the tombs of Spanish conqueror Pedro de Alvarado and his wife Beatriz, along with the first bishop of Antigua and other distinguished citizens.

The entire south side of the plaza is taken up by the Palace of the Captains-General, seat of the colonial bureaucracy, first built in 1558 and restored in its present form after 1773. The facade of the two-story palacio is a series of twenty-seven consecutive archways running the length of the block. The building now houses the police department and tourist information center as well as offices for the department of Sacatepéquez, of which Antigua is the capital. Visitors are welcome to tour the interior courtyard and second-floor public rooms.

Facing the palace on the north end of the plaza is the solid-looking Ayuntamiento (City Hall), built of thick adobe in 1740 to house the municipal government and prison. The city offices are still there—note the coat of arms hanging out front—but the jail has been turned into the Museo de Santiago, which displays paintings, cannons, and other artifacts from the colonial period. It is open daily from 9:00 a.m. to noon and 2:00 to 6:00 p.m. for a nominal admission fee. Next door is the Museo del Libro Antiguo, operating with the same hours. This "old book" museum contains examples of centuries-old printing and paper-making processes. It was in these rooms that the first Central American printing press began operating in the 1660s. A replica of Guatemala's first book is on display here.

Finally, on the west side of the Parque Central, is a long *portal* (covered walkway) where vendors often sell fruit, candy, art objects, and souvenirs. The buildings behind them, representing the commercial face of secular society, are occupied by restaurants, bookstores, a pharmacy, and a travel agency.

West of the Parque

If you come to Antigua by bus, you will be let off at the terminal on the western edge of the city, at the foot of 4a. Calle Poniente (Calle del Ayuntamiento), 3 blocks west of Parque Central. Daily buses leave here for Guatemala City (every 45 minutes during daylight hours),

The monument to Rafael Landivar, one of colonial Guatemala's greatest poets, located near his home in Antigua (Photo by Richard Mahler)

Chimaltenango (with connections to the western highlands), Escuintla (with Pacific Coast connections), and nearby villages. Departing buses line up along 4a. Calle all the way to 8a. Avenida (Alameda Santa Lucía) and sometimes around the corner in front of the Pollo Campero restaurant, where you can also find taxis.

Across from the buses along the north side of 4a. Calle is the public market, selling everything from fruits and vegetables to handmade textiles and inexpensive jewelry. The market operates every day, but there tend to be more vendors on Mondays, Thursdays, and Saturdays. The selection is fairly extensive, and prices (with hard bargaining) are reasonable.

Opposite the mercado and around the corner on 8a. Avenida is the baroque Monument to Rafael Landívar, a colonial Jesuit poet who died in Italy in 1793, twenty-six years after all Jesuit priests were expelled from the Americas on orders of the Spanish king, who felt they were becoming too powerful. Landívar's beautiful Antigua home is behind the monument on 5a. Calle Poniente. Nearby, at Calle Recoletos 55 (near Alameda Santa Lucía), is Casa K'ojom, a private music museum with an excellent collection of native instruments and folkloric recordings. There are daily tours at 10:30 a.m. and occasional concerts in the evening. The museum and gift shop are open every day except Sunday from 9:30 a.m. to 12:30 p.m. and 2:30 to 6:00 p.m. (tel. 323-087). Following the street in the opposite direction, 2 blocks west of Parque Central at 7a. Avenida, one passes the ruins of the Iglesia de San Agustín, a convent destroyed by the quakes of 1773 and never rebuilt.

North of the market and bus terminal, at the corner of 8a. Avenida and Calle de la Recolección, are the ruins of the Iglesia de San Jerónimo, a large church and religious school built in 1739 and once used as a customshouse. Next to San Jerónimo are the magnificent ruins of San José de Recolección, built in 1701, from which there are good views of all three of the nearby volcanoes.

Walking back to Parque Central on 4a. Calle Poniente, you pass the ruins of La Compañía de Jesús at the corner of 6a. Avenida. Completed in 1626, the crumbling brick walls of this Jesuit-run church and monastery housed Antigua's public market until the 1976 earthquake sent tons of debris crashing down. Many of the stalls have since been taken over by vendors selling inexpensive and unremarkable artesanía to tourists.

North of the Parque
Heading north from Parque Central on 5a. Avenida Norte (Calle de Santa Catalina), you will pass many of Antigua's best restaurants and most fashionable shops, passing under the arch of Santa Catalina, which is all that remains of a convent built here in 1609. The arch was constructed in 1697 so that nuns could walk from one convent building to another without being seen by the public. This is a favorite spot for photographers, who can frame Agua volcano within the bow of the arch on a clear day.

A half block northward, 5a. Avenida dead-ends at 1a. Calle (Calle de la Real Aduana). Turn west (left) at this intersection, and you will run into the church of La Merced, one of the most impressive religious buildings in Guatemala. A huge structure with an ornate Churrigueresque facade, La Merced has suffered little earthquake damage and has been in almost continuous use since its construction in the late 1760s. The baroque cloisters, fountains, and gardens next to the church did not fare so well, however, and mostly lie in rubble. There is a small fee for visiting the interior rooms and open ramparts, from which there is a nice panorama. The convent fountain is considered the most sumptuous in the city. La Merced houses an enormous wooden carving of the Virgin Mary and a splendid image of Jesus Nazareno carved by Alonzo de Paz in 1650. The latter is paraded through the streets of Antigua every Palm Sunday. In front of La Merced is a lovely park with several tall shade trees.

Walking back toward the Parque, at the corner of 1a. Calle Oriente (Calle de Platerías) and 4a. Avenida Norte (Calle del Obispo Marroquín), you will pass the convent of Santa Teresa. Built centuries ago by a Lima philanthropist to house Peruvian nuns, it now functions as the city jail. Two blocks farther south, on 3a. Calle Oriente (Calle de los Carros) are the ruins of El Carmen, a church built in 1638 that completely collapsed during the 1976 earthquake.

Two blocks to the east, at 2a. Avenida Norte (Calle de Capuchinas) and 2a. Calle Oriente (Calle de Santo Domingo), is the church and convent of Las Capuchinas, dating from 1736. Also called the convent of Zaragoza, this is one of the largest and best preserved of Antigua's colonial buildings, with eighteen nunnery cells extant and a curious two-story circular Retreat Tower (looming above a round courtyard). The convent, which originally housed Capuchin nuns from Madrid, was considered opulent in its day, boasting a sewage system, running water, and private toilets.

East of the Parque
The great colonial schools of Antigua were built immediately southeast of the plaza, facing the cathedral. Across 5a. Calle Oriente (Calle de la Universidad) from the church is the Seminario Tridentino, a seminary built in the early 1700s that is now used as private residences. It is one of the few buildings to survive Antigua's many earthquakes unscathed. Next door is the University of San Carlos, founded in 1681 as Guatemala's first public college (the third-oldest in the Americas). The school was eventually moved to Guatemala City, and this building now houses the Museum of Colonial Art. The

collection mostly consists of religious paintings, along with some carved wooden saints (*santos*) and depictions of student life in early Antigua.

Continuing east of the Parque on 5a. Calle Oriente, between 2a. and 1a. Avenidas Sur, is the Bernal Díaz del Castillo House. Castillo was a soldier who served under Alvarado during the conquests of Guatemala and Mexico. Dissatisfied with official accounts of those campaigns, he wrote his own critically acclaimed versions after retiring here.

At the corner of 5a. Calle Oriente and 1a. Avenida Sur is La Casa Popanoe, a wonderfully and authentically restored colonial mansion full of antiques and artifacts collected by its expatriate owners. Wilson Popanoe, a North American botanist who died in 1972, left explicit orders that his home be kept open to the public part-time. As of late 1992, it was open from 2:00 to 4:00 p.m. Monday through Saturday, except holidays.

The Church and Monastery of San Francisco is 2 blocks away on 1a. Avenida Sur (Calle de la Nobleza) at 7a. Calle Oriente (Calle de Chipilapa al Pensativo). Construction of a huge religious center was begun here in 1579 by Franciscan friars, but earthquakes wreaked havoc over the centuries, and it was not until 1960 that any significant restoration work was started. Not everyone in Antigua likes the idea of pressing ruined churches back into service, but that is exactly what has been done at San Francisco, and the visual results are splendid. Fray Pedro de Bethancourt, founder of Antigua's colonial hospital, is buried in the Chapel of the Third Order, rebuilt next to the main church in 1817.

Also on the east side of town, on 6a. Calle Oriente (Calle de los Peregrinos) near 2a. Avenida Sur (Calle de Santa Clara), is the Church and Convent of Santa Clara, founded by Mexican nuns in 1699 and rebuilt after a 1717 quake. The exterior walls are very ornate, and there is a large courtyard in the building's interior. Daughters of the most affluent families of colonial Antigua often spent time here, apparently praying and meditating in considerable comfort.

The Mesoamerican Regional Investigations Center (Centro de Investigaciones Regionales de Mesoamérica) maintains an excellent library and photo collection at 5a. Calle Oriente 5. The facility is open to the public Monday through Friday from 9:00 a.m. to 5:00 p.m. and Saturday until noon.

South of the Parque

The southern quadrant of Antigua contains a number of churches— several in ruins but most still functional—and twelve small crumbling chapels representing the Stations of the Cross. They culminate at the far end of town at El Calvario, a formidable-looking church kept in daily use. There is a beautiful carved fountain outside El Calvario, next to a small tree-shaded plaza.

Walking directly south of Parque Central on 5a. Avenida Sur (Calle de la Sin Ventura) you pass the haunting ruins of the Hermitage of San José el Viejo, completed in 1761. This baroque church, in ruins for over two hundred years now, was built to house an image of Saint James, Antigua's patron, carved by sculptor Alonso de la Paz. It is between 9a. Calle Poniente and 7a. Calle Poniente.

One of the few reminders of "ordinary" life in colonial Antigua is the Pila de la Unión, a public clothes-washing basin on 2a. Avenida Sur that has been used continuously, in one form or another, since 1553. It was given its name in 1920 in tribute to Central America's labor movement. Indian women can be seen scrubbing their clothes here by hand, as their maternal forebears have done for centuries.

Holidays and Fiestas in Antigua

The week before Easter, Semana Santa, is like no other in Antigua, or anywhere else in Latin America. For 7 days, the streets are filled with religious processions and spiritual pageantry, as hundreds of men, women, and children don multicolored robes and costumes to carry enormous Catholic icon platforms (*andas*) across carpets (*alfombras*) made of pine needles, hand-dyed sawdust, and flower petals. Some of the andas weigh several tons; all are carried by hand. They are followed by orchestras and men burning containers of copal incense. Early in the week the churches of Antigua are filled with pilgrims attending solemn prayer vigils. Events reach a climax on the morning of Good Friday with a reenactment of Pontius Pilate and his Roman soldiers arresting and condemning Christ, then leading him to his crucifixion, as a marching band plays funereal music behind

Carpets of flowers and colored sawdust decorate the cobblestone streets of Antigua during Holy Week (Photo by Richard Mahler)

them and clouds of incense fill the air. The procession always stops in front of the city jail, where one or two prisoners are chosen to join the spirtual quest and shoulder crosses heavy with chains. The custom dates back to the seventeenth century, when all the cell doors of the old prison are said to have miraculously opened as the procession passed by.

Antigua's population sometimes swells to 80,000 or more people during Holy Week, and wary visitors make room reservations as much as a year in advance. Most hotels (illegally) increase their rates, sometimes charging twice the standard fee. For those who have not made advance bookings, or would just as soon avoid the crowds, a practical option is to stay in Guatemala City and commute to Antigua for the various Semana Santa processions, which last 6 hours or more. Another idea is to rent a room in a private home, something that is also best arranged in advance. Antigua's INGUAT office and larger language schools can help in this regard.

If your visit to Guatemala coincides with Holy Week, you should plan to spend at least one full day observing the Antigua celebration, exceeded in size and scope only by the Semana Santa festivities of Seville in Spain. The days with the largest processions in Antigua are, in descending order of size, Good Friday, Palm Sunday, and Holy Thursday. For a more thorough description of Semana Santa, see the aforementioned Antigua guidebooks or any of the local English-language weekly newspapers, such as the *Antigua Times* and *The Classifieds*, which publish a detailed rundown of events. Processions start at main churches throughout the city, including La Merced and San Francisco, but times and routes change slightly from year to year. There are similar religious processions during the Lenten season, the festival of Corpus Christi, and the weeks leading up to Christmas.

Other important fiestas are held in Antigua on July 25 (the feast day of St. James), All Saints' Eve and Day, and All Souls' Day (October 31-November 2).

Shopping

Shopping for handmade textiles, ceramic pottery, wood products, and jewelry in Antigua is recommended. You will almost certainly find lower prices farther away from tourist areas like this, but the selection and quality are likely to be much more limited, although the public markets of Quetzaltenango and Guatemala City are both very good.

Several shops in Antigua are set up to maximize profits and support for the Indian craftworkers whose work they sell. For example, Ojalá (4a. Calle Oriente 35, tel. 320-064) is a showroom for the nonprofit Proyecto Artesanal, which seeks to preserve, protect, and stimulate the ethnic heritage of more than five hundred contributing artisans (mostly women) throughout the central and western highlands. In general, try to support stores that are either operated by or affiliated with cooperatives, which have helped strengthen the economic power of Guatemala's indigenous people. One of the biggest federations of co-ops, Artexco, sells handmade goods throughout the country. Another group called Cooperación para el Desarollo Rural Occidental (CDRO) distributes profits from its textile products into health, education, and agricultural development.

Antigua's INGUAT office can provide a complete list of local studios specializing in ceramics, woodworking, weaving, candle-making, and bronze sculpture, as well as information on cooperatives.

The finest jade jewelry is available from the shop and factory of Jades S.A. (4a. Calle Oriente 34, tel. 320-109 and fax 320-752), operated by former Indiana steelworker Jay Ridinger and his Texas-born, Mexico-reared, archaeologist wife, Mary Lou. During the mid-1970s the couple helped discover and reopen an ancient Mayan jade mine in the rugged Sierra de las Minas east of Guatemala City. Their company hauls out jade boulders by helicopter and mule, then cuts them to produce black, green, and white jewelry at their factory in Antigua. A number of Guatemalans have subsequently started their own jade businesses, and the industry is now an important part of the local economy. Stop by La Casa del Jade (4a. Calle Oriente 3, tel. 320-834), Jades J.C. (5a. Avenida Sur 6, tel. 320-677), or the studio of Julio Hernández (9a. Calle Poniente 2).

Antigua also has a silver factory, Platería Típica Maya, at 7a. Calle Oriente 9 (tel. 322-883). Owner José Luis Barillas sells good-quality rings, chains, and other jewelry. Custom furniture is built by Francisco López at his studio (tel. 322-853) across the street from the Hotel Ramada. Ceramic specialists in the city include La Familia Montiel and Florencio Rodenas (see chapter 12). Fine art books are being produced by several letterpress printers in the city, whose work is sold at Galería El Sereno and other locations. Paintings by local artists are available at Galería de Arte Estipite (6a. Avenida Norte 2).

Some of the other Antigua retailers selling high-quality artesanía include Casa de los Gigantes (7a. Calle Oriente 18), Concha's Foot Loom (7a. Calle Oriente 14), and Casa de Artes (4a. Avenida Sur 11). Jades S.A. has a very good textile outlet at 4a. Calle Poniente 12A, next to Restaurante Doña Luisa.

Hotels and Restaurants

Antigua is used to accommodating visitors and has an amazing range of places to stay, whether for one night or one year. Many of the best restaurants in the country are also found here, offering everything from teriyaki to wienerschnitzel.

At the high end of the accommodations spectrum is the Ramada Antigua (9a. Calle Carretera a Ciudad Vieja, tel. 320-011). At 156 rooms, this is by far the biggest and most modern hotel in the city. The architecture is dull, and the rooms look like any other in the

Ramada chain, but potentially useful amenities include a pool, health club, restaurant, gift shop, horse stables, and travel agency. It is located on the outskirts of town, about a 15-minute walk from Parque Central. Slightly less expensive and considerably more attractive is the Hotel Antigua (5a. Avenida Sur and 8a. Calle Poniente, tel. 320-288). This is a sort of Spanish colonial country club with a fine restaurant, a bar, and a pool. Outsiders can eat and swim here (for a fee), although the ambience is decidedly upper crust.

More moderate in price and pretension is the Posada de Don Rodrigo (5a. Avenida Norte 17, tel. 320-291, or in Guatemala City 318-017), a lovely, recommended lodge in a restored colonial mansion near the center of town. An excellent restaurant looks out on a colorful courtyard and rose garden. Equally charming, on a quiet edge of town next to a convent and coffee finca, is the Mesón Panza Verde (5a. Avenida Sur 19, tel. 322-925). The 6 rooms (2 with views and fireplaces) are in a modern but faithfully executed re-creation of a colonial home. Hartmut Zersch, the friendly German owner, operates a very good (though pricey) restaurant in the lower part of the building.

Across the street from the Panza Verde is El Rosario Lodge (5a. Avenida Sur 36, tel. 320-465), which rents pleasant rooms at a serene location. Furnished apartments with kitchens can be leased long-term, and there is a decent Guatemalan-style eatery, Café Ana, next door at 5a. Avenida Sur 14. Both are recommended.

Another reliable, moderately priced hotel, much closer to the action, is the Aurora (4a. Calle Oriente 16, tel. 320-217). A family-run establishment in an old home, this 16-room *posada* is a good value, though not especially flashy. All rooms have private baths and hot water. Breakfast is included, and secure parking is available.

Less costly lodging can be found at La Casa de Santa Lucía (Alameda Santa Lucía Sur 5). The place is small and clean, near the bus terminal and market. Noise and dust can be a problem on this busy street, and there is no phone. El Plácido (Avenida El Desengaño 25) is a family-run hotel built with rooms facing a flower-scented courtyard. Weekly rates are available, and the kitchen and laundry facilities may be used by guests. One disadvantage is its location, on the road to Chimaltenango, traversed by buses all day long. If full, try the Casa Sol-Mor across the street at Avenida El Desengaño 26. There are good eateries nearby. Hotel Villa San Francisco (1a. Avenida Sur 15) is also recommended by budget travelers.

Antigua suffers an embarrassment of fine restaurants, serving almost every cuisine imaginable. Favorites include the following. Restaurante Ahumados Katok (4a. Avenida Norte 7) is a pleasant, moderately priced café with an unusually diverse menu specializing in beef. The owner raises his own cattle on a ranch near Tecpán, where there is also a branch of this restaurant. Located a block north of the Central Park, but surprisingly quiet and uncrowded, with excellent service.

Quesos y Vino (5a. Avenida Norte 32) serves tasty low-cost Italian pastas and cheeses, along with one of Guatemala's best selection of wines. If you can stand the loud music and slow service, this is a great place to spend an evening. A block over, at 6a. Avenida Norte 25, is Caffè Opera, serving the best coffee drinks in Antigua or, for that matter, Guatemala City. Two multilingual gentlewomen from Verona operate this friendly place, which offers good Italian sandwiches and sinfully rich pastries.

Oasis del Peregrino (7a. Avenida Norte 96), in a quiet part of town near La Merced, has an extraordinarily diverse menu, good food, and reasonable prices. You can take your meals in the colonial-style posada or outdoors in the pretty courtyard.

The legendary Doña Luisa's (4a. Calle Oriente 12) deserves at least one visit by everyone who comes to Antigua. Run by Dennis and Luise Wheeler, former Peace Corps workers who contribute generously to Guatemalan social welfare programs, Doña Luisa's incorporates a justifiably renowned bakery and restaurant, plus the best bulletin board in the nation announcing everything from caving and snorkeling expeditions to yoga and shiatsu massage classes. The upstairs dining rooms offers Antigua's best tableside people-watching and fine views of the volcanoes.

For pizza, try Restaurante Roma (6a. Avenida Sur and 6a. Calle Poniente), where patrons may eat in or take out. If you are in the mood for a real splurge, perhaps the most elegant and romantic restaurant in the city is El Sereno (6a. Avenida Poniente 30), located in a perfectly restored colonial mansion that does double duty as a fine art gallery. The French food is very good, though expensive. Fair Japanese and Chinese meals, respectively, are served at Zen (3a. Avenida Norte 3) and La Estrella (5a. Calle Poniente 6). Mediocre American food is produced by the cafés around the main plaza. Higher quality ethnic fare is available at the German restaurant, Welten, at 4a. Calle Oriente 21.

Nightlife in Antigua centers around the restaurant and bar scene, with an occasional lecture, gallery opening, or concert thrown in. Some bars have discos and live music; others show foreign movies on video. These establishments come and go with such frequency that you are better off discovering them on your own. Most are clustered along 7a. Avenida and 5a. Calle Poniente near the center of town.

Services

Banking is relatively fast and simple in Antigua, one apparent blessing for having so many foreign students and visitors. Most popular are Lloyds Bank, at the northeast corner of Parque Central (4a. Calle Oriente 2), Granai & Townson Bank on the west side of the park, and Banco del Agro (north side of the park and Alameda Santa Lucía at 5a. Calle Poniente).

The post office is at the corner of Alameda Santa Lucía and 4a. Calle Poniente. Packages over 2 kilograms must be sent from the main branch in Guatemala City. The Pink Box (5a. Avenida Norte 14, tel. 322-922) handles everything from air parcels to money transfers, car rentals to airport shuttle services. Jades S.A. can also arrange overseas courier shipments and money transfers from either of its retail outlets on 4a. Calle Oriente.

The Guatel office is on the southwest corner of Parque Central, at 5a. Avenida Sur and 5a. Calle Poniente. There are pay phones next to the San Carlos restaurant under the portal on the north side of the park, outside the police station, and at Doña Luisa's.

The best bookstore in Antigua is Casa Andinista, at 4a. Calle Oriente 5A, opposite Doña Luisa's restaurant. Mike Shawcross, the expatriate Brit writer who owns the place, stocks an impressive selection in many languages, with an emphasis on English-language mate-

The arch of the Convent of Santa Catalina in Antigua. The cloudy peak of Agua Volcano is in the background. (Photo by Richard Mahler)

rial on Guatemala's politics, indigenous cultures, and natural attractions. Detailed maps are sold here, and information on volcano treks and similar adventures is posted. Good book selections (in English and Spanish) are also found at Un Poco de Todo and Galería Librería, both open daily on the main plaza. Film and one-hour photo processing are available at Foto Solís, 5a. Avenida Norte 13 (tel. 320-753). Supermarket Aylin (6a. Avenida Norte 1) has the best selection of groceries, cheeses, wines, and liquor.

Viajes Tivoli (5a. Avenida 10A, tel. 323-041) is a computerized, full-service travel agency, handling international and domestic excursions, including sailing charters and rental of bicycles, horses, motorcycles, and cars. Turansa (inside the Ramada Hotel, tel. 320-011, and at 5a. Avenida Norte 17, tel. 322-664) is another recommended agency providing a similar range of services. Both can arrange shuttle transportation to and from the Guatemala City airport and onward shuttles to Chichicastenango and Panajachel.

Several bus companies have departures for Guatemala City as frequently as every 15 minutes between 5:00 a.m. and 7:00 p.m. Buses leave about every half hour for Chimaltenango and Escuintla, more often to San Antonio Aguas Calientes and other nearby villages. Service to all destinations is less frequent after 7:00 p.m. and on Sundays and holidays. The bus terminal is at the foot of 4a. Calle Poniente (Calle del Ayuntamiento).

Taxis wait for fares near the bus station and Parque Central. Ask at INGUAT about appropriate fares to Guatemala City and surrounding villages. Budget and National car rentals can be arranged at the Ramada (both 320-011). Avis has its office at 5a. Avenida Norte 22 (tel. 320-291). Motorcycles can be rented at the Posada Refugio (4a. Calle Poniente 30).

Horses can be rented at the Ramada Hotel or the office of R. Rolando Pérez at San Pedro El Panorama 28 (tel. 322-809). Señor Pérez offers tours of nearby villages and mountains, including overnight trips. If you don't know how to ride, he will teach you.

Camping and mountaineering gear may be rented at Casa Andinista at 4a. Calle Oriente 5A. Guides can be secured through the INGUAT office, travel agencies, or Club Andinista de Antigua at 6a. Avenida Norte 34.

Day Trips from Antigua

Several villages close to Antigua are worth visiting. All are easily reached by car, taxi, or public bus and, in some cases, bicycle or horseback. The closest destinations are only a short walk from Antigua by paved road or footpath.

Ciudad Vieja
The old capital, literally wiped off the face of the earth more than 450 years ago, has little to interest the casual visitor aside from the massive white church next to the small plaza, which was built during the colonial era and has been nicely restored. Only a few crumbling ruins, including the original city hall, date from before the catastrophic mudslide of 1541. A plaque in the plaza commemorates the first mass ever said in Guatemala, beneath a tree that is still standing. Most residents of this area are descendants of the Mexican Indians who were brought by the Spanish to help conquer Guatemala's highland tribes

and given land around Ciudad Vieja as their reward. Buses leave Antigua many times a day for Ciudad Vieja, or you can walk the 3 miles in an hour or so.

San Antonio Aguas Calientes

This village, about 4 miles southeast of Antigua, has an informal and highly regarded market that sells a wide variety of fine handmade textiles, including particularly beautiful huipiles and tapestries. Local artisans are known throughout Guatemala for the tightness of their weave and their colorful combinations of floral and geometric designs, usually on an orange background. If you are interested, some of the women work part-time giving weaving lessons. Among those who have been recommended are Rafaela Godínez, Felipa López Zamora, and Carmelo and Zoila Guarn. Their rates are very reasonable, about a dollar or two an hour.

You can get to San Antonio Aguas Calientes from Antigua by bus via Ciudad Vieja or walk from there in about an hour. As the name implies, there are several hot springs in the area, although recent volcanic eruptions have shifted things underground and lowered their temperatures to the lukewarm range.

San Felipe de Jesús

The main attraction here is a whitewashed Gothic church that contains an image of Christ that some Guatemalans believe can cure their diseases. Many pilgrims journey here on the first Friday of Lent, and a major procession begins at the church on the afternoon of Good Friday. There is a silver jewelry factory a couple of blocks off the main plaza where you can watch craftspeople at work and then buy their creations. You can walk to San Felipe in about half an hour via 6a. Avenida Norte or take one of the many buses leaving the Antigua station.

San Juan del Obispo

The palace of the first bishop of Guatemala is in this village, a few miles south of Antigua. Bishop Francisco Marroquín's mansion is enormous, giving you some idea of the wealth and splendor enjoyed by members of Guatemala's colonial Catholic hierarchy. There are regular buses from the Antigua terminal, or you can walk here in about an hour via Calle de los Pasos. The town is slightly higher than Antigua and affords a good view of the city.

Santa María de Jesús

Located a few miles up the slope of Agua volcano from San Juan del Obispo, this is a picturesque village with good views of all three volcanoes. The trail to the top of Agua starts here, just beyond the cemetery. Fine huipiles are made in Santa María and can be purchased directly from the women who make them. Buses run several times a day from Antigua, or you can take a taxi. You must leave Antigua at about midnight if you expect to see the sunrise from atop the volcano.

Antigua's Volcanoes

The three volcanoes closest to Antigua vary considerably in accessibility. Agua is the easiest to climb—a communications array near the summit is served by a dirt road—and Acatenango is the most arduous. Fuego is quite active, venting lava, ash, and steam with some regularity.

As on all Guatemalan volcanoes, security has become an important issue for prospective climbers. In recent years several foreigners have been assaulted in the vicinity of Agua: you should inquire locally about the best routes and guides before heading up this or any other volcano. A good place to start is the Club Andinista in Antigua at 6a. Avenida Norte 34 or Casa Andinista at 4a. Calle Oriente 5A.

The trail (a road most of the way) to the top of Agua (12,356 feet) begins at the village of Santa María de Jesús, which can be reached by bus or taxi from the Antigua terminal. There is a small pensión, with meals available.

The peaks of Fuego (12,346 feet) and Acatenango (13,042 feet) are reached by trails starting at the La Soledad coffee finca, near Ciudad Vieja, or the village of Alotenango. These climbs are recommended only for experienced hikers in good condition. Experienced guides are advised.

For further details on climbing these and other volcanoes, consult the Spanish-only *Guía de los Volcanes de Guatemala* (Guide to the Volcanoes of Guatemala) by Carlos E. Prahl Redondo of the Club Andino Guatemalteco.

7

The Western Highlands

The western highlands, in the view of many travelers, is what a journey to Guatemala is all about. Indeed, it is hard to imagine any first-time visitor leaving the country without spending at least a few days among the "living Maya" in the towns and villages of these rolling hills and towering mountains, a land of eternal springtime.

The Spanish easily conquered this area in the early 1500s, a time when the long-feuding highland tribes were in decline. But the conquistadors failed to find the gold and silver they were hoping for, and, except as a source of cheap Indian labor, the area was pretty much ignored by European immigrants. By leaving the villages of the western highlands alone, the Spaniards enabled the Maya to carry on their traditional way of life, which they have done to the present day.

Besides the strong indigenous cultures, regional attractions include Lake Atitlán—dubbed "the most beautiful lake in the world" by English novelist Aldous Huxley—and the colorful market center of Chichicastenango, a justifiable must-see on the itinerary of most visitors to Guatemala. If you have time, visits to the historic cities of Quetzaltenango and Huehuetenango, with side trips to Todos Santos and other picturesque villages in the Cuchumatanes range, the country's highest mountains, are also highly recommended.

The most heavily populated parts of the western highlands range in altitude from about 5,000 to 8,000 feet above sea level, although some river valleys dip lower and a few volcanoes rise to over 13,000 feet. The temperature averages 60 degrees Fahrenheit all year long.

The Western Highlands

The vast majority of residents are indigenous people who have kept their native dress, religious beliefs, and customs, with Ladinos concentrated in the major towns and cities or coffee fincas. The rural peasants mostly earn their living from farming, plantation labor, and the sale of handcrafted goods such as textiles, masks, furniture, and blankets.

Buses are the main form of transportation in the western highlands, and here, as elsewhere, the aisles are no wider than a foreigner's hips and the vehicles are crowded with many more passengers than they were ever intended to carry. It is normal to cram four or five adults in a seat designed to hold two or three American schoolchildren. There are no sanitary facilities and few, if any, rest stops.

If traveling for a distance of 75 miles or more, it is worth taking a first-class bus, or *pullman*, as they are known in Guatemala. The tickets are slightly more expensive, but for only a few extra dollars the comfort level is astronomically improved. A pullman offers assigned seats in Greyhound-style vehicles, usually with a bathroom, air conditioning, and comfortable reclining seats.

Be advised that robberies occur with relentless regularity on Guatemala's public buses, and roadblocks are sometimes put up on even the main highways by armed outlaws who demand money, jewelry, and other valuables. Stops and searches by police and soldiers are not uncommon. It is always a good idea to check with someone familiar with local conditions before heading out on your own—and to avoid traveling at night.

Chichicastenango

Chichicastenango, situated in a high mountain valley about 90 miles (2½ hours) west of Guatemala City, is a Quiché Maya community famous for its dazzlingly colorful markets, held every Thursday and Sunday morning in the main plaza. This is one of the largest markets in Central America: textiles, wooden masks, leather goods, hand-embroidered huipiles, jewelry, pottery, and other craftwork are found here in great abundance, along with flowers, fruit, vegetables, and other domestic items. Even Spanish colonial coins and ancient pottery shards are sold. Since the 1200s, Chichicastenango has been a trading center, mainly because it historically occupied a kind of neutral zone between the domains of the frequently squabbling Quiché, Cakchiquel, and Tzutuhil Maya.

Although heavily touristed, the "Chichi" market is a marvelous place to mingle with the full-blooded Maya of the twentieth century whose faces could be models for the stone carvings at Tikal and whose clothing patterns are often the same designs found in paintings created a millennium ago. The marketplace itself is laid out according to a precise, age-old system: flowers sold on the steps of the Church of Santo Tomás, food sold around the plaza fountain, and so on.

Preparing for market day begins the night before, and good bargains can be found at this uncrowded time, when poles and canvas are erected to shelter the individual stalls. Prices tend to go up with each passing hour on market day, especially after tourist buses begin discharging their affluent passengers around 9:00 a.m.

Flower vendors of Chichicastenango on the steps of the Church of Santo Tomás during Sunday's market (Photo by Sue Dirksen)

The main attraction on the plaza is the whitewashed Church of Santo Tomás, built in 1540 on the site of a Mayan temple and still in daily use, primarily by the Maya. Non-Indians should enter the church only through the side entrance, never through the front, since the Quiché believe that permission must be obtained from the guardian spirits of the massive front door—something you will see each Indian do as he or she approaches the doorway, while a holy man swings a coffee-can censer full of smoking *pom* (copal incense) or tends a perpetual fire in a concrete altar called a *quemada*. If you decide to sit in the pews of Santo Tomás, it is recommended that you also follow the custom of men on the left side, women on the right. Notice the blaze of candles throughout the church lighted in honor of the saints, ancestors, and Mayan deities. Photography is not allowed inside Santo Tomás without permission.

A few steps away from the church, on the south side of the plaza, is a museum housing the collection of hundreds of Mayan artifacts and jewelry pieces presented to Father Ildefonso Rossbach, a well-loved, American-born priest at the church from 1894 until his death in 1944. There is a nominal admission fee to the museum, which is open from 8:00 a.m. to noon and 2:00 p.m. to 5:00 p.m., every day except Tuesday.

Facing Santo Tomás on the opposite side of the plaza is El Calvario, a smaller Catholic church used exclusively by the Maya for special prayers and services, particularly during Holy Week. Traditionally closed to outsiders, it should not be entered without permission or accompaniment by an Indian. The convent garden attached to it encloses the plaza on the west.

Indigenous and Roman Catholic customs are mixed freely and openly in Chichicastenango, and you will see the devout burning incense and lighting candles on the steps of both churches, then crossing themselves as they step inside to pray or attend mass. During Semana Santa the commingling of traditions is especially evident, as parish priests and Indian religious leaders from the ancient brotherhoods known as cofradías join in the ritual parading of Christian icons from the cathedral through the streets of the village.

Because the expense of the community's many elaborate religious ceremonies is too great for a single individual or family to bear, the cofradías provide a means for villagers to work together to keep these important rituals alive. The brotherhood's members, called *cofrades*, are dedicated to the service of various Christian saints, whose images also symbolize sacred spirits or gods from the Mayan religion. Throughout the western highlands, each god's distinctive dominion—the sun, moon, rain, clouds, and even corn—is inextricably woven with Christianity's Holy Trinity and the saints of Catholicism. Each year the most respected men of the village proudly take turns serving in the cofradías and carrying out the special spiritual and secular duties associated with them. In Chichi, the cofradía has fourteen members, each with six to eight cofrades, who in turn look after the image of a particular saint.

Among the Maya the gods have always required a yearly round of sacrifice and prayer to perpetuate the miracle of life. Today the cofradía and shaman participate in the rites of baptism, fasting, supplication, and incense burning that give their followers a sense of seamless infinity. The Maya view Catholicism as something foretold in their ancient prophecies, which said that a day would come when bearded men would arrive from the ocean bringing new forms of religion.

Next to Santo Tomás, enclosing a small courtyard, is a former monastery built in 1542 which is now used as a church office. It was here that the Spanish priest Francisco Ximénez became the first foreigner to see the Popol Vuh, the rarest and most sacred book of the Quiché. A kind of cross between the Bible and the Bhagavad Gita, this document revealed Quiché history and many details about traditional Mayan spiritual beliefs and practices dating back to the Classic era. Unlike other Catholic officials, who destroyed such materials whenever they found them, Father Ximénez became fascinated by the Popol Vuh and in 1680 translated it into Spanish. His manuscript is preserved in Chicago's Newberry Library; the original text was lost over two hundred years ago. It was Father Ximénez's enormous respect for Quiché traditions that convinced Indian leaders in Chichicastenango to incorporate their own forms of worship into the Catholic faith.

Some of the original Quiché shrines and rituals have been maintained as well. The most accessible of these is Pascual Abaj, a pre-Columbian monument located atop a small hill within walking distance of the Chichicastenango plaza. Ceremonies involving chicken sacrifices and incantations are regularly held here in front of a carved stone Mayan face next to which a Christian cross has been placed. Flower petals, candles, and incense can usually be found scattered amid the bones and ashes surrounding these altars. If a ceremony or sacrifice is in progress as you approach the shrine, it is best to stay back unless you are beckoned forward.

To get to Pascual Abaj, follow 5a. Avenida, the street that runs downhill (south) from Santo Tomás, and turn right at the first corner, 9a. Calle. The road eventually becomes a trail and is marked by signs and arrows pointing the way to Pascual Abaj. You will pass through a pine forest and patches of thorny bushes along the way. (Chichicastenango means "the place of the purple nettles.")

The path to Pascual Abaj also traverses the yard of the man who repairs and stores the village's ceremonial costumes, which you are welcome to photograph and examine. Masks, souvenirs, and cold drinks are sold here.

There are other Mayan shrines and sacred caves in the hills around this area, but they are all off-limits to non-Indians.

Located on a bluff northwest of the plaza, behind the Mayan Inn, is the Campo Santo or public graveyard. At the front of the cemetery is a small chapel, surrounded by the large tombs of the prosperous. Toward the rear are much simpler grave markers and a small yellow tomb that holds the remains of Father Rossbach. Like other Guatemalan cemeteries, El Campo Santo comes alive on November 1 and 2, All Saints' and All Souls' days, when families come to clean the graves and honor their dead with flowers, candles, food, and drink.

Another occasion of great religious fervor is the fiesta of Santo Tomás, held between December 14 and December 21. It is a week full of music, singing, dancing, processions, merrymaking, and fireworks. The crowning event is the Palo Volador, in which costumed men dangle by ropes from a 60-foot maypole. On the last day of this festival, all the babies born during the previous year are brought en masse to the church of Santo Tomás for a group christening.

As for the Thursday and Sunday markets, you are best off discovering them on your own. Merchandise and prices change slightly from week to week, but quality is uniformly high. Bargaining is considered mandatory and a fair price is often about two-thirds of the figure first quoted by the seller. Do not overlook the small shops near the plaza selling carved masks and other artesanía: some of them are particularly interesting and well worth a few minutes of your time.

Getting There

Chichicastenango is about 15 miles northwest of Los Encuentros, the high, windswept junction on the Pan American Highway where buses also turn off for Sololá and Panajachel. Unless you are on one of the few direct buses to Chichi from the capital or Panajachel, you will need to change here for one of the frequent local vehicles making the trip (about 30 minutes). There are a couple of buses every hour for Santa Cruz del Quiché and points north.

Buses leave Chichi from various points around the market and plaza, usually stopping to pick up passengers near the post office on 7a. Avenida if they are headed south to Los Encuentros.

Besides driving a private car, another option is to book passage on one of the many tour buses that go directly to Chichicastenango on market days. These are comparatively expensive ($15 and up) but may be the fastest and easiest transportation for those on a tight schedule. Check with hotels or see chapter 13 for a list of local travel agencies. Yet another alternative is booking a seat on one of the tourist minivans that head to Chichicastenango from Panajachel, Antigua, and Guatemala City, also for about $15.

Hotels and Restaurants

The Mayan Inn (8a. Calle and 3a. Avenida, tel. 561-176) is a 30-room hotel stuffed with colonial antiques and built around a pleasant Spanish-style courtyard full of beautiful flowers. The expensive Mayan Inn is known for its excellent dinners, served by Indians dressed in traditional Quiché clothing and accompanied by a fine marimba orchestra. The Mayan Inn was built in 1932 by the American-Guatemalan family that owns Clark Tours. Each room has a fireplace, private bath and hot water. The elegant bar and restaurant are pricey but worth a visit.

The Mayan Inn should not be confused with the much more modest Maya Lodge, on the plaza, which has received consistently mixed reviews from travelers and is not recommended.

Hotel Santo Tomás (tel. 561-061, or 21-560 in Guatemala City) is an expensive, modern hotel on the road coming into town from Guatemala City. Built in a colonial style around a central courtyard, it has a pleasant bar and restaurant. Many of its 43 rooms are furnished with antiques. Credit cards are accepted.

Pensión Chugüilá (5a. Avenida 5-24, tel. 561-176) is a moderately priced 23-room hotel about 2 blocks north of the plaza near the Arco Gucumatz, a distinctive arch across the nearby roadway. Rooms, most with baths and some with fireplaces, overlook a courtyard and restaurant. Both the pensión and café are good values, highly recommended.

There are some cheaper and more basic accommodations not

visited by the author. These include the El Salvador (10a. Calle 4-47) and Pensión Girón (opposite the vegetable market). Rooms are taken quickly in Chichicastenango on evenings before market days, and the prudent course is to make a phone reservation well in advance.

Hotel restaurants serve the best food in town (at the highest prices), but there are also some inexpensive eateries along the sides of the plaza. Try Tapena, at 5a. Avenida 5-21, or El Torito, on the second floor of the Girón Building, above the interior courtyard, where produce is sold. Tziguan Tinamit, 5a. Avenida and 6a. Calle near Pensión Chugüilá, serves decent typical Guatemalan meals.

Services
There is a Banco del Ejército on 6a. Calle, a block off the plaza, and, for a fee, the Mayan Inn will also change money for nonguests. The Guatel station and post office are on 7a. Avenida near 8a. Calle, about 10 blocks from the plaza. Besides the market vendors, several small stores sell food, drinks, and sundries. There are also a couple of pharmacies in town.

Around Chichicastenango

Santa Cruz del Quiché
The capital of the department of Quiché lies a half hour (14 miles) north of Chichicastenango on a paved road that passes the Laguna Lemoa, a small lake said to have been formed by the tears wept by the wives of Quiché leaders after their husbands were killed by the Spanish.

Santa Cruz, called simply Quiché by the locals, is a pleasant town and good base for exploring the surrounding villages or catching a bus into the Ixil Triangle and beyond. There are fine markets here on Thursday and Sunday: palm-woven hats are a local specialty (often made by women while they amble down the street!), and high-quality textiles are sold at excellent prices. The large colonial church on the plaza was built by the Dominicans with stone blocks taken from the nearby Mayan ruins of Utatlán (Utatlán's ornamental stonework is also embedded in the walls of the nearby courthouse). Inside the

Members of the Chichicastenango cofradía carry an image of Christ through the old monastery on Palm Sunday (Photo by Sue Dirksen)

church is a poignant memorial to the many Catholic padres in the department who lost their lives during the unrest of the 1970s and 1980s. The violence became so severe that all priests were withdrawn from Quiché for a time.

Military presence in the northern part of the Quiché department remains strong in the face of alleged guerrilla activity and widespread resentment toward government resettlement programs. The Quiché Maya were the most culturally advanced of the highland people at the time of the conquest and have always resisted attempts by outsiders to dominate them.

There are several basic but adequate *hospedajes* (simple lodgings) in Santa Cruz. These include Hermano Pedro (next to the bus terminal) and Tropical (1a. Avenida 9C). More upscale are the Posada Calle Real (2a. Avenida 7-36) and San Pascual (7a. Calle 0-43). There are several simple restaurants on or near the plaza serving typical native food. Recommended is the Santa Clara, which also rents rooms. A branch of Banco de Guatemala is also located on the plaza.

Daily buses run from the terminal on the edge of Quiché to Guatemala City (via Chichi), Joyabaj, Nebaj, Uspantán, Quetzaltenango, and San Marcos. There is no pullman (first-class) transportation, and local buses are especially crowded on market days. There is a fiesta on May 3 and another around the middle of August.

Utatlán Ruins

Only 2 miles outside of Santa Cruz del Quiché are the unrestored ruins of the ancient Quiché Maya capital, the most powerful city in the highlands before it was razed by the Spanish in 1524. Founded in the early 1400s as Gumarcaaj (sometimes spelled Kumarkaah), the site was renamed Utatlán by Pedro de Alvarado after he proudly sacked and burned the town.

Utatlán was never rebuilt after its destruction, and only a few temples, palaces, and stone monuments are still recognizable amid the mounds of pine-forested rubble and badly eroded foundations. Visitors may notice various trenches dug by archaeologists, treasure hunters, and local residents. Only the walls of two ancient temples remain standing.

About 50 feet beneath the main plaza are man-made tunnels (bring a candle or flashlight) that extend about 100 yards. These and other sacred monuments at the site are still used by local Mayan shamans and *brujos* (lay priests) for devotions to ancestors and the earth deity that include animal sacrifices and the burning of incense, candles, and sugarcane alcohol. Reportedly, the tunnels still serve as tombs for members of the Quiché elite. You will probably notice chicken feathers, ashes, and flower petals from these ceremonies strewn about the tunnels and aboveground ruins. Be careful as you explore the catacombs, as there are several vertical pits that sink to great depths. There is a small museum near the entrance with a scale model of Utatlán as it originally appeared. Camping is permitted at the site, which is open (by a small admittance fee) from 7:00 a.m. to 6:00 p.m. daily.

You can easily reach Utatlán from Santa Cruz del Quiché by car, or taxi, or on foot (in about 40 minutes). From the plaza head south on 2a. Avenida to 10a. Calle, then turn right and follow the road all the way to the ruins.

North and East of Santa Cruz del Quiché

A winding road (Route 15) continues north through the hills from Quiché to the outskirts of Cunén, where one branch (Route 3) heads north to Nebaj and another east (Route 7-W) all the way to Cobán, via Uspantán and San Cristóbal Verapaz. The latter road is seldom traveled by foreigners, although it passes through beautiful mountain country and some very traditional Quiché villages.

On the way to Cunén, Route 15 passes through San Pedro Jocopilas, Rancho de Teja, and Sacapulas, where there is a turnoff (Route 7-W) for Huehuetenango. A hot and dusty town on the Chixoy River, Sacapulas has an interesting colonial church dating from 1554, and some geothermal hot springs are located nearby. There is a good market here on the plaza (beneath the big ceiba trees) every Thursday and Sunday. You will see local women in lace huipiles who tie their hair with fancy pompoms. If you get stranded here, there are a few basic pensiones and comedores. Near Cunén, 10 miles northeast of Sacapulas on Route 7-W, there is a small cave that has been used by the local Maya since ancient times. It is often flooded by a swift-flowing river but may be accessible during the dry season.

A separate road (Route 2) heads directly east from Santa Cruz del Quiché through scenic hill country to the villages of Chiché, Chinique, Zacualpa, Joyabaj, and eventually, Guatemala City. Other than the Saturday market at Chiché, the most interesting destination is Zacualpa, where small shops sell exquisitely woven wool bags. The women also weave (and wear) an unusually good-looking red and purple huipil. Pretty huipiles are also made in Joyabaj, where the men of the village are suspended from a 60-foot Palo Volador during fiesta time (the second week of August).

The Ixil Triangle

Although not many tourists take the trouble to visit this remote part of Guatemala, it is one of the nation's richest areas in terms of indigenous culture and natural beauty. These highland valleys of Quiché are the last stronghold of the Ixil people, who suffered tremendously during the social unrest of the 1970s and 1980s. Some of the Indians displaced by the civil unrest and government policies are gradually returning to their homeland. One of the most effective projects started on their behalf is the nonprofit Shawcross Aid Programme for Highland Indians (Apartado Postal 343, Antigua), which helps install potable water systems, build schools, buy vegetable seeds, and pay teachers. You can write to this worthy group if you would like to volunteer time, expertise, or money on behalf of the Ixil Maya. Weavings are sold at their headquarters in Nebaj.

The Ixil originally occupied a roughly triangle-shaped region bounded on the north by the Río Xaclbal basin, on the east by the Río Chixoy, and on the west and south by the rugged Cuchumatanes Mountains. The territory of this tight-knit ethnic group has shrunk to only three main villages. Many of the men still seasonally migrate to the coast to harvest coffee on the many large plantations there.

Nebaj

The southern gateway to the Ixil-speaking area, Nebaj is 55 miles from Santa Cruz del Quiché in the corner of a long, isolated valley. Almost all the women still dress in the traditional manner, as do a few older men. The huipiles worn here are particularly stunning, with embroidered dancing figures of birds and animals. A twisted and braided strip of colored cloth is worn as a headdress, and a bright red skirt completes the outfit. Some of the men still wear a short red jacket that imitates the design worn by Spanish officers stationed in Nebaj three or four centuries ago.

The quality of the weaving in Nebaj is excellent, and traje can be purchased at good prices during the Thursday and Sunday markets or from craftspeople in their homes. Well-made crocheted cloth bags are also for sale. Some of the young girls and women sell huipiles to foreigners, and at least one, Juana Marcos Solís, is known to give weaving lessons from 1 day to 6 months duration. Look for her at Cantón Simacol.

There is not much to see in Nebaj beyond the daily routines of Indian life, although there is an interesting colonial church on the plaza. There are also some modest and unrestored pre-Columbian ruins just outside the town which are still the site of sacred rituals. About thirty mounds and pyramid structures were excavated by the Carnegie Institution in 1947, yielding lovely ceramics, jade, and alabaster artifacts, some of which are now on display at the Museum of Archaeology in Guatemala City and the British Museum in London. Mayan occupation took place between A.D. 600 and 800, and the site is noted for the explicit historical scenes found painted on polychrome burial pots. Curiously, no stelae or wall panels have been found here.

The mountain trails around Nebaj are very lovely, especially one leading to the remote village of Acul. The morning crispness is well suited to trekking. Do not forget that the locally grown apples are famous throughout Guatemala for their delicious flavor.

The best place to stay in Nebaj is Las Tres Hermanas, a pensión that consists of several basic sleeping rooms clustered around an interior courtyard. Good meals are prepared by the friendly sisters who run the place. If this place is full, try either the Pensión Las Clavellinas or the Little Corner Hostel a few blocks away. Private rooms with families are also available. The restaurants of Nebaj are very simple and are clustered on or near the plaza. There are no telephones.

There are several buses a day to and from Santa Cruz del Quiché via Sacapulas. It is a 2½-hour bus ride from Santa Cruz del Quiché to Sacapulas and another 1½ to Nebaj.

There is a large annual fiesta in Nebaj the second week of August, culminating with several processions and much drinking and dancing on August 15.

San Juan Cotzal

The town of San Juan Cotzal is 11 miles (2 hours by infrequent bus) east of Nebaj over a scenic mountain road that is often very muddy. Cotzal is even more traditional in its dress and customs than Nebaj. The residents grow maguey cactus and weave ropes and bags from the plant's stringy fibers. The women wear elaborate green huipiles. Other than what may be offered in private homes, there are no accommodations or services, except for a pharmacy that is said to rent rooms and serve meals to Cotzal's infrequent visitors.

Chajul

Along with Nebaj and San Juan Cotzal, Chajul is the only sizable community in Guatemala where the Ixil language is still widely spoken. It was established during colonial times through the forced merger of eleven separate villages. As in Nebaj, the women wear gorgeous huipiles decorated with fanciful animal figures and brilliant red skirts. They also wear earrings made from strands of cloth to which colonial era coins have been affixed. The red coats of the men are a stylistic adaptation of those worn by the Spanish conquistadors. Some of the men and boys still hunt with blowguns, a practice that dates back to pre-Columbian times.

An intriguing Christ of Golgotha figure in the Chajul church is flanked by two carved figurines dressed a bit like vigilant soldiers and is the object of pilgrimages on the second Friday of Lent, when there is a communitywide fiesta. Like San Juan Cotzal, Chajul receives few visitors, and you will have to ask around to find a sleeping room and meals. Inquire at the post office for the owner of a small pensión on the south side of town.

There is no bus service. Unless you drive or hitch a ride, you will have to walk 2 hours from Cotzal to Chajul. Several other traditional Ixil villages north of Chajul can only be reached by long hikes through the mountains. They include Bisich, Visiquichum, and Batzchocola.

Lake Atitlán and Panajachel

A two-lane paved road winds for over an hour (some 25 miles) through the mountains from Chichicastenango to the town of Panajachel, on the northeast shore of Lake Atitlán, about 70 miles west of Antigua and 90 miles west of Guatemala City. The zigzag route heads first to the four-way intersection of Los Encuentros, then along the Pan American Highway for a short distance before the turnoff to Sololá and Panajachel.

The famous 50-square-mile Lake Atitlán, dominated by the three towering volcanic peaks and the sheer granite cliffs that surround it, changes colors and moods by the minute. A few glimpses of Lake Atitlán can be seen along the Pan American Highway, but it must be seen close up to be fully appreciated. Atitlán means "abundance of waters," and the lake more than lives up to its name. It is over 11 miles long, nearly 8 miles wide, and more than 1,000 feet deep in some places.

Santiago Atitlán, wedged at the base of the volcanoes, is the most accessible village on the shoreline, but most of the hotels, restaurants, and services are across the lake in Panajachel, which can be easily reached by public bus, private car, or tour van. There is no airport.

If you are planning to spend more than a few days at Lake Atitlán, you may prefer staying at one of the handful of small hotels located outside of Panajachel. The most comfortable of these are around the villages of Santa Catarina and San Antonio Palopo on the northeastern shore, but there are also pleasant pensiones on the west and south sides of the lake in Santiago, San Pedro, San Pablo, and Santa Cruz. All are much more isolated communities than Panajachel, which means you will have a chance to see a more traditional indigenous community close up. These locations are also considerably quieter and less touristy than Panajachel.

Nicknamed "Gringotenango" on account of its touristic image and substantial expatriate community, Panajachel is home to many foreign-born exporters and entrepreneurs. Many Guatemaltecos also maintain vacation homes here, and the streets are full of *turistas* and "locals" alike on weekends and holidays.

There are few specific attractions in the town of Panajachel itself,

Massage and "nature center" in Panajachel (Photo by Richard Mahler)

beyond the well-stocked daily market and a nicely restored colonial church containing a statue of St. Francis of Assisi, patron saint of the city (a festival is held in his honor October 1-7). Panajachel is an ideal place to relax, however, particularly for those who have been shuttling around Guatemala in overcrowded buses on kidney-busting roads. The laid-back ambience, comfortable accommodations, and wide variety of restaurants may be a welcome indulgence.

The main market for artesanía is along Calle Santander above the public beach, although street vendors seem to be everywhere. Be prepared to bargain aggressively if you want to avoid paying tourist-targeted prices.

Panajachel is also a good base for participating in the many forms of recreation available on and around Lake Atitlán, which maintains a year-round average water temperature of 65 degrees. The lake is well suited for swimming, fishing, sailing, canoeing, kayaking, water-skiing, and even scuba diving. Conditions for each of these sports are excellent. The steep cliffs above Atitlán are also considered ideal for hang gliding: many national and international championship competitions are held here. On the placid waters below, regattas and sailboat races are regularly scheduled. And, of course, there is always volcano climbing.

If you stay for more than a day, a visit to one or more of the eleven villages around the lake is in order. Some can be reached on foot or by private car, motorcycle, or bicycle, others by public boat, bus, or horseback.

Getting There

There are hourly buses shuttling daily between Panajachel and Guatemala City from 5:00 a.m. to 2:00 p.m. The trip takes a minimum of 3 hours on a second-class bus. A more comfortable option is to take a first-class Quetzaltenango bus as far as the Pan American Highway turnoff at Los Encuentros, where there is frequent local service to Panajachel (although some buses go only as far as Sololá). There are no direct public buses between Antigua and Panajachel: you must transfer at Chimaltenango en route, and possibly again at Los Encuentros. Tour companies run direct shuttles on a daily basis.

From Panajachel, there are several direct buses each day to Quetzaltenango, Chichicastenango, and around the lake to San Lucas Tolimán and Cocales, and from there on to the Pacific Coast. Avoid traveling on the "old road" to Patzún that approaches the lake from the southeast: many robberies have been reported along this route, and the roadbed is in poor repair.

There are several public boats each day leaving from docks along the beach between 9:00 and 10:00 a.m. for Santiago Atitlán. Check in front of the Hotel Tzanjuyu and Brisas del Lago restaurant. Some of the boats continue on to San Pedro la Laguna and other lakeside villages. Or you can be taken to these smaller communities directly by smaller craft. The bigger boats return from Santiago between 12:30 and 1:30 p.m.

Because schedules, watercraft, and prices change fairly often, it is best to ask around to get current information about boat trips. Individual boats can be chartered to specific destinations, but the price may be steep unless spread among several passengers. Try not to schedule any boat trip after 3:00 p.m., because the breeze from the coast inevitably kicks in and can make the lake's surface very choppy.

Hotels

The Hotel Atitlán (Finca Buenaventura, tel. 621-416 or 621-441) is an expensive resort isolated from the main part of Panajachel by a ridge along the Sololá road. It has 45 well-appointed rooms, a restaurant, bar, private beach, and gift shop. If you do not mind being a long walk from town and cocooned in a rarefied upper-class atmosphere, this may be the place for you. Credit cards are accepted.

Somewhat less pricey is the Cacique Inn (Calle del Embarcadero, tel. 621-205), which has 33 rooms, a bar, and a restaurant. This pleasant lodge on the western edge of town is popular among tour operators. Rooms are large, and each has a fireplace.

Hotel Rancho Grande (Avenida Rancho Grande, tel. 621-554, or in Guatemala City 764-768); located on one of Panajachel's more pleasant side streets, is a moderately priced establishment and includes a large breakfast in the tab. There are 9 rooms, several with fireplaces. The staff is well informed and helpful. Credit cards are accepted. Highly recommended.

El Rosario (tel. 0621-491) is an inexpensive hotel set back from the public beach, with 8 bungalows surrounded by lawns and gardens. A friendly Indian family runs the place. Other inexpensive rooms are available at the Paradise Inn (Calle del Río, tel. 621-021), which has a bar and small café; and the Regis (Calle Santander, tel. 621-149), a simple 18-room hotel on a rather busy street. In the center of town is Hotel Galindo (Calle Principal, tel. 621-168), with 18 rooms. All have private baths, and several offer spacious suites. Also inexpensive and popular is Mario's Rooms on Santander, where you can order crepes for breakfast.

At the bottom end of the price scale are bungalow-style accommodations, marked by simple hand-painted signs on the back alleys of town. There is a public campground near the beach across the Panajachel River from the city itself, next to the cemetery and a residential area called Jucanyá.

Rooms with kitchens or small houses can also be rented by the day, week, or month in Panajachel. Look for posted signs, or simply ask around. Rates vary considerably depending on what is being offered and whether it is high season.

Restaurants

Panajachel ranks with Antigua and Guatemala City in the great diversity and quality of its restaurants. The roster tends to change frequently, as in any resort destination, but the following have earned reliable reputations in recent years. El Bistro (Calle Santander) serves excellent Italian food and salads; the portions are large, but unfortunately so are the prices. Much less expensive and almost as satisfying is El Cisne (Avenida Rancho Grande), which has a typical Guatemalan menu that includes fresh lake fish. Local fish is also well prepared at Manchón Típica Atitlán, a simple eatery on Calle Santander.

At the foot of Avenida Rancho Grande, opposite the beach, is Tocoyal, which looks expensive but really is not: the food and drink are fine, and the views of the sunset are spectacular. Several other restaurants along the public beach have second-floor bars or dining rooms where you can see the sun's orange disk slip behind San Pedro volcano, a sight not soon forgotten.

A couple of popular spots near the center of town are La Posada del Pintor (Calle los Arboles), serving good pizza and mixed drinks, and Al Chisme, an expatriate hangout farther up the same street that serves simple food of consistently high quality. Two of the few vegetarian restaurants in Guatemala are in Panajachel: Hsieh, on Calle los Arboles near the market, and Café Xomil, on Calle Principal; both are recommended.

Services

There is an INGUAT office next to the Mayan Palace Hotel, on Calle Principal next to the main bus stop and the intersection of Calle Santander. Transportation schedules are posted, and the well-informed staffers speak English.

The public market is past the city hall at the far end of Calle Principal. The main market day is Sunday, but you can buy fruits, vegetables, and incidentals here throughout the week. The police station is half a block down Principal in the direction of the beach, next to the town plaza.

Packages can be shipped to the United States and Europe from Get Guated Out, a well-run parcel service on the second floor of the building next door to Café Al Chisme. The same office handles overseas mail, fax, and telegrams. Adjacent is the Gallery, one of Guatemala's best bookstores and an informal message center. Américos Exports on Santander (622-064) also provides parcel and air cargo service. There is a post office and taxi stand opposite the main church and a Guatel office on Calle Santander. The only bank in town is Banco Agrícola Mercantil, in the center of Panajachel next to the Mayan Palace Hotel.

A number of outfits rent bicycles and motorcycles for reasonable hourly rates: Moto Servicio Quiché on Calle Principal, the main street, or Bicicletas Gaby, off Santander. Make sure you check the machine out and inquire about road conditions before going anywhere. Entrepreneurs at the beach and larger hotels rent sailboats, canoes, kayaks, motorboats, and other water recreation equipment. The Atitlán and several other large hotels can arrange horse, car, and boat rentals.

Around Lake Atitlán

A road goes around the eastern and southern sides of the lake but does not reach all of the eleven villages. Some can be reached only on motorbike, bicycle, or foot by way of narrow trails. The villages on the northwest shoreline are the most difficult to reach because the trail becomes very steep and arduous; it is not recommended for motorcycles or bikes. Each community can be reached by boat, however, and you might consider walking for part of your journey, then returning by water. INGUAT publishes a detailed map of the Lake Atitlán area, which is distributed free in Panajachel at hotels, shops, and restaurants as well as the local INGUAT office.

Santa Catarina Palopó
Located only 5 miles east of Panajachel, this village has shifted from an economy based on fishing and freshwater crab collection to one geared to textile production, mostly for the tourist market. The women's costume is made up of 3 panels, its waistline displaying geometric figures hand woven in a brocade of bright colors, with violet

dominating. The men's clothing repeats the pattern in a tighter brocade. There are many summer homes here now, but the only hotel in town is the highly regarded Villa Santa Catarina (621-291, or 319-876 in Guatemala City), which has 31 rooms and a restaurant at a spectacular location overlooking the lake. Fiesta day is November 25.

San Antonio Palopó

Two miles beyond Santa Catarina (by boat or road), San Antonio is a larger and more traditional village where some hostility toward foreigners has recently been reported. The people dress in traditional costumes of red shirts and wool skirts, sometimes accompanied by a turban-style hat. They tend terraced hillside gardens of onions, anise, beans, and corn, also working maguey and reed fibers into ropes and mats. The 8-room Hotel Terrazas del Lago (tel. 621-288, or 28-741 in Guatemala City) and nearby 14-room Bella Vista (374-303, or 26-807 in Guatemala City) are beautifully located and highly recommended. Both serve meals and are relatively expensive. The fiesta is held June 13. A lovely suburb of San Antonio called Agua Escondida is also worth visiting.

San Lucas Tolimán

A largely Ladino village in a heavily cultivated area (mostly coffee) on the southeast tip of the lake, San Lucas has little to recommend

The Catholic Church of Santiago Atitlán (Photo by Richard Mahler)

it except for a colonial church, Friday market, and the trailhead to the top of Tolimán volcano. The paved road from the Pan American Highway branches here, with one fork heading to Santiago and the other to Cocales and the Pacific Coast. A small dirt road also continues 2 miles northwest to the tiny village of Cerro de Oro, whose church has an unusual mural showing Christ dressed in the purple-and-white costume of the local Maya.

Santiago Atitlán

The largest of the lakeside towns after Panajachel, Santiago is famous for its Friday market and beautiful textiles. Other popular souvenirs are wood carvings of St. James, the town's patron saint, and oil or tempera paintings with naturalistic themes. The traditional dress of its residents is white and purple-striped short pants for the men, intricately embroidered huipiles for the women, some of whom still wear a tightly wound halo of red cloth on their heads. (It is tempting to photograph the older people in full regalia, but many of them resent picture-taking and either cover their faces or ask to be paid a small amount of money. Please respect their wishes.)

Santiago is the traditional capital of the Tzutuhil Maya (also spelled Zutuhil), a fiercely independent tribe who have been at odds with would-be conquerers since Pedro de Alvarado arrived with guns blazing nearly five centuries ago. More recently, the Tzutuhiles have had a series of violent conflicts with the Guatemalan military, commemorated by a shrine in Santiago's colonial church to the village's many dead, disappeared, and wounded. The roster includes Stanley Francis Rother, a popular American-born priest who has become a local martyr after his 1981 assassination in the church by unknown assailants, probably members of a right-wing death squad. Santiago was occupied for 11 years by the Guatemalan army, which was barred from the town after a 1990 massacre.

As in many highland villages, Santiago's religious customs mix indigenous beliefs with Catholic ideology. For instance, residents still pay their respects to the puppetlike image of Maximón, a figure dressed in Western clothing and a fedora that is paraded during Holy Week alongside solemn statues of Jesus and the Virgin Mary. This is one of the few places remaining in Guatemala (Zunil, near Quet-

Indian man wearing the traditional striped trousers and multicolored belt of Santiago Atitlán (Photo by Richard Mahler)

zaltenango, is another) where this curious, cigar-smoking, rum-drinking native deity is openly worshiped. Maximón's exact origins are shrouded in Mayan antiquity, but today he is an embodiment of the god of love and good fortune. On his own feast day, just before Easter, members of the village cofradía remove the wooden figure from his chapel, located in front of the town's Catholic church, stuff a cigar in his mouth, set a drink in his hand, and march Maximón in procession through the streets of Santiago. At the end of Holy Week he is returned to the house of a specially chosen cofrade, who is responsible for his well-being for the following year.

The walls of the Franciscan church, built in 1568, are lined with wooden statues of Catholic saints, clothed in shawls embroidered by the women of Santiago. Carvings on the wooden pulpit include the peculiar image of a quetzal reading a book and Yum-Kax, the Mayan god of corn. (According to the Maya, human beings were created from sacred corn.)

Besides visiting the market, Maximón's chapel, and the Catholic church, visitors can take a walk along the southern shoreline to San Lucas and beyond. There is a circuitous trail behind San Pedro volcano to the town of the same name. Boats also make frequent trips to San Pedro la Laguna and other nearby villages.

Local canoes can be hired to visit the nearby Atitlán Grebe Nature Reserve. The flightless water bird called a *poc* is found at Lake Atitlán and nowhere else on earth. The creature is very endangered, and extinction could result from the continued destruction of its nesting habitat (made up of marshland reeds that are used to make baskets) and the killing of its hatchlings by the aggressive black bass that were introduced to the lake during the 1950s. In fact, some bird experts believe there are already no true pocs left, due to crossbreeding with the more common pied-bill grebe, which it strongly resembles. Underwater fences have been installed to screen a few remaining reed beds from the marauding fish. The birds themselves are rather nondescript, but a boat ride to the reserve is a pleasant excursion and you may also see some of the lake's majestic migratories, the American widgeon and the ruddy duck.

There are several small and inexpensive hotels in the village of Santiago and an assortment of restaurants catering mostly to day visitors. The best accommodations are offered by Hospedaje Chi-Nim-Ya, which has 12 rooms (only one with private bath). Across the street is Restaurant El Gran Sol, with a nice view of the lake and good food. Some private homes rent rooms by the day, week, or month; ask around. Posada de Santiago (tel. 627-167) rents basic rooms and serves meals.

Large passenger boats leave daily between 9:00 and 10:00 a.m. for Santiago from Panajachel's public beach and the Hotel Tzanjuyu dock, returning between 12:30 and 1:30 p.m. The trips take about an hour and 15 minutes in either direction. Some vessels continue to San Pedro. There are several direct buses a day to Santiago from Cocales, but none from Panajachel (you must connect in San Lucas Tolimán).

Santiago' s annual feast day, to its patron, Saint James, is July 25.

San Pedro la Laguna

Quiet San Pedro la Laguna, a Cakchiquel Maya village located on the opposite side of the San Pedro volcano from Santiago, receives relatively few visitors and is mainly oriented toward the cultivation of coffee, corn, avocados, and produce, as well as the manufacture of shirts, rugs, and Maya-style curios for the tourist market. Some of the men still carve *cayucos* (canoes) out of the trunks of large cedar trees growing on the slopes of the nearby volcano, which can be climbed from here in about 4 or 5 hours (see chapter 12 for details). With widespread adoption of evangelical Protestantism, many residents have discarded their traditional folkways, although a modified form of Indian dress is still worn.

You can visit rug-making workshops in San Pedro, and some of the women teach foreigners how to weave on their back-strap looms; Rosa Cruz has been recommended. The rocks near the beach called Chuazanahi are a good place for swimming. Fiesta in San Pedro is June 29.

There are several small hotels and restaurants in San Pedro. Try Pensión Chuazanahi or Pensión Balneario for rooms, Comedor Ranchón or Restaurant Chez Michel for meals. Several boats head directly each day for San Pedro from Panajachel and indirectly via Santiago. The town can also be reached on foot via a steep trail or by vehicle over a rough road that goes behind the volcano.

San Juan la Laguna and Beyond

This small fishing and farming village, less than a mile beyond San Pedro, specializes in the weaving of lake-reed mats called *petates*.

There is a market on Tuesday and Saturday where these and other locally produced crafts are sold at good prices.

Continuing on foot for several miles along rough, steep trails, you can continue, in order, to the tiny and rarely visited settlements of Santa Clara, San Pablo, San Marcos, Tzununa, Jaibalito, and Santa Cruz la Laguna. This area is considered relatively free of political violence and banditry, although accommodations and services are very limited. Camping is permitted along the lakeside, but finding even a small patch of unused level ground can prove difficult.

The people of Santa Clara and San Pablo produce and sell cane baskets, hammocks, ropes, bags, and clothing from local materials. San Marcos is well known for its weavers of fine reed mats and maguey ropes. In the last of these villages, near the Santa Cruz dock, is El Arco de Noé, an inexpensive little hotel and restaurant run by a knowledgeable and friendly Austrian couple, Wolfgang Kallab and Annegret Kallab-Welzel (write Apartado Postal 39, Panajachel). They also sell beautiful Ixil weavings and can make suggestions on unusual things to see and do in the highlands. Although not visited by the author, both the hotel and the restaurant have been recommended by other travelers. Here and elsewhere in Santa Cruz you can

An Indian child walks the cobblestone streets of Santiago Atitlán (Photo by Richard Mahler)

sample local fish, freshwater crabs, and snails, which locals (distinguished by their bright red traje) collect for their own consumption and sale. There is an impressive sixteenth-century church in the village, surrounded by very old homes.

There are daily boats between San Pedro, Santa Cruz, and Panajachel, or you can walk between the latter two towns in about 3 hours.

San Jorge la Laguna

A lovely village located just below the paved road that connects Panajachel and Sololá, San Jorge was settled by refugees from the 1773 Antigua earthquake, who were subsequently forced to move from the Atitlán shoreline after a catastrophic flood.

The skyline of the village is dominated by a pretty whitewashed church. You can take a bus to the village and hike back to Panajachel via a steep trail that follows a river valley to the lake. Inquire about safety before setting out: San Jorge has been the scene of violent confrontations over land reform, and in 1992 there was a major demonstration by San Jorge farmworkers near Lake Atitlán which resulted in mass arrests by the authorities.

Sololá

One of the major market centers of the western highlands is Sololá, perched on a ridge high above Lake Atitlán. The plaza and streets fill up every Tuesday and Friday morning with sellers from throughout the area. The traditional costume, still very much in evidence, is very colorful. Men are dressed in red-striped pants with blanket aprons and waist-length woolen coats modeled after those of Spanish colonial officers. Women wear multihued long skirts and red pinstriped huipiles.

Founded in 1547, after the Spanish destroyed a nearby Indian settlement, Sololá is the capital of the department of the same name and a stronghold of Cakchiquel Maya traditions, as indicated by the distictive bat-shaped emblem on the back of the men's jackets, the symbol of the last ruling clan of the Cakchiquel nation. The ancient cofradía brotherhood is still strong here, and on Sunday mornings shortly before 10:00 you can see its members walking to the magnificent colonial cathedral in their elaborate costumes. Outsiders have tried for many years to fathom the rituals and traditions played out in Sololá, but the local residents have been jealous of their secrets and share little information with non-Indians. A colorful fiesta is held here every August 15 on Mim Ajij Sololá, which translates as "the great day of Sololá." The town is served by frequent daily buses from Panajachel and Los Encuentros, both about 6 miles away and where connections can be easily made to Chichicastenango, Quetzaltenango, and other cities.

Santa Lucía Utatlán

Santa Lucía is a good-sized, Quiché-speaking town, 9 miles beyond Sololá, surrounded by pine and oak forests. Seldom visited by outsiders, it can be reached by a branch road off the Pan American Highway. There is a good market each Sunday. A few miles farther down the road are the communities of Santa María Visitación and Santa Clara la Laguna. The latter is a basket weaving village with an excellent view of Lake Atitlán and a long, steep trail to San Pablo far below.

Nahualá and Santa Catarina Ixtahuacán

These twin towns, about 3 miles apart from each other along the Pan American Highway, are noteworthy in that they have deliberately and successfully resisted the influence of the non-Indian world. At one point during the last century the entire able-bodied male population walked the 100 miles to Guatemala City and confronted the president face to face about government land confiscation. Today only a handful of Ladinos live here, although casual visitors of any nationality are welcome.

Set in cool, high mountains, Nahualá and Santa Catarina Ixtahuacán (known collectively as Los Pueblos Chancatales) are coffee, weaving, furniture, and sheep-raising centers. Folk Catholicism is especially strong in this mountainous region, and ancient ceremonies are often carried out on the steps of the churches.

Nahualá is at Kilometer 155 on the Pan American Highway, between Los Encuentros and Quetzaltenango. Santa Catarina is about 3 miles to the southwest. Their jointly held fiesta day is November 25. Highly recommended markets take place every Sunday in Nahualá, where excellent textiles are made and sold.

You can take a bus to Puente Nahualá on the Pan American Highway, then walk to either village in a half hour or so. Accommodations and services are very limited, so consider this a day trip.

The Iximché Ruins

About 30 miles east of Los Encuentros and about 30 miles west of Antigua on the Pan American Highway is a well-marked turnoff to the town of Tecpán and nearby ancient Mayan ruins of Iximché. Tecpán is only a few hundred yards beyond the highway, and the archaeological site is about 2 miles farther south at Pueblo Viejo.

Founded in about 1470 by the Cakchiquel Maya as a defense measure against the aggressive Quiché Maya to the north, Iximché is on a strategically located promontory surrounded on three sides by steep pine-covered ravines. This site was the capital of the Cakchiquel when the first conquistadors arrived in the early sixteenth century. The Spanish and Cakchiquel formed an alliance against the Quiché and other rival Indian tribes in the area, and a provisional Spanish colonial capital was established at Iximché in 1524. After a few months the Cakchiquel revolted against the European invaders, forcing them to retreat first to the nearby village of Tecpán and then to the Almolonga Valley, where they founded Ciudad Vieja and, 16 years later, Antigua.

The Cakchiquel were defeated by the Spanish about 1530, and their capital was ransacked and burned. The destruction was not absolute, however, and some of the original plaster and paint remain on a few buildings. Still extant are several temple pyramids, a main plaza complex, a couple of ball courts, and some uncovered mounds, plus the foundation of the royal palace. Unfortunately, many of the original building materials have been hauled away for construction projects in nearby Tecpán.

The setting is very peaceful (it was purposely chosen as a ceremonial center to be used for sacrifices and other religious rituals), and today Iximché makes a good place for quiet contemplation. At any given time, you are likely to be the only foreign visitor present.

As you enter Iximché, there is a small museum on your right where you can obtain a pamphlet describing the results of research done here from 1959 to 1961. The ruins are open daily from 9:00 a.m. to

4:00 p.m. You can walk there in about 45 minutes from Tecpán or drive from there to Iximché in a few minutes by car.

The town of Tecpán was severely damaged in the 1976 earthquake, and there is not much to see except for a partially collapsed colonial church, now replaced by a new structure next to it. An ancient oracular stone, highly prized by the Maya and later placed on the altar of the older church, was lost in the disaster. There are no services or accommodations in either Tecpán or Iximché. Use caution in the area: some violent robberies involving tourists have been reported.

Quetzaltenango

Guatemala's second-largest city is more commonly referred to locally as Xela (SHAY-lah), an abbreviated version of its original Indian name, Xelajuj, a Quiché word referring to the ten principal gods this Mayan tribe worshiped. The sprawling community, 130 miles from Guatemala City, is a major trading center for the western highlands. Coffee, wheat, cotton, fruits, and vegetables, along with cattle and sheep, are brought here for processing, sale, and distribution. Xela is located in one of the coldest parts of the country, and temperatures can drop into the 30s during the dry season, although daytime highs usually reach a balmy 70 or 80 degrees.

Capital of the department of the same name, Quetzaltenango is about 10 miles off the Pan American Highway on Route 9-S. To get there, turn southwest at the crossroads called Cuatro Caminos. In terms of miles, it is actually a slightly shorter distance from Guatemala City to Quetzaltenango via the Coastal Highway, turning north at Mazatenango, but that route is much less scenic.

Mountains and volcanoes surround Quetzaltenango, which is located in a large flat plain at about 7,700 feet. For an excellent view of the city, climb to the top of the hill called El Baúl where there is a monument in tribute to Tecún Umán, the Quiché emperor who defended this area against the Spanish conquerors. A look at Xela from this perspective is a good way to get your bearings before heading out to explore the city on foot.

Xela is famous for having many of the oldest colonial buildings in the country, as this is where the Spanish conquerors first settled. There are also many nineteenth- and early-twentieth-century structures in classical, neoclassical, and Italian Renaissance style, most built from local volcanic stone with detailing by expert Indian stonecutters.

Among the best examples of Xela's fine colonial and neocolonial architecture are the deteriorating facade of the Espiritu Santo Cathedral, built in 1535, facing the tree-shaded main plaza—Parque Centro América—and the adjacent Church of the Los Altos Diocese, completed in 1899. Fronting the same plaza, also called Parque Municipal, are the Corinthian-style Palacio Municipal (City Hall) and the Greek revival Casa de Cultura del Occidente, where INGUAT, a recital hall, a library, and the Museo de Historia Natural (Museum of Natural History) are located. The museum is highly recommended for its eclectic assembly of artifacts, ranging from pickled or stuffed Guatemalan animals (including dogs!) to dramatic photographs of the severe damage sustained by Xela during volcanic eruptions in the 1920s. Exhibits are poorly marked, in Spanish only.

Parque Centro América, Quetzaltenango (Photo by Richard Mahler)

The downtown Parque Centro América is a great place for people watching, especially on balmy summer evenings. Unlike most Guatemalan cities, in Xela many of the townspeople proudly wear traditional Indian dress as everyday clothing and love to promenade each evening beneath the shade trees and monuments. The Municipal Theater (1895), at the corner of 1a. Calle and 14a. Avenida, is another good example of solid neoclassical style. The inside of the building is very fancy: theatergoers can rent private boxes equipped with individual vanities for the women. Other attractions near the city center include the Pasaje Enriquez, an old shopping complex with pretty stained-glass windows, and the Iglesia de San Nicolás (4a. Calle and 15a. Avenida), a neo-Gothic perpendicular structure with concrete flying buttresses and other eccentricities, now used as an evangelical church.

On the west side of town, near the bus terminal in Zone 3, is Parque Minerva, where the neoclassical Templo de Minerva has been erected to inspire Guatemalan youth to study hard. Minerva was the Roman goddess of wisdom and has always been revered in Xela, home to many of Guatemala's foremost musicians, artists, and intellectuals.

The large La Democracia municipal market, located between 16a. and 15a. Avenidas near Calle Rodolfo Robles in Zone 3, sells craftwork from throughout the highlands and offers high-quality goods, especially textiles, at reasonable prices. It is open every day. Do not confuse this with the "new" municipal market, a much smaller and less interesting collection of shops and stalls at the southeast corner of Parque Centro América, where there is also a three-story shopping mall catering to tourists. A worthwhile handicraft market takes place on the main plaza the first Sunday of every month.

One of Guatemala's biggest federation of weaving and textile cooperatives is based in Quetzaltenango and sells handmade products through its Tejidos Guadalupanos store. Artexco represents over 2,000 artisans whose work is of exceptionally high quality. Profits from Artexco's sales support a weaving and dyeing school that is open to foreigners.

After you have seen the markets, museums, and dignified public buildings of Xela, there is not much else for a casual visitor to do here.

Unless you have the time and inclination to enroll in one of the city's several fine language schools (see chapter 12), you are best off using Quetzaltenango as a base for day trips into the marvelously beautiful countryside where there are many villages, hot springs, volcanoes, and other interesting destinations.

Getting There

Xela is easily reached by bus from Guatemala City, Antigua, Panajachel, Huehuetenango, and other major towns. From Chichicastenango and Panajachel there are few direct buses, so you will probably have to change at Los Encuentros. Passengers from Antigua change in Chimaltenango. The main bus terminal is in Zone 3 near Parque Minerva, a 10-minute taxi ride from the main plaza, where there are always cabs. Several companies run first-class buses every day between Xela and Guatemala City, with arrivals and departures from their own private terminals near Parque Centro América. This option is highly recommended for long-distance travelers. The trip takes about 5 hours.

Hotels

Pensión Bonifaz (4a. Calle 10-50, Zone 1, tel. 614-241 or 612-959) was built in the early 1930s yet radiates colonial elegance. It is expensive by Guatemalan standards. Each of its large, comfortable suites has a sitting room, TV, and private bath. There is a good, moderately priced restaurant and comfortable bar off the lobby. Recommended.

Hotel del Campo (Km. 224 Carretera a Cantel, tel. 612-064) is difficult to reach without a car. This is a pleasant lodge with a restaurant and swimming pool, located a few miles outside of town.

Hotel Modelo (14a. Avenida A 2-31, Zone 1, tel. 612-529) is an old-fashioned, centrally located establishment that is popular among Guatemalan travelers. The rooms and meals are an unusually good value, and both are recommended. Hotel Centro Americana (Boulevard Minerva 14-09, Zone 3, tel. 614-901) is another medium-priced, 14-room hotel near the central market, with a restaurant and bar. The 13-room Gran Hotel Americano (14a. Avenida 3-43, Zona 1, tel. 618-188) is located on a busy downtown street. It is moderately priced and serves meals.

Looking south over the skyline of Quetzaltenango, with the Santa María volcano in the distance (Photo by Richard Mahler)

Hotel Casa del Viajero (8a. Avenida 9-17, Zone 1, no phone) is a good, low-priced hotel in the downtown area. Casa Kaehler (13a. Avenida 3-33, Zone 1, tel. 061-2091) is a small hotel located in a cozy, converted old house. The accommodations are clean and inexpensive. Some of the 6 rooms have private baths; others share. The owner is a German woman who has lived in Guatemala for many years.

Popular among budget travelers are the Casa Suiza (14a. Avenida A 2-36, Zone 1, tel. 614-350) and Hotel Río Azul (2a. Calle 12-15, Zone 1, no phone). Both are clean, inexpensive, and centrally located.

Restaurants

Café Baviera (5a. Calle 12-50, Zone 1) is an excellent bakery and coffeehouse run by a German-Guatemalan man (who speaks no German and little English), serving probably the best coffee drinks in the country. The specialty breads and pastries are highly recommended. You can leisurely read the morning paper while sipping a café latte and listening to George Winston.

Hotel Modelo (see above) serves excellent fixed-price meals in a pleasant colonial-style dining room. Pensión Bonifaz (also above) has the most elegant restaurant in town, and the prices are not excessive. Quality and service are first-rate. High tea is served late afternoons, with lots of blonde German-Guatemalan ladies chatting each other up. For less expensive fare, try Cafetería El Kopetin (14a. Avenida 3-31, Zone 1), serving good Guatemalan fare and Spanish-style tapas. Pollo Frito Albumar (4a. Calle 14-16, Zone 1) offers tasty fried chicken and grilled beef.

Services
There is an INGUAT office at 9a. Calle and 12a. Avenida, in the Casa de Cultura, and Guatel is just across the street. Both are in Zone 1. The post office is at the corner of 4a. Calle and 15a. Avenida, also in Zone 1. There are several banks around Parque Centro América and the main public market.

The colorful Quetzaltenango Fair takes place September 12-18. As in most other Guatemalan towns, Holy Week and Christmas are also occasions rich in tradition, with high-spirited ceremonial processions through the streets of the city.

Around Quetzaltenango

Most of the sights of Quetzaltenango can be taken in over 2 or 3 days. Beyond that, the city is a good springboard for day trips to nearby villages and hot springs. Most can be easily reached by public bus, private car, or taxi. In some cases, the destinations are even close enough to reach on foot. The area has generally been free of political unrest and banditry in recent years, although commonsense precautions should be taken.

During the annual fairs and fiestas mentioned below, colorful Indian dances are often performed in the village plazas. These may include performances of the popular La Conquista Española (the Spanish Conquest), El Mono (the Ape), and El Venado (the Deer).

Almolonga
Only 2 miles southeast of Xela, this Quiché town is known for its delicious fruits and vegetables as well as the nearby Aguas Amargas (Bit-

ter Waters) and El Rosario hot springs. The latter have been developed as a family-oriented attraction. High-quality textile and leather goods are also made and sold in Almolonga. Market days are Wednesdays and Saturdays, with a fiesta June 27-29.

Zunil and Fuentes Georginas

Zunil is on a dirt road a short distance beyond Almolonga and 6 miles from Xela, on the banks of the Río Salamá. The indigenous people of Zunil wear traditional clothing made using pre-Columbian weaving techniques and designs representing objects from their environment. The women wear an unusually long purple shawl. Textiles are sold at the artisans' cooperative in town and at the colorful markets held every Monday.

Seven miles away by a rough but scenic road are the Fuentes Georginas mineral hot springs, which emanate from the dormant Cerro Quemado volcano and are said to have curative properties. Guatemala's largest geyser is also located nearby. There are outdoor pools here, surrounded by cedar and pine forests. Simple meals are served at the modest 7-room Fuentes Georginas Hotel (no phone). You can also camp on the grounds for a nominal fee.

There is a local fair on November 25. A stunning old white church with an ornate facade dominates Zunil, which along with Santiago Atitlán is one of the few remaining places where the "pagan" image of Maximón is still openly revered with pomp and ceremony, especially during Holy Week. Also known as San Simón or Alvarado (after Spanish conquerer Pedro de Alvarado), Zunil's Maximón is a comical-looking, plastic tailor's dummy dressed in ski wear, gloves, and sunglasses.

There are regular buses from Xela to Zunil, but you will have to walk, drive, or take a taxi to Fuentes Georginas. You can also walk between Zunil and Almolonga in about 1½ hours.

Los Vahos

Only 15 minutes (12 miles) from Xela by car, these hot sulfur and mineral springs have been used by local people since the days of the Maya. Today there are several bathhouses and bungalows available at Los Vahos for use by day and overnight visitors. Like the nearby springs at Georginas, Aguas Amargas, and El Rosario, the Vahos spa is situated in a scenic mountain setting. Like the others, however, it is neither particularly clean nor private.

Olintepeque

About 6 miles northeast of Xela on the old road to Huehuetenango, Olintepeque is the place where the proud Quiché Emperor Tecún Umán is said to have been killed in 1524 during a fierce Indian battle against the forces of Pedro de Alvarado. The story that has been handed down claims that the nearby Xequijel River was tinted bright red by the blood of the Indian warriors, hence its name, which means "blood" in Quiché. Markets are held here on Tuesdays, and the local fair is June 24. Hand weaving of silk and cotton textiles is the main occupation. There are frequent buses to Olintepeque from Xela.

Salcajá

A few miles east of Olintepeque on the road to the Pan American Highway, this very old and mostly Ladino village is famous for its *jaspe* cloth, handwoven from tie-dyed yarn for subsequent use by weavers throughout the highlands. Salcajá is also renowned for its delicious alcoholic beverages: *caldo de frutas* is a powerful fruit punch, and *rompopo* is a bit like eggnog. Worth seeing here is the stately Church of San Jacinto, said to be the first colonial building erected in Guatemala. Market day in Salcajá is Tuesday. A local fiesta takes place on August 25.

San José Chiquilaja

Located about 10 minutes by car from Xela on the Salamá River, this village comes alive every January 15 for a festival venerating the Black Christ of Esquipulas (see chapter 10).

San Juan Ostuncalco

This Mam-speaking trading center is 9 miles northwest of the provincial capital and is a good place to buy wicker furniture, musical instruments, and regional weavings, especially during the Thursday and Sunday markets. (Unless you wish to carry these often fragile goods with you for the remainder of your Guatemalan tour, it is

Man and child from Todos Santos. (Photo by J. W. Smith)

▲ San Pedro Volcano looms over Lake Atitlán. (Photo by J. W. Smith)

▼ The colonial capital of Antigua beneath Agua Volcano. (Photo by INGUAT)

Carved stela in the Maya ruins of Tikal. (Photo by J. W. Smith)

▲ Keel-billed toucan in the Petén jungle. (Photo by Kevin Schafer)

▼ "Hot lips" plant used as natural contraceptive. (Photo by Kevin Schafer and Martha Hill)

▲ Village in the Chuchumatanes Mountains at dawn. (Photo by J. W. Smith)

▼ Colonial-era church in the highland town of Zunil. (Photo by INGUAT)

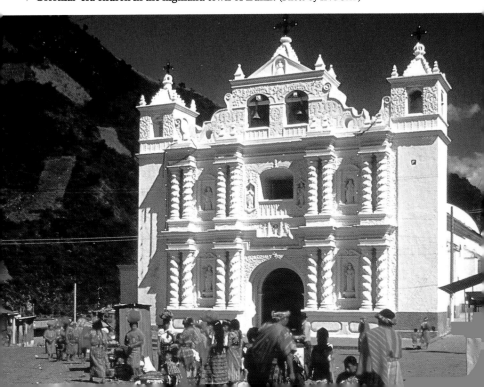

▲ Maya Indians wear masks of Spaniards during the dance of the conquerors. (Photo by INGUAT)

▼ Temple II looms above stone stelae along the Great Plaza of Tikal. (Photo by Don Usner)

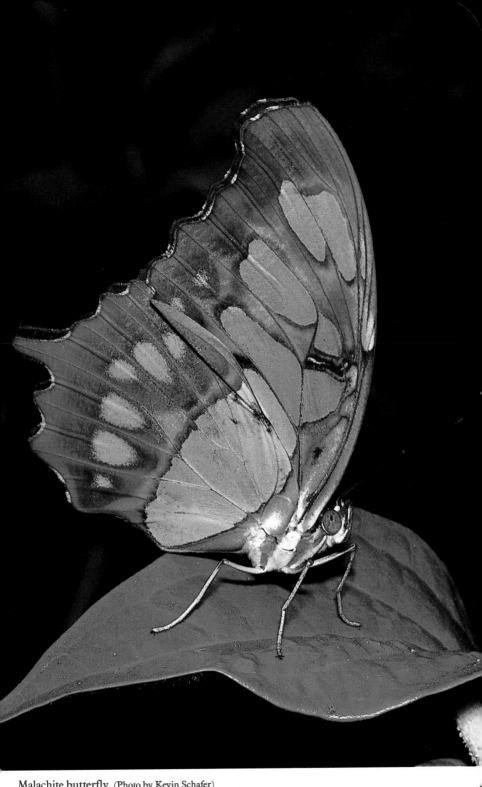

Malachite butterfly. (Photo by Kevin Schafer)

▲ A tight weave and bright colors characterize textiles made in the highlands. (Photo by Don Usner)

▼ A Quiché Maya woman sells handwoven clothing in a public market. (Photo by J. W. Smith)

advised that you send them home via one of the shipping specialists of Xela, Panajachel, Antigua, or Guatemala City.) San Juan is located in a picturesque mountain valley and holds an annual fair from January 29 to February 3.

Cantel

Cantel is justifiably famous for the quality of both its lovely textiles and its delicious fruit. In fact, Guatemala's largest textile company is headquartered here. Cantel is about 15 minutes by car from Xela on the paved road heading southeast toward the Pacific Coast. Market day is Sunday, and the annual fiesta is August 15.

San Martín Chili Verde

One of the most traditional villages in the region, San Martín is situated near Lago de Chicabal, a volcanic lake considered sacred by local Indians. Much of the land is devoted to cultivation of green chili peppers, and many residents are skilled basket weavers. San Martín is located about 25 minutes by car from Xela. There is a five-day fair that begins November 7.

San Cristóbal Totonicapán

An important center for the weaving of silk, wool, and cotton textiles, San Cristóbal has an outstanding Franciscan church with an unusual altar made of chiseled silver and crystal. The town is about 14 miles northeast of Xela on the Pan American Highway. Sundays are market days, and there is a week-long fair beginning July 20.

Totonicapán

The departmental capital of Totonicapán is about 17 miles northeast of Xela and well worth a visit, especially for those interested in Guatemalan native and colonial craftwork. Nestled in high mountains and surrounded by tall pine and oak forests, it is famous for its indigenous traditions and handicrafts, notably pottery, wooden toys, leather goods, ceremonial masks, and weavings. Markets are on Tuesday and Saturday, and there is a fair the last week of September. There are smaller handicraft markets each Sunday and Thursday.

INGUAT has prepared a guide to Totonicapán artisans and studios that is available at any of its offices as well as many travel agencies in Guatemala.

A rather unattractive public bath has been built around a hot spring on the edge of town (as elsewhere in Guatemala, a bathing suit is required). Totonicapán is about 8 miles off the Pan American Highway on Route 1 via San Cristóbal.

San Francisco el Alto

Friday is market day in this stunning highland village surrounded by tall volcanoes and pine forests. The view from the colonial church to the valley far below is quite spectacular. San Francisco is located on a steep mountainside about 12 miles northwest of Totonicapán (and about half hour by car from Xela).

The buying and selling of farm and hunting animals at the big San Francisco el Alto market every week is not to be missed. For tourists, there are particularly good buys on handmade woolen blankets bearing intricate geometric designs. A large fiesta is held October 5 and includes some especially big and exotic markets. There are a couple of basic hospedajes here should you wish to get to the market early (it starts at 4:00 a.m.). There are frequent buses from Xela that continue from San Francisco to Momostenango.

Momostenango

This village, roughly 20 miles (an hour by car) north of San Francisco on Route 2, is known throughout the world for its superbly made woolen blankets, scarves, and rugs, woven on large foot looms. Market day is Sunday, and a regional fiesta called Octava de Santiago is held from July 28 to August 2. Traditional Mayan rituals are also held throughout the year in Momostenango, which is one of the most traditional and spiritual communities in the western highlands. The ancient 260-day Tzolkin calendar is still in use here, and there are said to be as many as three hundred Indian shamans living in the area, each specializing in a different kind of practice. Located about 2 miles from the village is a hot spring used for bathing (by locals only) and the shrinking of newly made blankets. There are a couple of basic hotels and restaurants.

The Momostenango Riscos near the village of Momostenango (Photo by INGUAT)

The Momostenango Riscos are located in a rural area several miles from the town itself. They are an unusual set of eroded pillars and caves composed of consolidated volcanic ash from eruptions that probably took place thousands of years ago. Inquire locally for exact directions to the site, or hire a taxi for the one-hour ride through spectacular mountain scenery.

San Marcos and San Pedro Sacatepéquez
These twin cities (less than half a mile apart) are located about 50 minutes by car northwest of Xela in a Mam-speaking region of the western highlands. The San Marcos department's largest market, famous for its colorful Indian textiles, takes place in San Pedro every Tuesday, Thursday, and Sunday. A local fair is also held in San Pedro the week of June 24. On Tuesdays and Fridays there are markets in the town of San Marcos, noted for its natural hot spring bathing center, called Agua Tibia. Another local attraction is the Maya Palace, a strange-looking building between the two towns that is governmental headquarters for the department. The outside of the structure is elaborately decorated with imitation Mayan friezes, and a sculpted pair of roaring jaguars guard the entrance. A fiesta takes place in San

Marcos April 22 through April 27. There are several basic hotels and restaurants, most of them in San Pedro. Buses run each hour to Xela, and several first-class *pullmanes* leave for Guatemala City every day.

Santa María, Santiaguito, Tajumulco, and Tacaná Volcanoes

One of these peaks—Santiaguito—is still active, and current conditions should be checked before climbing it. The crater of Santiaguito is about a 2- or 3-hour hike from the Llanos de Pinal, about 10 miles directly south of Quetzaltenango. Santa María, the higher peak of the same mountain (at 12,376 feet), is a fairly arduous climb. Tajumulco and Tacaná, located north of San Marcos near the Mexican border, are not especially difficult climbs, but the altitude takes some adjustment. At 13,846 feet, Tajumulco is the highest mountain in Guatemala (and all of Central America). Tacaná checks in at 13,429 feet. (See chapter 13 for details volcano-climbing excursions.)

Huehuetenango

This small, nondescript town is 90 minutes by car (about 50 miles) northwest of Quetzaltenango. Affectionately referred to as Huehue, it is a good encampment for day trips to the many surrounding Indian villages, each with its own distinctive Mayan markets and fiestas (see below). Bus connections can be made here to scores of tiny settlements of the Cuchumatanes mountains, the highest range in Guatemala, where life has changed very little in the last several hundred years.

Huehue is 4 miles off the Pan American Highway, at the base of the Cuchumatanes. It is an important trading center with one of the best public markets in the highlands (open daily) and has an interesting neoclassical church overlooking its main plaza. The Iglesia de Chiantla has a statue of the Virgin made entirely of silver that was mined locally. The silver mines were exploited by the Spanish during colonial times using Indian slave labor.

Most of the activity is on the east side of Huehue, along 1a. Avenida. Besides subsistence farming, residents of the area are active in sugarcane and coffee production as well as textile crafts.

Huehue is most easily reached from Guatemala City by first-class bus, several of which depart each day from the capital. If arriving by car, turn north from the Pan American Highway on Route 9-N for the short drive north into Huehue. If heading for or from Mexico, the border is an easy 52 miles to the west. Guatemala City is 160 miles southeast.

There are a number of inexpensive hotels and restaurants in Huehuetenango, most of them clustered around the city plaza and none of them exceptional. Try Hotel Maya (3a. Avenida 3-53, Zone 1, no phone), the slightly fancier 23-room Hotel Zaculeu (5a. Avenida 1-14, Zone 1, tel. 641-086), or Mary (2a. Calle 3-52, Zone 1, tel. 641-569), which has 25 rooms and a comedor on the premises. The best restaurants in Huehue are in the hotels, or you can try Ebony (2a. Calle 5-11, Zone 1), which serves Guatemalan and "international" cuisine in a youth-oriented atmosphere. Also recommended is Pizza Hogareña on 6a. Avenida between 4a. and 5a. Calles.

The Huehuetenango post office is at 2a. Calle 3-54, the Guatel station is next door, the Mexican consulate is on the plaza at 5a. Avenida and 4a. Calle, and Banco de Guatemala is at 5a. Avenida and 4a. Calle. All are located in Zone 1.

Zaculeu

These restored ruins, located a few miles west of Huehuetenango, date from the pre-Conquest period and are all that remain of the former capital of the Mam, one of the main highland Maya tribes. There are a few large temples, plazas, and a ball court, laid out in a strategic defense pattern. Unlike the Mayan archaeological sites familiar to most visitors, the walls of the constructions contain no hieroglyphic writing, and there are no stelae or figurative objects, possibly because of clumsy restoration work carried out by the United Fruit Company in the late 1940s. In fact, Zaculeu has a rather sterile, characterless quality, as if its benefactor had purposely swept away all potsherds and stone monuments in order to give the site a well-scrubbed look. Admission is free, and a small museum is open from

8:00 a.m. to noon and 1:00 to 6:00 p.m.

Several buses and minivans head this direction each day from Huehuetenango, or you can take a taxi. Walking to Zaculeu from Huehue takes about an hour.

Around Huehuetenango

Todos Santos Cuchumatán

Located about 30 miles northwest of Huehuetenango via the Paquix junction, Todos Santos is an isolated valley town ringed by very tall, forested mountains. Its Mam-speaking residents have kept to their traditional ways of life, including unusually colorful patterns of dress: men wear red-and-white striped pants, black woolen breeches, and elaborately embroidered collars; women clothe themselves in dark blue skirts and brilliant red blouses.

The elevation of Todos Santos is 8,154 feet, so temperatures are always fairly cool. A good time to visit Todos Santos is during the local All Saints' Day fiesta, from October 31 to November 5, when an unusual kind of all-day horse relay race and other traditional forms of celebration can be observed, all with the accompaniment of marimba orchestras. Among other attractions are the high-quality traje sold at the Saturday market, along with locally made pottery and woolen goods.

The 260-day Mayan calendar is still used in Todos Santos, and many brujos continue their ceremonies and rituals at nearby ruins. Nights can get very cold in the upland pastures where men tend their sheep. You will sometimes see the shepherds wearing a traditional overdress of long-haired black monkey skin.

Basic lodging is available at Pensión Lucía, Los Olguitas, and Hospedaje La Paz, all near the bus stop. There are a few simple comedores on or near the plaza. A pathway next to one of them, Comedor Katy, leads to the small Mayan site of Tojcunanchén above the village. Two buses run each day between Todos Santos and Huehuetenango. They continue up the valley to smaller communities where there are no services or accommodations.

San Mateo Ixtatán and Aguacatán

Markets are held each Thursday and Sunday in the village of San Mateo, with a good selection of well-made textiles and other típica, including the warm woolen cape called a *capixay*. San Mateo is at a high altitude (above 8,000 feet) where wheat is grown and sheep are grazed; there is a communal salt works here, too. The community is about 8 hours by bus northeast of Huehuetenango.

Thursday and Sunday are also market days in Aguacatán, the garlic center of the highlands (and Central America), where the ethnically distinct residents speak their own language. Aguateca is spoken here and in the surrounding countryside and nowhere else on earth. The Spanish colonials tried to integrate the Aguateca Maya with the nearby Quiché but with little success. There are ruins of an early colonial church here, and nearby is the historic site of Pueblo Viejo, a pre-Columbian village with several unexcavated burial mounds. It is here that the Indians are said to have brought gold bricks to the conquistadors from their neighboring mines in the vain hope that the king of Spain would allow them to keep their lands.

Aguacatán has a large Sunday market (which actually begins Saturday afternoon), and this is an excellent place to both shop and people watch. The women of Aguacatán are distinguished by their headdress, a fanciful embroidered ribbon of bright reds, yellows, greens, and blues. It looks a lot like the pom-poms used by American cheerleaders during football games.

Aguacatán is about a 1-hour (17-mile) bus ride east from Huehuetenango, from which there are several daily buses, some continuing along Route 7-W to Sacapulas. There are a few basic hotels and restaurants in the village but not much else. Just outside Aguacatán is the source of the Río San Juan, which bubbles out of the ground from a hidden limestone cave.

Chiantla

The village church in Chiantla, three miles north of Huehuetenango, is famous for its silver image of the Virgin Mary, which is said to have special restorative powers. Pilgrims come from throughout the country every February 2 to pay homage to the Virgen del Rosario. This is a spectacle worth seeing, although there are no hotels or restaurants in the community itself. The silver for the icon was mined locally during the colonial era by Indians enslaved by the Spanish.

The High Road to Nebaj and Cobán

From Huehuetenango, Route 7-W twists and turns through the Cuchumatanes Mountains to Aguacatán, Sacapulas, and, after it intersects Route 3, the Ixil-speaking town of Nebaj. It is a scenic (usually 2-day) bus ride along this road through eastern Quiché department and into the lush Sierra de Chuacús and Chamá of Alta Verapaz. Route 7-W eventually meets the Cobán Highway north of Tactic. It is about 10 more miles from that intersection to the city of Cobán. This road is seldom taken by travelers, but there are a few hospedajes and comedores along the way in Cunén, Uspantán, Chicamán, and San Cristóbal Verapaz. The adventurous would do well to inquire about local transportation, guerrilla activity, and services before heading east of Cunén along Route 7-W. Several bicyclists have recommended this route as a scenic alternative to the Guatemala City-to-Cobán highway.

The High Road to Barillas and Beyond

Route 9-N continues north from Huehuetenango into the Sierra de los Cuchumatanes and through beautiful mountain villages that are among the most traditional and undisturbed communities in all of Guatemala. It takes at least a full day (preferably two) to travel the 90-odd miles to Barillas, where the road runs out in a steamy lowland jungle that stretches deep into Mexico. There is talk about extending the one-lane road all the way to Playa Grande, on the Río Chixoy in Alta Verapaz, but further construction is unlikely while this remote region remains a guerrilla stronghold. This northernmost part of Huehuetenango department has experienced much military and guerrilla activity in recent years, and inquiries should be made before proceeding beyond the Todos Santos turnoff on Route 9-N.

The Mexican Border and Beyond

La Mesilla

There are buses every 90 minutes or so between Huehuetenango and La Mesilla, on the Mexican border, a journey of about 2½ hours. The border is open from 6:00 a.m. to 9:00 p.m. and sometimes even later. Mexican tourist cards are always issued here, but if you are coming from the other direction, there are sometimes no Guatemalan tourist cards or visas available at this frontier, so you are advised to get those documents in advance (i.e., from the Guatemalan consulate in Comitán).

Buses for San Cristóbal de las Casas and other Mexican cities start leaving Ciudad Cuauhtémoc, the village on the Mexican side of the border, about noon each day. Going the other way, you can catch a direct bus to Quetzaltenango and/or Guatemala City from La Mesilla starting at 6:00 a.m.

Chinkultic

This small Mayan site rises out of the flatlands just north of the Mexican border and a few miles south of the town of Comitán. Unattended and largely unexcavated, Chinkultic features two small, unrestored pyramids and a tall acropolis, also covered by earth and rubble. Visitors will find sacrificial pools, carved stelae (depicting jaguars and the ubiquitous god Chac), stone bridges, altars, and temples.

A chain of iridescent jungle lakes begins here, variously known as Lagunas de Montebello or Las Encantadas, which seem to dramatically change color during the course of the day due to a combination of mineral and algae content. These attractions, as well as the deep and impressive Sumidero Canyon, are now incorporated in the Lagunas de Montebello National Park.

Chinkultic can be reached by turning east from the Pan American Highway at a point 9 miles south of Comitán. Look for a sign designating the Lacandón Rainforest/Lagunas de Montebello turnoff. The ruins are about 12 miles down this narrow dirt trail, marked by a small sign pointing to the left. Only four-wheel-drive vehicles should attempt this route, especially during wet weather. You can either camp in the national park or stay at a hotel in the nearby towns of Comitán or La Trinitaria, both on the Pan American Highway.

The dirt road continues beyond Lagunas de Montebello National Park all the way to Frontera Corozál, on the Río Usumacinta, but this route is not recommended during the rainy season. From Corozál, connections can be made by boat, land, or plane for Yaxchilán, Bonampak, Piedras Negras, Palenque, and other ancient Mayan sites (see chapter 11). The Lacandón rain forest is one of the largest stands of primary forest remaining in subtropic Mexico, but access is intentionally limited to preserve wildlife habitat and the sacred homelands of the dwindling Lacandón Maya.

8

The Pacific Coast

Guatemala's hot, humid Pacific coast is understandably low on the destination list for most visitors, although it does have some secluded beaches, ancient ruins, and nature reserves to recommend it. The Costa Sur (or South Coast, as it is otherwise known) is heavily cultivated, with a largely Ladino resident population and a sizable number of migrant Indian plantation workers who come from the highlands to the area's labor camps during harvest times. There are many sugarcane fields, tropical fruit orchards, and food-processing plants. Coconut, rice, manioc, coffee, and corn are also important crops. In pre-Columbian days, cacao, dye-plants, and cotton were grown here.

The Pacific Coast has beaches that are sometimes scenic and empty but also frequently hot (due to their black volcanic sand) and treacherous (because of strong currents). The resorts of the region cater primarily to Guatemalan families, most of whom come from the capital on weekends and holidays. At these times the beaches—and the roads leading to them—tend to become very crowded.

Best bets for foreign travelers include the several archaeological sites and wetland reserves described below. There is also excellent deep-sea fishing offshore, and some opportunities for bird-watching, camping, volcano climbing, and kayaking.

Many destinations along the Pacific Coast are within an easy day's drive or bus trip of the capital, Antigua, Quetzaltenango, or Lake Atitlán. In addition, most major tour operators have regular and reasonably priced trips to Pacific Coast attractions by car or minivan.

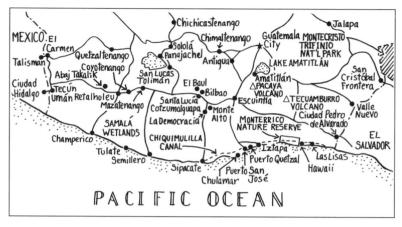

The Pacific Coast

When to Go

The lowland Pacific Coast is warm and damp throughout the year but hottest and rainiest from May to November. If you must travel during those months, be advised that malaria and dengue fever are common and precautions should be taken. Use of antimalarial pills, mosquito nets, and fine-mesh window screen will help reduce the likelihood of contracting these potentially fatal maladies. Consult your physician for advice concerning other endemic diseases, such as typhoid and cholera. The best time to travel here, in terms of weather, is December through March.

Getting There

Buses serve all the major coastal towns with frequent and reliable schedules. As in the rest of the country, these vehicles are small by American standards (except for first-class coaches) and are usually uncomfortably crowded.

From Guatemala City's Zone 4 terminal there are several buses each day departing for the coastal communities of Puerto San José,

A mixture of western and traditional clothing styles among the men and boys of Santiago Atitlán (Photo by Richard Mahler)

Las Lisas, and Escuintla (which is also served from Zone 1). Connections on buses serving smaller communities can be made via Escuintla.

There is daily passenger rail service—cheaper and much slower than the bus but just as crowded—from the Mexican border at Tecún Umán to Guatemala City, with stops in Coatepeque, Retalhuleu, Mazatenango, Santa Lucía Cotzumalguapa, Escuintla, and other towns along the way.

By auto, the main road through the region is the Pacific Coast Highway (also called the Coastal Highway), marked on signs and maps as CA-2, which runs roughly parallel to the Pacific from the Mexican frontier to El Imposible National Park in El Salvador. The road is actually some distance northeast of the ocean, but most of the way there are feeder roads connecting it to virtually every community on the coast. From Guatemala City, take CA-9 southwest to meet the Coastal Highway at Escuintla. From Panajachel and Lake Atitlán, head south through San Lucas Tolimán on CA-11. From Quetzaltenango, the coast route is reached by heading south on 9-S, which continues to the seaport town of Champerico.

Entering / Leaving Guatemala from Mexico

The northern part of Guatemala's Pacific Coast region is easily reached by several paved highways that enter the country from Mexico. Although intended for those traveling by car or bus from the Mexican state of Chiapas, information on the frontier crossings below may also be useful to those heading to or from Mexico via the western highlands, Antigua, and Guatemala City.

El Carmen—A 24-hour Guatemalan border crossing of CA-2 over the Río Suchiate into Talismán, Mexico. Besides the customs and immigration post, only a small number of services are available. It is best to plan your trip so that you will be able to stay overnight or change buses in a larger town, such as Malacatán or Huehuetenango in Guatemala or Comitán in Mexico. There are better first-class bus connections here than farther south in Tecún Umán.

Tecún Umán—A traffic-clogged village opposite the town of Ciudad Hidalgo, Mexico, with railroad and highway connections north as far as the United States. There is a 24-hour customs and immigration office, plus several small restaurants and hotels. The best of the latter is called Vanessa 2. Buses head into the interiors of Mexico and Guatemala in a steady stream.

La Mesilla—Located on the Pan American Highway in the state of Chiapas, Mexico. It is best to have tourist cards in hand before arrival, since the customs and immigration offices here are sometimes inefficient. Bus connections can be made several times a day for Huehuetenango and San Cristóbal de las Casas, Mexico.

Pacific Coast Towns From North to South

Escuintla

This is the largest of the coastal towns, located at the junction of the Pacific Coastal Highway and the main road between Guatemala City and Puerto San José. Despite its size and strategic importance, Escuintla is a dull commercial center that has little to recommend it beyond a bustling daily market, convenient bus connections, and easy access to the archaeological sites around Santa Lucía Cotzumalguapa, some 12 miles west on the Coast Highway.

The biggest hotel in town is the Sarita (Avenida Centro América 15-32, Zone 3, tel. 380-482) with 34 rooms, a bar, a restaurant, and other amenities. Down the street is the 26-room Motel Texas (Avenida Centro América 15-04, Zone 3, tel. 380-183), which also serves meals. Both charge moderate rates.

Along 4a. Avenida, Escuintla's main street, you can find plenty of inexpensive eateries serving everything from decent Chinese fried rice to excellent fresh seafood.

Puerto San José

Located about a 2-hour drive south of Guatemala City (and about 25 miles south of Escuintla), this city is a major cargo port for the capital and surrounding areas, although it has been somewhat overshadowed by the new Puerto Quetzal a few miles to the east. Nearby also are the beach resorts of Chulamar and Likin, which tend to be crowded and noisy on weekends and during school vacations. San José and these holiday retreats are separated from the beach by the Chiquimulilla Canal, a man-made inland waterway that runs from Sipacate, 15 miles west of San José, all the way to the Salvadoran border. There are plenty of small boats and ferries transporting beachgoers across the canal throughout the day and evening. You can also hire a boatman to transport you along the canal in either direction, dropping you at the secluded beach, campground, or resort of your choice.

Be advised that prices at all of the better hotels in the San José area vary dramatically, depending on whether it is a weekend or a holiday (expensive), weekday or slow season (moderate). Be prepared to bargain if you visit during a down time, especially if you wish to stay more than a day or two.

In descending order of services, major hotels include the 24-room Agua Azul (Km 106½, tel. 741-887, or in Guatemala City 315-858), the 18-room Posada del Quetzal (Avenida 30 de Junio, no phone), and the 37-room Turicentro Martita (5a. Calle y Avenida del Comercio, no phone). The larger hotels have reliable restaurants, and there are a number of inexpensive comedores around San José serving good shrimp dishes and other seafood.

Chulamar, Likin, and Puerto Quetzal

Chulamar, a self-contained, moderately priced resort a few miles west of San José, has several restaurants, swimming pools, and beaches. Its 52 rooms are usually filled on weekends and holidays, when the rates often triple (tel. 313-801 in Guatemala City). Balneario Chulamar, a 12-bungalow complex next to the Chulamar resort, is moderately priced, except on weekends and holidays (tel. 23-836 in Guatemala City).

Farther east, past the container cargo and cruise ship terminal of Puerto Quetzal, is the fully planned (and security-conscious) community of Balneario Likin. There are boats that can shuttle you to the beach, but otherwise there is not much to do here. The homes are mainly weekend and holiday residences for prosperous city dwellers. Try the Turicentro Likin Hotel, which has bungalows and a small restaurant.

Iztapa and the Chiquimulilla Canal

The main road east of San José along the beachfront ends at the town of Iztapa, a quiet old port used by the early Spanish as the main Guatemalan naval station. There are hourly buses from Guatemala City and two low-priced hotels worth considering: the Brasilia and María del Mar. You can take the car ferry across the Río Naranjo to Pueblo Viejo and a bus from there to the national park at Monterrico, or hire a boat and follow the Chiquimulilla Canal, which winds its way for another 25 miles to Las Lisas on a course roughly parallel to the ocean. Unfortunately, what could be a peaceful journey with plenty of bird-watching is often interrupted by noisy speedboats. You can camp on the beach at Iztapa, but the environs are rather dirty and polluted. You will have better luck near El Cenacaste and Madre Vieja, beach villages farther along the way to Monterrico.

Las Lisas

Another favorite vacation destination of Guatemaltecos, the beach town of Las Lisas is about 14 miles northwest of the Salvadoran border and about the same distance down a branch road from the Coastal Highway. The beach is separated from the town by the Chiquimulilla Canal, and boats can be hired to cross the waterway or make excursions to smaller villages nearby. Despite its popularity, hotels and services are limited. Buses to Las Lisas leave several times a day from Zone 4 in Guatemala City.

Ruins

Unlike other parts of Guatemala, the archaeological sites of the coastal piedmont are spread out and in some cases difficult to get to. A few are on private land, surrounded by cultivated fields of sugarcane and other crops. Many of the remarkable stone monuments for which the region is famous have eroded considerably over the years or have been carelessly disassembled. A good number have also been carted off to museums and private collections. Because of these circumstances, visitors may be better off taking an organized tour from Guatemala City or hiring a local guide (even a well-informed taxi driver) than trying to find some of the archaeological sites on their own.

Monte Alto and La Democracia

Little is known about the origins of the huge Olmec-style structures that are strewn about the fields of the Monte Alto Archaeological Park, located in the town of La Democracia on Route 2 about 6 miles south of the Pacific Coast Highway and just east of Santa Lucía. The park, in the La Democracia plaza, features colossal heads from the Late Pre-Classic era (300 B.C. to A.D. 300) which are believed to have been created by the Olmec. The collection also includes enigmatic potbellied stone figures that were hauled in by Europeans from their original location 4 miles away at Monte Alto, where there are no longer any ruins. Smaller specimens are found in the city's archaeological museum (open 9:00 to noon and 2:00 to 5:00 p.m., Tuesday through Sunday, except holidays). Also on display are obsidian blades and carvings of mushrooms, which lead some observers to speculate that hallucinogenic fungi may have been used in ceremonial rituals by these early residents.

Other Buddha-like heads and eroding zoomorphs (carved animal-like figures) are scattered throughout the rolling hills of this area. Some are still used by local descendants of the Maya in ceremonial rituals that involve the anointing of the rocks with sugarcane liquor (which is then burned) along with incense, flower petals, and sacrificial blood.

Many archaeologists believe that Mexico's ancient Olmec Indians, in addition to the Maya, occupied this part of Guatemala for some time. These experts point out that some of the carved figures wear Mexican-style clothing and headdresses or have faces that resemble Olmec gods, such as those represented at the Monte Alban site near Oaxaca, Mexico. Other scientists disagree, preferring to more closely connect these ruins with the highland and Petén Maya of Guatemala, although no Mayan glyphs have yet been found here. Still others feel that these sculptures may be the work of neither group. Whatever the case, some of the carvings may be well over 4,000 years old, which would put their creation during the most formative years of the Mayan civilization. Most, however, appear to have been made between 300 B.C. and the birth of Christ. A few stelae from after this time imply that there was a gradual transition from Olmec to Maya domination of the area, with closer ties between coastal and highland Indians.

A good hotel and restaurant complex in the area is Caminotel Santiaguito (Km 90½, Santa Lucía Cotzumalguapa, tel. 745-435). Rooms are moderately priced, and there is a large pool. Fresh seafood and paella are usually available, along with cold drinks and sandwiches. A less expensive but perfectly decent alternative is the Hotel El Camino across the street.

El Baúl, El Bilbao, and Las Ilusiones

Each of these sites contains monumental sculptures of the little-known Cotzumalguapa-Pipil culture, which flourished here during the Classic era and was apparently linked to both the highland Maya and the Mexican Olmec.

The El Baúl site is about 3 miles north of Santa Lucía on a sugar plantation and is the most accessible to visitors. There are two stones at the top of a hill, both still used in animal sacrifices, flower offerings, and the burning of incense. The tallest of these is a fertility symbol, used in supplications for pregnancy and safe births. Another carved stone resembles an enormous head, blackened now by count-

A tire is changed on an old American school bus, the most popular form of public transportation in Guatemala (Photo by J. W. Smith)

less burning rituals. Yet another stelae shows a presumed ruler in ritual paraphernalia holding a wavy-bladed flint knife. As at other Indian ceremonial centers, you should stay away when the shrine is in obvious use unless specifically beckoned forward by participants. A number of sculptures, some with non-Maya glyphs, have been stacked haphazardly next to a sugar refinery.

El Bilbao is just to the north of Santa Lucía and consists of four sets of stelae, all that remains of a much larger ceremonial site that was shipped off nearly in its entirety to Germany in the 1880s. The stones were carved by artisans of the Pipil culture between A.D. 400 and 900. The glyphs bear some resemblance to others found in southern Mexico from the same era. The monuments are well hidden by sugarcane, and the services of a local guide are strongly advised.

Las Ilusiones is a mile or so east of Santa Lucía, also surrounded by sugarcane fields. The attraction here is a jumbled but impressive collection of stone carvings and artifacts, some with Olmec characteristics, others that look like Mayan creations. You will have to ask at the main house of the finca for someone to unlock the building that houses this eclectic private museum. Particularly interesting are the finely carved Mayan stelae and zoomorphs. The site can be visited for a small fee between 8:00 a.m. and 5:00 p.m. Again, a local guide is recommended.

Three other ancient Pipil sites are within a few miles of Santa Lucía. They are Pantaleon, El Castillo, and Santa Rita. Ask locally for directions to these stone monuments.

Abaj Takalik

Monumental structures at the Abaj Takalik site, also known as El Asintal (the name of the town where it is located), include some structures with Olmec and others with Pre-Classic Mayan characteristics. Apparently both groups lived here at different times. Some stelae found here bear hieroglyphic dates in the Long Count notation corresponding to A.D. 200. Others, which have been damaged, may be older. Researchers believe this is one of the first places along the coast where carved stone stelae became a public and religious art form, at about 100 B.C. The site is located between Coatepeque and Retalhuleu, near the Pacific Coast Highway. All together there are about 50 stone monuments at Abaj Takalik, the 12 largest averaging nearly 15 tons each.

Parks and Nature Reserves

Monterrico-Hawaii Biotope

This is the only part of Guatemala's Pacific lowlands that enjoys specific environmental protection, although a move has been under way to grant the Río Samalá wetlands near Champerico similar status. This may have occurred by the time of your visit.

Located near the village of Monterrico, the 7,000-acre Monterrico-Hawaii Biotope includes several miles of pristine coastline, a stretch of inland mangrove swamp, and some lowland forest. This is an extremely important habitat for many species of waterfowl, such as herons and egrets, plus the many small fish, crabs, insects, worms, and other creatures they feed on. Quite a few migratory birds also make this their winter home. The maze of mangrove roots provide a kind of underwater nursery, where hatchlings can grow to adulthood with plenty of nutrients and some measure of protection from predators. Raccoons, opossums, anteaters, weasels, iguanas, and other water-loving animals can be found here, especially at night.

Sea turtles, along with iguanas, are raised and released at Monterrico in the hope of increasing their numbers, which have been devastated by human hunters. Sea turtles nest and lay their eggs along the beach before returning to the ocean. Farther inland, the reserve protects the habitat of freshwater turtles. If your visit corresponds with the winter hatching period, you can help the newborn turtles make their successful escape to the Pacific.

The Monterrico reserve has a self-guided nature trail and a swimming hole. It is bisected by the meandering Chiquimulilla Canal, which offers good opportunities for bird-watching. The reserve extends south to the fishing village of Hawaii, accessible only by boat, the site of a few vacation homes and *cabañas* (but no hotel).

Monterrico can be reached by boat from La Avellana, a small town not far from Taxisco. Both communities are served by regular buses and minivans via either the coastal or the inland roads.

The Hotel Baule, run by an American expatriate and former Peace Corps worker, offers rooms and meals at budget prices. Although not visited by the author, the lodge and its services have been recommended by other travelers. Tours of the reserve by cayuco, foot, or horseback can be arranged through Nancy, the hotel's friendly and knowledgeable owner. Beach cabañas and campsites can also be inexpensively rented on the black sand beach, which has good surfing.

Montecristo National Park

This national park, some distance inland from the coast, is jointly administered as part of the Trifinio-La Fraternidad Project by the governments of Guatemala, Honduras, and El Salvador. It encompasses a range of rugged mountains in the area where the borders of Guatemala, Honduras, and El Salvador intersect. Peaks here rise to nearly 9,000 feet and protect the last remnant of cloud forest in the region. These mountains are, in effect, ecological islands now surrounded by the farmlands that stretch in every direction below them.

The reserve bears the same name in El Salvador and is called Montecristo-Trifinio National Park in Honduras. As of late 1992, access and services were limited and visitor permits had to be obtained from authorities in El Salvador. You may check locally with officials in Esquipulas to see if the situation has changed. There is a dirt road into the park from the town of Metapán, El Salvador, which can be negotiated on foot or by four-wheel-drive vehicle.

There is an orchid garden, an apple orchard, and a campground at the end of the road (allow 2 hours to drive there from Metapán). For permits write or phone Dr. Adonis Moreira, Director; Centro de Recursos Naturales; Cantón El Matazano; Soyapango; El Salvador. Tel. 270-484.

Entering / Leaving Guatemala from El Salvador

Guatemala's Pacific Coast is a convenient access point for travelers entering or exiting El Salvador. The information provided below may also be useful for those heading into central or eastern Guatemala from El Salvador, or vice versa.

Check with your nearest Salvadoran embassy or consulate before making plans to visit El Salvador. As of late 1992, U.S. citizens were required to obtain a visa before entering the country. The procedure requires several passport-sized photos and may take up to 2 weeks. There is also a processing fee of about $4.

Ciudad Pedro de Alvarado—One of the less busy of Guatemala's four main border crossings with El Salvador. Most first-class buses cross on the Pan American Highway at San Cristóbal Frontera. Nonetheless, there are second-class buses passing here en route to and from Guatemala City and San Salvador about once an hour during the day. Services are limited. El Imposible National Park is only a few miles across the border in El Salvador.

San Cristóbal Frontera—The main border crossing for frequent pullman buses and much commercial traffic to San Salvador. The road continues to the Mayan ruins of Tazumal and Santa Ana, the largest city in western El Salvador.

Asunción Mita-Anguiatú—A small border crossing on the little-used road between Esquipulas and Santa Ana. Shortly after it crosses into El Salvador the road passes Lake de Güija, a good-sized body of water that forms part of the national boundary. There is reportedly good fishing and bird-watching in and around the lake.

Valle Nuevo—Another crossing without much traffic. It is located on CA-8, which eventually reaches Ahuachapán and Santa Ana, El Salvador. Limited accommodations and services are available.

9

Baja and Alta Verapaz

This seldom-visited part of Guatemala, the area immediately northeast of the central highlands, was one of the last to be brought under Spanish domination. Known as the Land of War in the early years of the conquest, this region was defended by fierce indigenous tribes who thwarted successive waves of conquistadors.

Finally, the king of Spain granted liberation theologist and pacifist priest Bartolomé de las Casas five years in which to peacefully convert the Quiché, Pokomán, and Kekchí Maya who inhabited the area. Las Casas distinguished himself among the Indians by allowing them to worship Christ in their own languages, something that was then unheard of in Guatemala. His gentle and respectful outreach worked, and the area was renamed La Tierra de la Verapaz (land of the true peace). Las Casas continued to fight for justice throughout the country and returned to Spain to argue against the enslavement of Guatemalan Indians, insisting that all human beings shared the same basic civil rights.

Even after its conversion to Christianity, the isolated Verapaz existed for centuries almost as if it were a separate country. Until relatively recently (the mid-1970s) there were no paved roads, and trade was via pack animals, forest trails, and river boats. A rail link to the Caribbean coast was abandoned earlier this century, and air traffic was infrequent.

The capital of the department of Alta Verapaz, Cobán, was founded by Bartolomé de las Casas in 1538, and by 1900 it had become like no

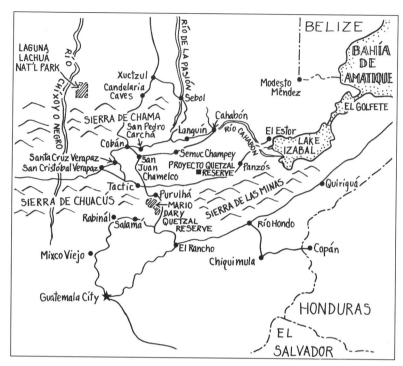

Alta and Baja Verapaz

other city in Central America. Many German coffee growers moved to the area beginning in the 1880s, with the promise of virtually free land and labor. They created a cosmopolitan, cultured society of their own in Cobán that dominated the coffee industry in Guatemala for more than half a century. Under pressure from the United States, the Guatemalan government eventually expelled most of the Germans during World War II and took over many of their coffee plantations. The departments of Baja (Lower) and Alta (Upper) Verapaz are still home to a handful of German-descended families, but much of the area clings tightly to its indigenous traditions and bloodlines. The Ladino presence is largely confined to larger towns and the most recently settled farmlands. Coffee is still the number one cash crop, although there is also much cultivation of cardamom spice (nearly all of it shipped to the Middle East), corn, cacao, allspice, and maguey.

There is now a paved highway to Cobán, which is of most interest

Slash and burn agriculture is now occurring even on the steepest hillsides of the Guatemalan jungle, as on this patch of land above the Río Cahabón in Alta Verapaz (Photo by Richard Mahler)

to the traveler as a base for touring local Maya villages, spelunking, hiking, whitewater rafting, and visiting the nearby nature reserves. En route you will pass a cloud forest reserve dedicated to the preservation of Guatemala's endangered national bird, the quetzal.

Baja Verapaz

Guatemala's department of Baja Verapaz is a land of steep mountains and rolling hills, some of these bare and studded with cacti, others thick with pines or hardwoods.

Most visitors enter the region by turning north off the Atlantic Highway at El Rancho, a hot and dusty town in the bottom of the Río Motagua gorge. The road immediately begins winding its way into the westernmost foothills of the Sierra de las Minas through a hot desert landscape that seems to have more in common with Arizona than Central America. Within minutes, however, the cacti become fewer as the air becomes cooler and more humid at the higher altitudes. Trees, mostly pines and other softwoods, become the rule rather than the exception. In less than an hour, the terrain has become lush and pastoral, suddenly looking like New England instead of the American Southwest. The view toward the provincial capital of Salamá, reached by a side road that heads from the main highway into the San Jeronimo Valley, recalls the wine country of California's Napa and Sonoma counties. In reality, olives, sugarcane, beans, corn, and cattle are the area's main products. The large colonial church at Salamá contains fourteen finely carved and gilded altars as well as a figure of Christ made by the celebrated Guatemalan artist Evaristo Zuñiga.

The Pokomchí village of San Miguel Chicaj, 6 miles from Salamá, is famous for the beauty and quality of its textiles. There is a fiesta there September 27-28.

A short distance farther west is Rabinal, known for the production of its pre-Columbian-style *nij* ceramics, unique musical instruments, and painted gourds. Nij is an unusual dye extracted from insects found in the area. On January 25 of each year, the town puts on its Rabinal Achí dramatic Indian ballet, which dates back to before the

Spanish conquest. Rabinal was the first village "peacefully" converted by the Dominicans under Fray Bartolomé de las Casas, in 1537. On a hill above the community is the Cahrup (also spelled Xecoc) archaeological site, the original Pokomchí capital, with its sweeping view of the Urrán Valley. A few miles to the northwest are the ruins of another pre-Columbian city and the quarries from which the Quiché hauled stones to build their capital at Utatlán. These and other ancient ruins in the Salamá Valley were excavated by the University of Pennsylvania between 1970 and 1974.

Also in Rabinal are the Los Chorros springs, an outdoor bathing complex. From Rabinal, Route 5 heads south through El Chol and Granados to Guatemala City.

Mario Dary Quetzal Reserve

One of Guatemala's rarest ecosystems, the tropical cloud forest, can be visited firsthand along the main Baja Verapaz highway, and, with luck, one may glimpse the elusive national bird. Only a small portion of the 2,849-acre Biotopo del Quetzal is open to the public to assure future generations of the chance to see this almost mythic bird. The quetzal is a notoriously shy creature, and this protected habitat may be one of its last hopes for survival in this country. Despite its sacred role in Mayan religion and symbolic importance in modern Guatemala, the bird is actually now more common in the cloud forests of Costa Rica and other parts of Central America where deforestation has been less severe.

There is ample parking at the reserve's visitor center, which encompasses a small museum, store, and picnic facilities. Adjacent to the center are rest rooms, hammock shelters, and campsites (bring plenty of insect repellent), plus several interpretive nature trails of varying lengths. An environmentally friendly sewage system processes human wastes in the reserve, and biodegradable materials such as tree-fern trunks are used in building trails.

Local guides can be hired for a small fee at the visitor center and are an excellent source of information about the plants and animals of the region. They can take you deep in the forest to such destinations as Xio Ua Li Che (Grandfather Tree), a living shrine said to be nearly five centuries old.

The reserve's shady pathways are well maintained and regularly patrolled, turning and twisting into the steep embankments and canyons of the nearby hills. An easy half-hour hike on Musgos (Mosses) Trail passes beneath tall orchid-covered trees and giant ferns and ends at a small but spectacular waterfall. Longer treks of up to 3 hours follow the Río Colorado toward its source on a ridge of the Chuacús Mountains, where spider monkeys, toucans, and parrots can sometimes be observed in the high canopy. Throughout the reserve the vegetation is lush and thick, with a profusion of vines, epiphytes (air plants), liverworts, mosses, lichens, palms, and ferns that thrive on the nightly mists cascading down from the surrounding peaks. Trees include varieties of oak, cypress, walnut, and pepper. Remember to wear good (preferably water-repellent) walking or hiking shoes, and bring along a bathing suit if you wish to dip into any of the reserve's several swimming holes.

Most visitors leave the park without having seen a quetzal, although many other bird species are in evidence. Quetzals are most active in the early morning, just after dawn, when they first stir from their perches, and even then, the birds spend most of their time in the highest tree branches. Your chances are slightly better during the March-April mating season, when the rites of courtship make the quetzal a bit bolder. You may also be able to see quetzals around the beginning of the rainy season, in May and June, when the young are being raised in nests that their parents have built in dead trees.

The reserve is open from 6:00 a.m. to 5:00 p.m. and has no telephone or hotel. A bust of Mario Dary commemorates the tireless campaign this University of San Carlos environmentalist waged to establish a cloud forest sanctuary for the quetzal. Dary was assassinated in Guatemala City in 1981, not long after the preserve was created by the government in cooperation with the environmental studies department he founded at the university. Some speculate that lumber interests, unhappy about his efforts to protect the highland forests, may have had a hand in Dary's still unsolved murder.

Despite its verdant appearance, the area encompassed by the reserve has only a thin layer of topsoil and is not productive for farming, which may be the main reason it has survived so long as a relatively pristine example of this lush microclimate, formed by a highly localized combination of altitude, humidity, and wind patterns.

Getting There

The reserve can reached easily by car, taxi, or bus, although it is almost too far for a comfortable day trip from Guatemala City. It is just south of the small village of Purulhá at Kilometer 162 on the Cobán Highway.

Public buses pass the quetzal reserve's entrance every hour or so throughout the day, passing to or from Cobán, El Rancho, and terminals as far away as Guatemala City and Flores. Tell the driver you want to be left off at the *biotopo*, as the turnoff is not posted very far in advance. When you wish to leave the park, simply flag down a bus passing on the highway in either direction. Taxis can be hired in Cobán, about 35 miles away. Many tour companies arrange trips to the quetzal sanctuary from Guatemala City.

Hotels and Restaurants

Posada Montaña del Quetzal (Km 156 Ruta a Cobán, Aldea La Unión, Purulhá, tel. 314-181 in Guatemala City). This moderately priced 18-room hotel is highly recommended. Located in pleasant surroundings 1½ miles south of the park, it has a bar, a restaurant, a pool, and laundry service. All cabins have fireplaces. Credit cards are accepted, and reservations are advised (especially on weekends). The views from the posada are wonderful, and there is considerable wildlife in the area. You can usually get a ride the short distance to the reserve or walk there in about an hour.

Pensión Los Ranchitos (also known as Hospedaje Los Ranchos) is a few hundred yards north of the reserve's entrance, on the way to the nearby village of Purulhá. These are simple accommodations in wooden huts, rented at an appropriately modest fee. If closed or full, try the farmacía in Purulhá, which reportedly has basic rooms to let. A number of quetzal sightings have been reported at this location.

Food is served at the Posada Montaña del Quetzal and the Pensión Los Ranchitos. Cold drinks and snacks are sometimes available at the visitor center. There are a couple of small *tiendas* and street vendors in Purulhá where you can buy fruit, crackers, and other basic supplies.

Two Kekchí Maya Indians proudly display their catch along the banks of the Río Cahabón, in the department of Alta Verapaz (Photo by Richard Mahler)

Alta Verapaz

Several miles beyond the quetzal sanctuary, heading north through spectacular mountain landscapes, travelers cross into the department of Alta Verapaz. Soon the road descends into a narrow, cultivated valley bracketed by steep, jungle-covered hillsides. At one point, near the town of Tactic, a large waterfall can be seen shimmering in the distance, surrounded by dense vegetation. Called Cascada Patal by locals, this is believed to be the headwaters of the Río Cahabón, one of Guatemala's longest and most scenic rivers. Rain that falls here will be carried by the Cahabón to Lago Izabal, then down the Río Dulce to the Caribbean Sea. A trail leads through cattle pastures and cornfields up a streambed to the waterfall.

Tactic
Tactic is a mostly Pokomchí-speaking center for the production of beef, cheese, and other dairy products, plus some silver jewelry, textiles, and other craftwork. The old part of the town is dominated by a colonial era baroque church built by the Spanish. Inside there are some paintings showing Byzantine influence in addition to some interesting altars. The Maya of Tactic have traditionally kept in their homes small clay animals, ancient protective symbols for humankind.

There are a couple of basic places to eat and sleep on the main street. On the side of a hill overlooking the settlement is the strikingly picturesque Chi-ixim chapel.

Near Tactic, at the end of a dirt road that begins opposite the Esso gas station, is a dubious attraction called *el pozo vivo*: the living well. This is a small pool fed by an underground spring that seems to bubble up from nowhere. Local legend holds that the pozo is perfectly calm until human beings begin to approach, when the spring suddenly swirls into action. It is far more likely that the effervescent spring is the outlet for a natural aquifer. Another spring-fed pool and swimming hole, Balneario Cham-che, is located nearby.

Beyond Tactic a road branches west at Santa Cruz toward San Cristóbal Verapaz, situated on the banks of Lago Cristóbal. This small lake is said to have been created in 1590 when heated disputes between local Pokomán and a Spanish priest caused the earth to shift, entombing the Indians and flooding the area with water. It is now used for fishing, boating, and swimming, mostly by Guatemaltecos. In the past, San Cristóbal was an important center for the production of achiote paste, used as red dye in foodstuffs, and was also the home of Guatemala's largest shoe factory. In 1992, the 48-room Hotel del Parque (Km 197, Santa Cruz, tel. 512-142) opened near Lago Cristóbal.

The road, Route 7-W, continues for about 60 miles beyond this coffee and sugarcane producing village to Cunén. From there travelers can go on to Nebaj and, by a separate highway, Huehuetenango.

Continuing on the main road, about 14 miles beyond Tactic, the mountainous terrain becomes more gentle and rolling, with large coffee fincas on either side of the highway. There is a gradual descent into Cobán, set on the edge of a small valley ringed by tree-covered ridges.

Cobán

The largest town in either of the Verapaces, Cobán has a laid-back atmosphere that confirms its status as capital of one of Guatemala's more isolated departments. Navigating the almost empty streets, one has the sense that busier times have come and gone here, and that no one cares.

At the invitation of then-president Barrios, hundreds of German immigrants came to this area in the 1880s and 1890s, creating huge plantations of coffee, tea, jute, cardamom, vanilla, and sarsaparilla. They also cut down thousands of acres of hardwood, shipping lumber down the Río Polochic to Lake Izabal, and from there down the Río Dulce and across the Atlantic to Germany. It is said that until an airport and road were built here in the 1930s, the self-sufficient residents of Cobán had stronger ties to "the old country" than to the rest of Guatemala.

When World War II broke out, the Allies pressured Guatemala to take action against the approximately 3,000 Cobán-area Germans who retained their citizenship in the old country. About two-thirds were deported to Germany or sent to prison camps in the United

States, and many of their fincas were confiscated by the Guatemalan government, which had asserted that the land was being held under "alien control." Today the main evidence of German influence here is the blonde-haired, blue-eyed, Spanish-speaking Ladinos one encounters and the occasional Teutonic surname. The owners of the nearby fincas, some still foreign-born, are now mostly based in Guatemala City, and many of the local men leave for months at a time to work in parts of the country where jobs are more plentiful. Except for a handful of new houses around town and a modern bank on the plaza, Cobán probably looks pretty much the way it did thirty years ago. Unfortunately, there is not much for the traveler to do here, beyond visits to the centrally located (but undistinguished) market, cathedral, and triangle-shaped park. The colonial era El Calvario Church, located on a hill on the edge of town, is interesting for the carved tiger cubs guarding its entrance, placed there in tribute to a local Indian legend.

Getting There
There are buses (some first-class) leaving about once each hour for Cobán from Guatemala City between 5:00 a.m. and 5:00 p.m. Travel time is about 4 hours. There are also daily buses to Cobán from El Estor (via the Polochic Valley), Huehuetenango, Nebaj (the latter two towns requiring connections in Sacapulas), and Flores, via Sayaxché and Sebol. Only the route from Guatemala City is paved, and the others may be subject to suspension during the rainy season or periods of civil unrest.

Driving time to Cobán from Guatemala City by private vehicle is about 3 hours. There are several tour companies that offer excursions to Cobán and the surrounding area. See chapter 13 for details.

Hotels and Restaurants
La Posada (1a. Calle 4-12, Zone 2, tel. 511-495) is a wonderful colonial-style inn, consisting of 14 rooms clustered around a beautifully landscaped courtyard. Prices are moderate, and the staff is friendly. Highly recommended. The Rabin Ajau (1a. Calle 5-37, Zone 1, tel. 512-296) is a 12-room, moderately priced hotel on the main street. Meals are available.

The low-priced, 15-room Hotel La Paz (6a. Avenida 2-19, Zone 1, tel. 511-358) has a small restaurant attached to it. The building also houses Proyecto Quetzal, which operates a guest house on a private reserve in the Polochic Valley (discussed later in this chapter). The 14-room Central (1a. Calle 1-79, Zone 4, tel. 511-442) is a budget pensión near the cathedral with 14 rooms. Another low-priced accommodation is Hotel El Recreo (10a. Avenida 5-01, tel. 512-160), which has 16 simple rooms.

The previously mentioned La Posada is recommended for typically Guatemalan food. Also reliable are Pizzeria El Molino (in the Hotel Rabin Ajau), Pastelería Mus Mus Hab, on the main plaza in Zone 2, and Tico's Pancakes at la. Calle 4-40, Zone 3. Cheap meals are also available around the main market about a block north of the plaza and from numerous sidewalk vendors who do business in the evening.

Services

The local Guatel office is on 1a. Calle between 1a. and 3a. Avenidas. Telephone calls and cables can be sent from 7:00 a.m. to midnight, seven days a week. There is a Banco de Guatemala on the plaza and a post office at the intersection of 2a. Calle and 2a. Avenida, Zone 2. Two movie theaters are located near the center of town. There are also a few taxis on the plaza next to the bus stop.

Around Cobán

A few miles beyond Cobán on the main highway is San Pedro Carchá, a good-sized town that is referred to locally simply as Carchá. This is one of the few communities in Guatemala with a long history of Indian self-government. The Kekchí-speaking majority has been pretty much in control of its own affairs since Carchá was founded in the mid-1500s by Dominican friars from nearby Cobán.

There is a small museum, Museo Regional de la Verapaz, across the street from Radio Imperial. It is open weekends from 9:00 a.m. to noon and 3:00 to 5:00 p.m. Knock during the week, and you may be allowed to enter. The museum contains Mayan artifacts and samples of local craftwork. Also worth visiting nearby is a large colonial church. Locally carved masks and silver filigree jewelry, such as chains, bracelets, and Indian elder wands, are available from some of the shops in Carchá as well as the daily market. The annual fiesta is June 29.

There are only a couple of basic hotels and restaurants in Carchá. Many buses make the short commute to Cobán during the day. You can also walk the 5 miles from one town to the other in about 2 hours.

The Las Islas bathing resort is at a hot mineral spring on the road heading southeast of town. Also in this direction is Hostal Michels, an inexpensive lodge and campground run by some friendly European expatriates. They can arrange jungle treks of up to 5 days' duration and day-trip nature walks to such destinations as the Finca El Arenal waterfall, underground Río Uqueba (part of the San Juan Chamelco Cave system), and scenic Río Pasamulha canyon.

On a separate road from Cobán, about 7 miles directly south of that city, is the village of San Juan Chamelco. This is a perfect place to buy the renowned braided or twisted Tzy'bil textiles, showing images of ducks, pineapples, and butterflies. A nearby waterfall, La Presa, is also worth a visit.

The San Juan Chamelco Caves, located near the village, are part of a complex underground river system that seems to appear and disappear in a haphazard manner. Some of the galleries are quite large, but care should be exercised when entering the passageways during times of heavy rainfall because of possible sudden changes in water level. A flashlight and a sturdy pair of shoes are necessary.

Beyond Carchá the paved road narrows and turns to dirt, with slow going from here to Sebol and (in the dry season) on into the Petén. The countryside is beautiful, however, as you slowly wind through the lush Sierra de Chamá. In the distance are sweeping views of pristine forest, still too remote to be profitably farmed. On either side of the road much of the land has been turned over to coffee, cardamom, corn, beans, squash, wheat, and maguey. Happily, some reforestation has also begun and the results are visible along roadsides in the area.

Virtually all of Guatemala's cardamom is exported from here to the Middle East, where the spice is in demand among coffee drinkers and adds a sweet, pungent flavor to local cuisine. Cardamom is also used as a digestive aid and, in some places, an aphrodisiac. There are about ten thousand producers of the tall reedlike plant around Cobán, but most of the cardamom pods come from a few dozen large fincas. At a 1992 wholesale price of $6 per kilogram, it ranked as the world's third most expensive spice after saffron and vanilla.

Among the fields and pastures, occasional waterfalls can be seen in the surrounding ravines. There are many such cataracts in Alta Verapaz. The more noteworthy include Sepemech and Pelizempec, along the Cahabón.

From time to time, as the poorly maintained road snakes up and down steep mountainsides, you will pass deep sinkholes, places where limestone caverns or underground rivers have fallen in on themselves. The abrupt drop-offs give the terrain a jagged, unfinished appearance and underscore the fact that this part of the Verapaz has geologic underpinnings ideally suited for cave formation.

Lanquín Cave

Two hours (about 30 miles) past Cobán, an impossibly narrow and twisting road branches off from the main highway at Pajal and heads east toward the village of Lanquín. (The other branch continues north to the villages of Sebol and Fray Bartolomé de las Casas.) Just before the settlement, a sign points the way to Las Grutas de Lanquín, a cave complex from which flows the Lanquín River. These subterranean passageways are a national park and worth at least a brief inspection.

The main entrance to the Lanquín Cave is a short walk from a shaded picnic and camping area on the banks of the river where you can take a refreshing swim. On first glance, the Río Lanquín seems to burst forth from the side of a mountain. A closer look betrays an underground channel bubbling up beneath a rock face at the right side of the cave. On the opposite side is an attendant's hut where a small fee will be collected if you wish to have the cave's lights turned on (this covers the expense of firing up a diesel generator). If you bring your own candles or flashlights, admittance is free and you can explore beyond the short section illuminated by overhead bulbs. Be sure to bring extra batteries. (Candles are dangerous and not advised.)

Although Lanquín is a relatively small cave, it has a long, rich history. Stone altars located a hundred or so meters inside the cave have been used by local Maya for centuries in sacred ceremonial rites. At least one such altar is still regularly used in Mayan rituals, which include blood sacrifices of chickens and the burning of copal incense. Unfortunately, insensitive visitors have scrawled graffiti on some of the sacred stones and broken precious stalactites from grotto ceilings. Others have left empty bottles and litter. Nevertheless, a profound sense of majesty pervades these dark, dank rooms.

The Lanquín Cave is warm and humid, with the musty odor of bats throughout. Thousands of bats make this their home, and it is an extraordinary sight to see them stream out of the entrance en masse just after sunset. As in other Guatemalan caves, you may also encounter blind and unpigmented fish, crabs, spiders, crickets, and other creatures. Even some plants and fungi grow in the complete blackness of these chambers.

Precaution should be taken when entering this or any other Guatemalan cave during the wet season, when water levels may flood interior chambers. Even during the driest months of the year, Lanquín's well-marked trails and stairways are very slippery. Be sure to wear shoes with plenty of traction.

Rumors have circulated for years that Lanquín Cave is part of one of the largest cavern systems in the world; however, expert teams believe they have disproved that theory by following all accessible passages to their termination points. Lanquín's total length is no more than one or two miles.

A 7-room lodge and restaurant, Hotel El Recreo (tel. 512-160), opened near the caves in mid-1992, and there are other modest accommodations in the village of Lanquín, plus a couple small restaurants.

Semuc Champey
About 6 miles directly south of the village of Lanquín, across a ridge and in the canyon of the Río Cahabón, is a remarkable natural bridge and series of limpid freshwater pools called Semuc Champey. This amazing limestone structure stretches nearly a thousand feet across

a narrow mountain gorge. The river runs underneath the overhanging rock through a cave, reemerging a few hundred yards downstream.

Across the top of the bridge is a cascading series of deep, luminous lagoons filled with rainwater and stream runoff. An unusual interplay of minerals and light gives these pools a magical blue-green color. The setting is idyllic, and the warm, turquoise water is a soothing antidote to the strenuous hike to the top of Semuc Champey.

Besides its inherent beauty, Semuc Champey is a wonderful place to camp, picnic, relax, and swim. Be careful of the sharp edges around the sides of the water-eroded basins. Also keep in mind that at least one tourist has toppled to his death from the top of this high archway.

The traditional means of getting to Semuc Champey involves hiking from the Finca Arenal bridge over the Cahabón River. This is also a put-in point and campground for whitewater river expeditions heading down the Río Cahabón (see chapter 12 for details).

The government is improving access to Semuc Champey in the hope of making it a major tourist attraction, grading a road and building recreational facilities nearby. It is now possible to drive to the natural bridge directly by four-wheel-drive vehicle. No food or services are available, however.

Public transportation in the area consists of about three buses a day passing along the road between Pajal junction and Cahabón, a small village 14 miles east of Lanquín. About the same number of buses continue north toward Sebol-Fray Bartolomé de las Casas and the Petén province, depending on road conditions. Helicopter charters can also be arranged from Guatemala City.

Río Cahabón to Cahaboncito
The Cahabón is Guatemala's most popular whitewater river, offering about 30 miles of navigable stream and a drop of about 1,600 feet. There are many Class II and III rapids along this waterway and a few Class IV. At the Chulac dam site there is an unrunable rapid that must be portaged. Floating the Río Cahabón usually takes about 4 days from the put-in point above Lanquín, but you can cut a day or more

At El Paradiso on the Río Cahabón, a stream of hot mineral water cascades into a deep pool (Photo by Richard Mahler)

from the trip by putting in farther east at the village of Cahabón, at the end of a dirt road. Highly recommended for whitewater adventures is Maya Expeditions in Guatemala City (15a. Calle 1-91, Zone 10, tel. 374-666). The cost of such a 4-day Río Cahabón trip in mid-1992 was about $500, including all equipment, food, and domestic transportation.

The river trip takes visitors through some of the most beautiful jungle canyons of the Alta Verapaz, with many placid pools between the exciting rapids. The Lower Gorge is a particularly pristine portion of the waterway, where high limestone cliffs close in on either side. There are many waterfalls and several caves along the course of the Cahabón, plus several soothing hot springs. Bird life is particularly abundant, and otters, deer, coatimundi, and other large mammals may also be encountered. Large-scale cultivation is increasing along the river, but much of the Cahabon watershed is still inhabited by Kekchí Maya who survive as subsistence farmers and hunter-gatherers. The river widens and slows above the village of Cahaboncito, the usual pull-out point for transfer by vehicle to the town of El Estor and subsequent ferry ride across Lake Izabal to Mariscos and the nearby Atlantic Highway.

Río Polochic Valley to Lago Izabal

Travelers heading from Alta Verapaz to such east coast destinations as Lago Izabal, Río Dulce, Puerto Barrios, or Lívingston may want to consider the Tactic-El Estor road as an alternative to backtracking on the return trip via the Atlantic Highway.

The unpaved road follows the Río Polochic as it winds its way between the Sierra de Santa Cruz to the north and rugged Sierra de las Minas to the south. The valley floor has been cultivated, mostly with coffee and corn plantations, as well as cattle pastures. The steep hillsides are still heavily forested, and the distant Sierra de las Minas is now protected as a nature reserve. The Pokomán Maya are dominant in the area, although only a few now wear their traditional clothing.

Perhaps the main destination of touristic interest in the Polochic Valley is a private quetzal reserve near the village of Tucurú. For a fee of about $15, visitors can stay in a rustic cabin on a coffee finca where numerous quetzals have been observed in surrounding forests, especially during early morning hours. Only a few overnight guests are allowed at a time, and bookings must be made in advance. Contact Proyecto Quetzal at 6a. Avenida 2-19, Zone 1, Cobán, Alta Verapaz (office in front of the Hotel La Paz), or Roger Brenner at Expedición Panamundo in Guatemala City at 317-588 or fax 317-565 (6a. Avenida 14-75, Zone 9). The Proyecto Quetzal Preserve is financed by a combination of German and Guatemalan business interests, plus a European bird-watching society. The farm itself is owned by a coffee grower of German descent, Alfredo Schleehauf, who lives in Guatemala City. Also recommended is a side trip to the nearby coffee-growing village of Senahú, set in a spectacular mountain valley north of Tucurú.

Buses pass several times a day between Cobán and El Estor, stopping at farming villages en route. The road skirts the edge of Lago Izabal, passing a large nickel mine that was operated briefly by a Canadian company in the late 1970s.

From El Estor, about 20 miles from Cahaboncito, travelers can either hire a boat to continue their journeys or take the daily 6:00 a.m. passenger ferry (no autos) to Mariscos, where a paved road passes

Campers have set up their tents near the goal post on a soccer field in this Indian village in the mountains of Alta Verapaz (Photo by Richard Mahler)

through rubber plantations to connect with the Atlantic Highway near the Mayan ruins of Quiriguá (see chapter 10). Heading the other direction, from Mariscos to El Estor, the ferry leaves at 5:00 a.m. and 1:00 p.m. daily. There is a swimming beach at Mariscos, and boats can be hired for trips around the lake or along the Río Dulce as far as Lívingston. Inquire locally near the ferry dock. Buses wait for the ferry and continue to communities along the Atlantic Highway as well as Guatemala City.

The Candelaria Caves

These spectacular caverns are located 40 miles by rough road north of Cobán in the verdant Sierra de Chamá. To reach the entrance, you must first travel to the riverside village of Chisec, then take a side road 5 miles south to the cave entrance, located between the hamlets of Candelaria and San Antonio.

A French-Guatemalan team undertook a systematic exploration here in 1968 and counted more than two hundred separate small caves totaling at least 15 miles in length. A documentary film on the effort, *Cuevas y Siguanes de Guatemala*, was released in 1972. Many of the passages are what spelunkers call "technical caves," which should be explored only by experienced personnel with the proper equipment. A further complication is that much of the Candelaria network is perpetually flooded and must be explored on specially equipped, inflatable rafts.

The Candelaria River emerges from the main cave, within which there are rooms as large as 240 feet in height and 360 feet in diameter—big enough to hold a football field. These galleries were sacred to the Maya, who left pottery, paintings, and murals in some of them. A complete archaeological study of the complex has yet to be undertaken, and much of the cave network can be explored only by boat with the aid of a knowledgeable and experienced guide.

Near the caves there is a small lodge and campground operated by an expatriate Frenchman, where tours can be arranged. For details, contact Servicios Turísticos del Petén in Guatemala City, Expedición Panamundo, or Maya Expeditions (see chapter 12 for addresses and telephone numbers). If traveling from Guatemala City, allow at least 3 days for a round-trip visit to the Candelaria Caves.

10

East to the Caribbean

As you head south and east from Guatemala City, the character of the land and its people changes dramatically. The mountainous terrain almost instantly becomes barren and dusty, the climate desertlike: this is the driest terrain in Central America. The farmworkers, so proud of their colorful costumes in the western highlands, are replaced by nondescript cowboys in simple T-shirts, blue jeans, and broad-brimmed straw hats.

Natural and historical forces—deforestation, Spanish colonization, and fickle weather patterns—have conspired to create a region that is generally lacking in scenic beauty and cultural appeal. Powerful landowners and faceless companies seemingly have molded the departments of El Progreso, Jalapa, and Chiquimula into agricultural machines whose lands are to be exploited as much as possible and then abandoned after their exhaustion.

Traversing the heartland of this region is the Atlantic Highway, also known as CA-9 or Ruta al Atlántica. From the southeast suburbs of Guatemala City, the two-lane road winds through desolate cactus-studded mountains interrupted occasionally by villages or fincas nestled into the swaths of green vegetation that indicate year-round springs or streams. The road is often crowded with trucks and buses, shuttling between the capital and heavily populated areas near Zacapa and Morales.

Around Guastatoya the Atlantic Highway begins plunging steeply into the Motagua River valley, and a number of lumber mills appear

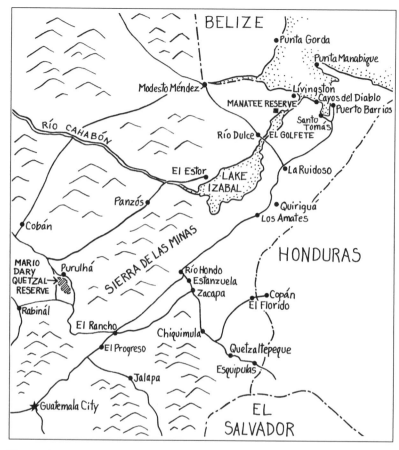

East to the Caribbean

along the sides of the road. These are processing centers for the truck-loads of pine logs hauled out each day from the forests of Alta and Baja Verapaz, along with some hardwoods brought in from the Petén. At El Rancho the highway intersects with the road to Cobán, capital of Alta Verapaz, and other points of interest in the northeast highlands (see previous chapter). Also at El Rancho you will pass an enormous pulp mill, built with financing from Spain in the late 1980s and subsequently abandoned.

The highway parallels the Río Motagua for most of the next 140 miles, through a series of dusty farm towns that have little to recommend them to the foreign visitor. At Km 126 there is a turnoff to Zacapa and Chiquimula, 8 and 21 miles away, respectively. From Chiquimula, separate routes continue onward to the Copán ruins in Honduras and the shrine of the Black Christ in Esquipulas (see details later in this chapter).

Even if you are not turning south, the Río Hondo's crossing of the highway is a good place to stop for a meal or swim. Especially recommended is the bungalow-style Longarone, a 54-room hotel at Km 126 with a popular bar, a restaurant, and a pool (tel. 417-126). Several other lower-budget establishments offer food and lodging at the same intersection, including the 20-room El Atlántico (tel. 417-160), the 25-room Nuevo Pasabien (tel. 417-314), and the 14-room Santa Cruz (tel. 417-112). The Pasabien also has a swimming pool. About 25 miles farther toward the coast, between Mestizo and Gualán near the Doña María Bridge at Km 181, is the Doña María Hotel, which also serves meals and offers 16 basic rooms (no phone).

North of Gualán the Atlantic Highway veers away from the river and hugs the foothills of the Sierra de las Minas, a long and forbidding chain of mountains that is being protected as one of the last best examples of pristine subtropical habitat in Guatemala.

Sierra de las Minas Biosphere Reserve

Saving the rugged wilderness of the Sierra de las Minas range is the main focus of the Guatemalan conservation group Defenders of Nature (Defensores de la Naturaleza). With assistance from Conservation International, World Wildlife Fund, Swedish Children's Rainforest, and other nonprofit organizations, Defenders of Nature and the Guatemalan government have been able to place much of these mountains into a protective status. This includes 26,000 acres owned directly by Defenders and 26,600 acres of land donated by the government's Institute of Agrarian Transformation. Another 90,000 acres in the reserve's "core area" are privately owned and are gradually being purchased by conservationists to prevent further extraction of timber. Logging concessions granted before the protective designation cannot be revoked, but a 1991 court decision dismissed claims by timber companies that they could still cut trees without employing sustainable-use techniques. Nevertheless, more than one-third of the reserve's original forest cover was removed between 1981 and 1991. Created in 1990, the Sierra de las Minas Biosphere Reserve was not readily accessible to casual visitors in 1992, pending approval of a long-term management plan. Those wishing to enter the reserve should contact Defensores de la Naturaleza at its Guatemala City office (tel. 325-064, 7a. Avenida y 13a. Calle, Zone 9).

Protection of this mountain range is especially important because it contains an estimated 60 percent of Guatemala's remaining cloud forest habitat, misty home of the elusive quetzal. Because of its geographic isolation and wide range of elevation, the Sierra de las Minas is home to at least 885 species of birds, mammals, amphibians, and reptiles—fully 70 percent of all the species from these groups known to exist in Guatemala and neighboring Belize.

Forest experts refer to these mountains as "an important tropical gene bank of conifer endoplasm," noting that 17 distinct species of pine trees are found here and nowhere else on earth. They are thus considered an irreplaceable seed source for reforestation and agroforestry throughout the tropics.

Besides its unique flora and fauna, the Sierra de las Minas plays an important role in providing fresh, clean water to the many farms and villages in valleys below. More than 63 permanent rivers drain from the reserve, making it the country's biggest water source and a potentially important resource for future hydroelectric power. The dense forests in the northern part of the reserve and on mountain summits naturally filter rainwater, prevent topsoil erosion, and inhibit river siltation. Unfortunately, timber harvesting and farming on the southern slopes of the range have made much of the land in that area unproductive and have already turned some of it into an infertile wasteland.

The reserve's managers are engaged in an environmental education program designed to convince community leaders of the project's value and teach soil conservation techniques to local farmers, many of them Kekchí Indians. The goal is to discourage their ongoing migration into the forest and to establish "sustainable" agricultural

activities—those that do no long-term damage to the environment—
in the buffer zone surrounding the reserve.

Because of their location, the peaks of the Sierra de las Minas help
divert rainfall into the lower Río Motagua valley, a rich agricultural
area that has been under intense cultivation for over a century. This
is where the United Fruit Company transformed thousands of acres
of jungle into banana plantations during the early 1900s, eventually
selling out to national and multinational interests that still dominate
the local economy. Whatever its transgressions—and there were
many—United Fruit left at least one positive contribution: it
provided funding for the study and preservation of the important
Mayan archaeological site of Quiriguá, located near the village of the
same name.

The Quiriguá Ruins

Located on a 75-acre forest preserve that once belonged to the United
Fruit Company, Quiriguá stands out as a green oasis amid miles of
cultivated fields and orderly Del Monte-owned banana plantations.
Much of this ancient site remains sheltered by lush jungle foliage, and
its huge, inscrutable carvings—the tallest ever found in the Mayan
lowlands—are well worth a visit of at least and hour or two.

Because its deep-relief, intricately carved stelae and altars are quite
similar to those found in nearby Copán, Quiriguá is believed to have
been a colony or outlier of that city, which was much larger. It may
also have been inhabited by a splinter group from the larger site,
which is only 30 miles away. Only here and in Copán have there been
found large boulders carved into bizarre, fearsome monsters. These
zoomorphs, as they are known, were all created in the brief period
between A.D. 780 and 795.

Recent translations of the hieroglyphics at Quiriguá suggest that
this was a trading center and perhaps an important source of cacao,
the rich chocolate bean the Maya used as currency. In A.D. 737, the
leaders of Quiriguá are believed to have taken the priest-king of
Copán prisoner and sacrificed him. The former dependency then
appears to have gone on a building boom and subsequently remained

The image of a Mayan god is carved into one of the magnificent stone monuments of Quiriguá (Photo by INGUAT)

autonomous for many years. Until further archaeological work is done, however, the true origins, demise, and purposes of Quiriguá are likely to remain a mystery. More than 50 distinct sites have been found in the area, but only 15 have been excavated.

The brown and red sandstone stelae found here are particularly massive, standing up to 35 feet tall and weighing as much as 65 tons, and the artistry is finely detailed. The Maya apparently moved them on wooden skids or rollers from a river quarry several miles away, then stood them on end like silent sentinels. They can now be viewed under thatched shelters that protect them from the torrential rain (use flash or high-speed photography). There is also a massive acropolis and central plaza at Quiriguá, plus an ancient stone ball court. The western platform of the acropolis once supported an elaborate mosaic wall, part of which remains. Discovered by a North American adventurer in 1840, the site was excavated bit by bit in the nineteenth century and partially restored by the University of Pennsylvania in the 1930s.

Modern bird-watchers can find a lot to look at in the big trees growing among the Quiriguá ruins. Parrots, toucans, kiskadees, motmots, parakeets, hawks, and woodpeckers seem to thrive in the high canopy here, having been driven out of the surrounding countryside by deforestation and human activity. Unfortunately, the removal of vegetation around the site has made the remaining trees especially vulnerable to the powerful tropical storms and hurricanes that sometimes sweep through this area from the Caribbean. This kind of structural damage to tropical forest "islands" is common throughout Guatemala, where deforestation has also led to considerable soil erosion and localized climate changes.

The site is open from 7:00 a.m. to 5:00 p.m. daily. There is a nominal admission fee, and vendors usually sell cold drinks and snacks near the entrance, along with maps and souvenirs. The ruins are often very hot, and it is advisable to carry water and wear a hat.

Getting There

Quiriguá is about 2 miles off the Atlantic Highway, roughly 100 miles east of Guatemala City and 67 miles west of Puerto Barrios. There are many daily buses traveling this route in both directions. Ask the driver to be let out at the Quiriguá access road rather than the regular stop in Los Amates, about 2 miles away. Taxis, buses, and motorbikes are available to the site, or you can walk there in about an hour from the villages of Los Amates or Quiriguá via the unpaved access road or railroad line, which passes very near the ruins. Traffic is sometimes stopped to let conveyor belts full of bananas go by. Wrapped in plastic to promote uniform ripening and discourage insects, they look more like dry-cleaned garments than America's favorite tropical fruit. Several tour companies offer one-day trips to Quiriguá from the capital, which may be combined with overnight excursions to Copán or Lívingston.

Hotels and Restaurants
There are two inexpensive hotels near the Quiriguá site and a number of simple comedores. The family-run Royal has very basic rooms with or without bath. At Kilometer 200 in the village of Los Amates is the newer Santa Monica, an unpretentious 8-room hotel next to a Texaco gas station and 24-hour convenience store. Neither accommodation has a telephone. You will also find several produce stands and a supermarket-gas station at the Quiriguá turnoff from the Atlantic Highway, where you can easily hail a passing bus.

Quiriguá to Copán
Many travelers combine a trip to Quiriguá with a visit to Copán, its much larger sister city across the border in Honduras. While it is possible to do this in the same day, serious thought should be given to breaking the trip into at least 2 days. Both sites are usually unbearably hot during the afternoon and are best seen in the early morning hours. In addition, much of the roadway between them is unpaved and subject to slow traffic. There can also be unforeseen delays crossing the border. Finally, be advised that there have been sporadic reports of bandits holding up cars en route between Quiriguá and Copán: proceed with caution.

The Copán Ruins

The Copán ruins, writer Shirley Slater once proclaimed in the *Los Angeles Times*, are "alive and buzzing with romance, a genuine Lost City of the Maya with spooky tunnels and mysterious carvings, blood

sacrifices and voices from the dead, and young archaeologists meeting over cold beer at the funky Tunkul Bar after a hot, dusty day in the digs.''
Indeed, the extensive Honduran site provides all this and much more. Located about 7 miles south of the Guatemalan border and about 30 miles northeast of El Salvador, Copán is a magnificent lowland city, abandoned for centuries to the scarlet macaws, green parrots, and keel-billed toucans that squawk in the Spanish cedar, ceiba, and acacia trees surrounding it. The area was last occupied around A.D. 830, although a few Mayan pilgrims continued to use it for religious purposes and farmers tilled their fields nearby. It was at Copán that the Classic Maya reached the heights of their artistry, and fortunately a good deal of this work has been preserved due to the area's relatively benign climate. Even some of the original paint remains on a few monuments and temples.

The site is dominated by the Great Plaza and brooded over by tall stone pyramids, carved Mayan baroque-style stelae, and an intricate 100-foot-high hieroglyphic stairway that is believed to be the longest pre-Columbian inscription in the hemisphere. Towering above it all is a lofty acropolis, from the top of which you can scan the lush, green Copán Valley. The ruins themselves are in mountainous terrain at about 2,000 feet above sea level.

On the back side of the acropolis, up a steep set of steps, is a royal compound that served as residence and burial place for the godlike priests who once ruled the Maya—and who were sometimes decapitated by their rivals from nearby Quiriguá. In the West Court, next to the acropolis, is the Jaguar Altar, where the sixteen priest-kings of Copán are carved in relief and where as many as fifteen live jaguars are believed to have been sacrificed in a single ceremony. The bodies of the rulers may lie beneath the altar, an area that has not been fully excavated. Clay offertory figurines found in a pyramid near Structure 16 suggest that members of the family of Yax K'uk'Mo' (Green Quetzal Macaw), the fifth-century founder of Copán's royal dynasty, may be buried in nearby tombs.

At the heart of the Great Plaza itself is a ball court, embellished by stone carvings, where opposing teams of four men each played a game best described as a cross between basketball and soccer. An important difference, however, is that members of the losing team were sometimes sacrificed.

Archaeologists from Northern Illinois University, the University of Pennsylvania, and the Honduran government have recently excavated portions of the site (see *National Geographic*, October 1989), but much of Copán still lies buried beneath enormous heaps of collapsed building material and tombs. Some of the piles are randomly strewn stones that were tossed carelessly by ill-informed researchers (and looters) in the nineteenth century. The entire site was leased from a local farmer in 1841 for $50 by American lawyer/explorer John Lloyd Stephens, who had "discovered" Copán with English illustrator Frederick Catherwood two years earlier. As a result, some of the most priceless artifacts wound up in museums or private collections in the United States and Great Britain. As in the rest of Mesoamerica, the sale or export of such items is now highly illegal.

During the late 1980s and early 1990s, the Honduran Institute of Anthropology and History tunneled into the heart of Copán's great acropolis and made a startling find: a smaller temple is entombed within, "mummified" 1,400 years ago by the Maya with a rough coating of plaster (see *National Geographic*, September 1991). Inside the temple's sealed chambers archaeologists found a cache of exquisite offerings, among them cloth-wrapped stone silhouettes painstakingly flaked from chert, one of the rarest art forms in the Mayan world. These "eccentric flints" were accompanied by other important ceremonial artifacts, including shark vertebrae, oyster shells, a jade bead, and a stingray spine. Hand-modeled stucco decorations on the outside of the underground chamber depict gods and celestial serpents from the complex Maya cosmology. Researchers are still uncertain as to the sealed tomb's purpose.

Visitors may notice repeated images of the bat (*zotz*), which plays a major role in Mayan mythology. Some experts believe the bat emblem was carried from Copán to the western highlands, where it is still used extensively by today's Cakchiquel Maya, most notably in the town of Solólá.

Knowledgeable local guides are available for hire at the Copán ruins, and there are vendors selling crafts, food, and drinks. Young boys with flashlights will help you find your way through the dark tunnels, corridors, stairways, and tombs. During the dry season there are usually archaeologists and their interns working here who may be willing to answer questions about their discoveries. The best times to visit are the dry months of December through April. On weekends Copán is often invaded by Honduran schoolchildren, for whom this is a mandatory field trip. Also, try to see the ruins during early morning or late afternoon hours, since the midday sun can be intense.

Getting There
Although Copán is only 30 miles from Quiriguá on a map, the terrain is such that it is three times that distance between the two sites by car or bus via Chiquimula. A secondary road to Copán begins 9 miles south of the latter community. A long journey from Guatemala City (150 miles and 5 or 6 hours each way), it is nevertheless possible to make it to Copán and back in one exhausting day. The trip can be made by private car; you will have to present appropriate documents at the El Florido border crossing. Buses are also available from Chiquimula to the frontier, where you must transfer to a Honduran bus for the onward journey to the Copán ruins. Be aware that the last public transportation from the ruins to the Guatemala border leaves Copán at 1:00 p.m. and that bribes may be demanded by officials on both sides of the border.

Special travel permits are issued at the border which enable visitors to enter Honduras, visit the ruins, and return to Guatemala without having to obtain a new Guatemalan tourist card or visa.

If you are coming from San Pedro Sula, the second-largest city in Honduras, Copán is about a 4-hour ride by bus or minivan. Flights from San Pedro Sula connect that city with Belize City, Guatemala City, the Bay Islands, and Tegucigalpa, which is Honduras's capital. Tegucigalpa can also be reached overland in about 4 hours from San Pedro Sula. Several Guatemala City-based tour operators may now be chartering direct flights between Tikal and Copán. Check with companies listed in chapter 13.

Hotels and Restaurants
All accommodations and services are in the nearby Chorti Maya village of Copán Ruínas.

The Hotel Marina is an old colonial-style pensión with 15 rooms, hot water, restaurant, bar, intermittent electricity, pool, and a new annex with private baths as well as air conditioning. This is the best place to stay in Copán and also the most expensive. Rooms can be reserved through the Honduras Travel Agency in Tegucigalpa by calling 31-10-03.

Cheaper accommodations are found at Madrugada, an old-fashioned adobe house formerly used to house archaeologists. It has 18 rooms, hot water, and ceiling fans. The popular Tunkul Bar is adjacent.

In the budget price range are Hotel Brisas de Copán (friendly and clean, but no hot water); Hotel Maya Copán (simple rooms with showers); Hotel Gemelos (basic with shared baths); and Hotel Paty (no services). Besides the barely passable hotel restaurants, there are a couple of comedores and stores in the village of Copán Ruínas.

There are no hotels in El Florido, on the Guatemala side of the border, although you may find places to camp there.

Zacapa, Chiquimula, and Esquipulas

Heading south from the Atlantic Highway, a paved road (Route 3) passes through a heavily cultivated area before entering Zacapa, seat of the department of the same name. This city is best known for its beautiful parish church, San Pedro Zacapa, and the nearby Santa María hot springs. Estanzuela, a village 6 miles north of the regional capital, is home to Guatemala's Museum of Paleontology, Archaeology, and Geology, containing a large collection of prehistoric animal relics, ceramics, and archaeological items. The same community is famous for the fine embroidery work produced by its resident artisans.

Chiquimula, 18 miles south of Zacapa, has one of the busiest and most colorful markets in the country, held every day and offering plenty of bargains. This commercial center is a changing point for hourly buses to Copán and Honduras, as well as Puerto Barrios, Guatemala City, and Esquipulas. There are several inexpensive hotels and restaurants if you need to spend some time here. The colonial era church was destroyed in 1765 and remains in ruins.

Located about 30 miles south of Chiquimula on CA-10, the town of Esquipulas is known throughout Guatemala and much of Central America as the home of the Black Christ, a venerated carved image housed in an impressive twin-domed basilica. Pilgrims converge on the shrine throughout the year but especially on January 15 and, to a lesser extent, March 9, when the Black Christ is said to embody its greatest powers. According to legend, those who visit may have their ills cured by praying and burning incense or candles within the aura of the carving, which takes its dark color from the balsam wood of which it is made. Miraculous powers have been ascribed to the Black Christ since its installation in 1595, but it has been particularly popular since a Guatemalan bishop claimed to have been cured in Esquipulas in 1737. Some nearby caves and hot springs are also said to have curative powers.

Esquipulas hosted a historic Central American summit meeting during the turbulent 1980s, which left it with the sobriquet City of Peace.

There is a Honduran border crossing a few miles south of Esquipulas, at Agua Caliente on Route CA-10. If you are going to Copán, however, it is much easier to take a bus from Chiquimula to the frontier at El Florido, on Route CA-11. Those with a private car may prefer this detour: it is longer but more scenic and with roads that are in better condition.

Hotels and Restaurants

Because it is such a popular destination for religious pilgrims, Esquipulas is blessed with an abundance of accommodations. The most charming (and expensive) of the lot are the 20-room Hotel El Gran Chorti (tel. 431-143) at Kilometer 222 on the Pan American Highway and the 56-room Payaqui (tel. 431-143) at 2a. Avenida 11-56 in Zone 1. Both have bars, restaurants, pools, and other amenities. More moderately priced are the 32-room Posada del Cristo Negro (tel. 431-482) at Kilometer 224 on the outskirts of town and the 39-room Los Angeles Hotel (tel. 431-254) at 2a. Avenida 11-94 in Zone 1, next to the Payaqui.

The restaurants of Esquipulas are unexceptional, and you would do well to stick to those in hotels. The better kitchens are at Payaqui downtown and El Gran Chorti, which is on a hill overlooking the city.

Quiriguá to Puerto Barrios

Once you rejoin the Atlantic Highway at Quiriguá, it is an additional 67 miles to the road's terminus at Puerto Barrios. The vegetation is lush and thick here, as the total average annual rainfall rises to more than 120 inches near the coast. Dense groves of bananas, citrus, and other fruits crowd the highway, interrupted from time to time by cattle pastures and cornfields. About 10 miles north of Quiriguá, at La Trinchera, is a turnoff that winds through rubber plantations to Mariscos, on the south shore of Lago Izabal. Daily passenger ferries (no autos) leave here at 5:00 a.m. and 1:00 p.m. for the one-hour trip across Izabal to El Estor, from which there is a rough road to Cobán and bus connections from there to Guatemala City, Huehuetenango, and Flores.

At La Ruidosa the Atlantic Highway intersects the road to Petén, Route CA-13, which is paved as far as the village of Modesto Méndez and then is dirt all the way to Flores. Most buses plying either route stop at the twin cities of Morales and Bananera, a hot, squalid agricultural trading center on the Río Motagua. The latter, not surprisingly, is the longtime headquarters of the infamous United Fruit (now Del Monte) banana empire in Guatemala, complete with private airstrip and golf course. The turnoff to these towns is just west of the Ruidosa intersection. You can also get a local bus from Morales to the village of Río Dulce (El Relleno or La Frontera on some maps), where it is easy to hire a boat to Lívingston or El Estor.

From this point on the Atlantic Highway it is a 33-mile drive through the foothills of the tree-covered Montañas del Mico (a federally protected rain forest ecosystem overseen by the University of San Carlos) to the broad coastal plain where Puerto Barrios sprawls in the tropic sun. The road divides on the outskirts of town, the left fork heading into Santo Tomás, the new port facility that has largely replaced Puerto Barrios as the main harbor for commercial vessels on Guatemala's east coast.

Puerto Barrios

Puerto Barrios (population 35,000) is nearly 200 miles east of Guatemala City and the capital of the department of Izabal. Founded in the 1880s by President Rufino Barrios as an eastern railroad terminus, this shabby city was Guatemala's chief port for much of the twentieth century. The United Fruit Company used it to ship bananas to the United States from its nearby plantations, and the country's coffee growers have sent tons of their product from these docks. Puerto Santo Tomás, just a mile across the bay, now handles about 75 percent of Guatemala's exports and half its imports (plus a good portion of El Salvador's foreign trade).

There are plenty of hotels in Puerto Barrios, many of them cheap, basic, and a little seedy. One of them, however, is a genteel relic of a bygone age and should not be missed; the Hotel Del Norte (7a. Calle Final y 1a. Avenida, tel. 480-087) has been remodeled and serves the best meals in town. As one would expect in a down-on-its-luck port city, there are also lots of bars, brothels, strip shows, and grubby restaurants. Other than checking out the lively market, marveling at a few stately Caribbean-style houses and patronizing a handful of movie theaters, there is not much for the foreign traveler to see or do in Puerto Barrios. The beaches north of town are one recommended diversion while waiting for transportation somewhere else, such as Belize (via the Punta Gorda ferry), Punta Manabique (by private launch), or Lívingston (by either mode of transport). Across the bay from Puerto Barrios is an expensive hotel and resort complex called Los Cayos del Diablo, which can be reached by land or sea (see below).

Getting There

About two dozen buses a day shuttle between Guatemala City and Puerto Barrios. Most are slow, crowded, second-class buses, and it is advisable to spend a couple of extra dollars for pullman coaches, with an assigned seat, a bathroom, and air conditioning. These *primera clase* buses also shave 4 or 5 hours off what might otherwise be an all-day trip. The best of the lot is the Litegua line, which departs from 15a. Calle 10-30 in Zona 1. Food and drinks are served on board.

Buses also leave the Puerto Barrios market hourly for the Esquipulas-Chiquimula area, and there is at least one bus each day from Puerto Barrios for the frontiers of El Salvador and Honduras, with connections to Copán and to Mariscos on Lago Izabal.

There is a worn-out passenger train from Guatemala City three times a week, returning from Puerto Barrios the following day. The journey, in filthy and windowless cars, can take more than 20 hours to complete.

The passenger ferry (no vehicles allowed) from Puerto Barrios to Lívingston leaves from the dock at the end of 12a. Calle Monday through Saturday at 10:30 a.m. (10:00 a.m. Sundays) and every day at 5:00 p.m. The same vessel departs Lívingston at 5:00 a.m. and 2:00 p.m. daily, taking about 90 minutes to make the trip. The boat fills up quickly, so be sure to get there at least 45 minutes before departure time. You are likely to be approached by the owners of *lanchas* (12-passenger speedboats) or slightly smaller, motorized cayucos asking if you would like to pay a little extra to get there faster. With enough people the cost can be negotiated down to a few dollars each, not much more than the price of the ferry. The option is worth considering if there is going to be a long wait for the latter. The smaller craft can make the trip in about 30 to 45 minutes, although you will probably get wet.

This is also a good place to hire private boats to Punta Manabique, the peninsula east of Puerto Barrios that is a fairly popular destination on weekends, and to Los Cayos del Diablo.

A few blocks away, at the foot of 9a. Calle, is the office of Empresa Portuaria, Agencia Líneas Maritimas, where tickets are sold for the Tuesday and Friday (7:30 a.m.) passenger ferry to Punta Gorda, Belize. The boat no longer berths at Lívingston en route. Round-trip tickets are about $6. Be sure to stop at the Guatemalan customs and immigration office on 9a. Calle in Puerto Barrios before paying your fare to Belize. The entire trip takes about 3½ hours. The returning boat from Belize leaves Punta Gorda at 2:00 p.m. every Tuesday and Friday. There is no food or water on board.

Hotels and Restaurants

The Del Norte (7a. Calle Final and 1a. Avenida, tel. 480-087) has 38 rooms, a bar, and a restaurant in an incongruous waterfront complex: a wonderfully ramshackle, clapboard British Caribbean-style edifice has been wedded to an uninspired modern stucco monstrosity. The mood inside suggests something out of a Somerset Maugham novel, and the view of the harbor is just the right backdrop. Moderately priced and uncrowded; in fact, you may very well be the only one there. Highly recommended.

The Hotel Europa (8a. Avenida between 8a. and 9a. Calles, tel. 480-127) is clean, comfortable, and inexpensive. Some rooms have private showers. Located not far from both the bus station and ferry terminal. Hotel Canadá (6a. Calle between 6a. and 7a. Avenidas, no phone) has private baths, ceiling fans, and low prices at a central location. Budget travelers have recommended the phoneless Caribeña, on 9a. Calle near the ferry terminal.

Puerto Libre (Km 292, at the turnoff for Santo Tomás, tel. 480-447) is the most luxurious hotel in town, with 34 rooms, air conditioning, TV, a restaurant, and a pool. The location is a little far if you are on foot. Credit cards are accepted.

Services

There are several banks on 7a. Calle between 6a. and 7a. Avenidas, and another at the corner of 7a. Calle and 2a. Avenida. The Banco del Café will change money for those traveling to or from Belize. The post office is at 6a. Calle and 6a. Avenida, the Guatel office at 10a. Calle and 8a. Avenida. Streets are poorly marked in Puerto Barrios, and the town is spread out. Ask locals for directions if you get lost; most are friendly and eager to help.

Los Cayos del Diablo

An upscale resort complex consisting of 50 beachfront bungalows, a restaurant, and a bar has been carved out of a lush jungle environment near Puerto Barrios and was opened by the Biltmore chain in 1991. Although not visited by the author, this hotel reportedly offers waterskiing, fishing, swimming, kayaking, bird-watching, and volleyball. A few small islands, Los Cayos del Diablo, lie a short distance offshore. Each cabaña has air conditioning, purified water, telephone, and private bath. Credit cards are accepted. Catering primarily to rich Guatemalans, this hotel and a smaller resort at Poza Azul have come under criticism from some environmentalists who are concerned about their possible negative impact on the area's fragile ecosystem, which is designated for federal protection. Contact Cayos del Diablo Resort Hotel, Santo Tomás de Castillo, Bahía de Amatique, or tel. 323-365 in Guatemala City, 800-327-3573 in the United States.

Punta Manabique
Several luxury hotel groups have expressed interest in developing fancy resorts on the unspoiled beaches of Punta Manabique, an arm of low-lying land (also called Cabo de Tres Puntas) that extends northeast of Puerto Barrios, forming the Bay of Amatique. Although the threat of large-scale construction on the point contradicts the stated government policy of preserving this pristine area, things may have moved forward by the time you read this. If not, your best bet for accommodations in the village of Punta Manabique is the Pirate's Point Lodge, which offers simple huts and hammock spaces plus three meals a day. The expatriate owner describes his modest establishment as "primitive but comfortable" (call 946-950 in Guatemala City for bookings and directions). Pirate's Point is an excellent place for swimming, beachcombing, sunbathing, snorkeling, and fishing. Boat trips can be arranged to the Canal de los Ingleses (an artificial waterway dug across the peninsula many years ago by English sailors) and Río Estero Lagarto (a small village on the Bay of Amatique shoreline), as well as Punta de Cocolí, Cayo Zapotillo, and Punta de Palma. You can be assured of seeing many species of marshland animals and water birds, possibly including pink flamingos, which have a rookery on the peninsula.

Another favored destination and possible day trip from Puerto Barrios is El Paraiso Beach, across from Punta Manabique near the fishing hamlet of Matías de Gálvez.

There is no regularly scheduled transportation to Punta Manabique. You must hire a boat from Puerto Barrios or Lívingston, a distance of an hour or so by motorized launch. Be sure to bring plenty of fresh water, something in very short supply on the peninsula. Food is available from local fishermen and villagers, however.

Livingston

Located about 16 miles—and a 90-minute ferry ride—north of Puerto Barrios, Livingston is one of Central America's true cultural oddities. With its coconut palms and brightly colored wooden homes, the community looks more like Belize or Jamaica than Guatemala, yet it is really a world unto itself. Most of the town's 5,000 residents are blacks or creoles whose ancestors include Jamaican slaves and Carib Indians brought to Guatemala in the seventeenth and eighteenth centuries. Livingston's name commemorates the contributions of a nineteenth-century American judge to refinement of the Guatemalan judicial system.

In Livingston one is as likely to hear the Garifuna dialect as Spanish. The melodic native language is a unique mixture of African, English, Dutch, French, and Indian words and grammar.

Also called Black Carib or *gariganu*, the Garifuna culture is a combination of African and indigenous Caribbean traditions, along with Spanish Catholicism, evangelical Christianity, and Mayan spiritualism. Garifuna history begins in the mid-1700s, when shipwrecked West African slaves escaped to the British-controlled islands of Dominica and St. Vincent in the West Indies. The freed Africans intermarried with Red and Yellow Carib Indians, sharing many customs and rituals from their various cultures. They remained staunchly independent, refusing to bargain with the Europeans who repeatedly tried to subdue them and take their lands. For many years they successfully resisted colonization, but in 1795 their chief was killed by an English soldier's bullet. The subdued Garifuna were rounded up and deported to the Bay Islands off Honduras, then a British colony. Over the next twenty-five years, small bands established settlements up and down the Central American coast, from Belize to Costa Rica. Today there are an estimated 120,000 Garifuna, most of them in Honduras. About 9,000 live in the greater Living-

A Garifuna drummer keeps the beat during a traditional Black Carib dance in Lívingston (Photo by INGUAT)

ston area, most descended from migrants who originally came from Puerto Barrios and southern Belize.

This hillside community is set in a rain forest environment and can be reached only by boat or chartered airplane. Besides subsistence farming, fishing, and tourism, the primary industries in Lívingston are trading and small-scale exporting.

Perhaps the best times to visit are during the Christmas season or May 13-15, when Garifuna dance festivals are under way and the Black Caribs reenact their arrival in Guatemala with much joy and celebration. The three days of hand-clapping, singing, dancing, and music-making culminate on the morning of May 15 with Yuriman, a simulation of the first farm plantings by the newly arrived Garifuna.

Other festivities are scheduled during Holy Week (with a live performance of the passion of Christ), November 26 (feast of San Isidro Labrador), and December 12 (the feast of the Virgin of Guadalupe, when local Kekchí Maya dance the sacred *pororo*). During these celebrations call-and-response singing and energetic costumed dancing is accompanied by musicians pounding out a rhythmic Afro-Caribbean beat on turtle-shell drums. Visitors can see the lively *punta* and Yacunú dances performed, the latter by men only.

Although more and more Ladinos and Kekchí have moved into Lívingston in recent years, along with some East Indians and Asians, the Garifuna culture still dominates. On side streets you can see families living in traditional windowless, single-door, palm-roofed houses with mud and cane reed walls. In their backyards you may also see women pounding and straining cassava root, a starchy potatolike vegetable that is a staple of the Garifuna diet. Its flour is used to prepare many kinds of breads and pastries. The cultural significance of cassava cannot be overestimated: in fact, the word *Garifuna* roughly translates as "the cassava-eating people."

With its gracious and friendly manner, Lívingston is a popular hangout for young backpackers, who take full advantage of the community's tolerant and relaxed atmosphere, lilting reggae soundtrack, and low-cost restaurants. Although there are no beaches in Lívingston proper, several are within easy walking distance north of town. Boat trips are a popular pastime, and many locals make a living using their cayucos to transport visitors to remote beaches, islands, or rivers. Excursions can also be arranged to each of the three Garifuna villages north of Lívingston: Cocolí, San Juan, and Sarstún.

Recreational drugs are also widely available in Lívingston, although police do arrest and prosecute foreigners for drug-related offenses. Some officers pose as dealers to snare unsuspecting buyers of marijuana and other illegal substances. Visitors should also be aware of a continuing problem of theft in hotels and dance clubs and on the beach. Rape and robbery of tourists has been reported as well, most often occurring at night.

Lívingston pastimes include sunbathing on the nearby Río Blanco beach, bird-watching in the jungle, and hiking about 3 miles north of town to Paraje de los Siete Altares (Resting Place of the Seven Altars) waterfalls, where you can swim in several idyllic freshwater pools or picnic by the bay. The hike to Los Siete takes about 90 minutes and requires good walking shoes. During the dry season the pools are sometimes virtually empty and hardly worth the effort. Litter and crime are recurring problems. Inquire locally about conditions and the best route to Los Siete Altares. About 15 minutes farther up the shoreline is La Chimiguilla, a small bungalow lodge near the village of Cocolí not visited by the author.

For more pristine swimming, try Cayo Zapotillo, a beach where you can camp and buy fish or shrimp from local fishermen (you will need to bring your own water and tent, however). Inquire at the Lívingston dock about launches to this and other isolated coastal destinations.

A quicker side trip is across the Lívingston harbor to the settlement of Buena Vista on the opposite bank. There are only a few houses here, linked by trails, but it is a good place to observe the birds and take a swim. Archaeologists believe that within the jungle near here may be the lost site of the ancient Maya village of Nito, one of the civilization's few coastal settlements and a transfer point for goods from the highlands. It is believed to have been inhabited when Hernán Cortés passed through the area in 1525 after his historic conquest of Mexico, but it has never been rediscovered.

Boats up the Río Dulce leave the dock every morning beginning at daybreak. Be sure to bargain for your fare, which will largely depend on how far you are going and how many passengers will be on board. Be prepared to pay at least $8 for a one-way trip to the village of El Relleno (often referred to as Río Dulce) that may include a half-hour stop at the manatee reserve en route. With a stop there and at Río Dulce hot springs, the journey takes about 3 hours. It is usually slightly more expensive to hire a boat in the opposite direction, from El Relleno back to Lívingston.

A Garifuna child returns from a successful fishing trip along Guatemala's tropical Caribbean coast (Photo by INGUAT)

The daily ferry from Lívingston to Puerto Barrios leaves at 5:00 a.m. and 2:00 p.m. daily, arriving 90 minutes later. The twice-weekly ferry between Puerto Barrios and Belize no longer stops in Lívingston.

The town has no bank, so you will have to change currency at a hotel, store, or restaurant.

There is no traditional market day in Lívingston, and informal stands are set up along the main streets of town each morning. Prices, because of the isolation, tend to be notably higher than in the rest of Guatemala. Shops close down on Sundays, when Lívingston is packed with churchgoers, mostly Catholics but some Protestant evangelicals.

Between June and November the area receives its heaviest rainfall, and traveling is discouraged. May is the hottest month, often exceeding 95 degrees at midday.

Hotels and Restaurants
Hotel Tucán Dugú (tel. 481-572, or 315-213 in Guatemala City) is an expensive (and often empty) 42-room hotel that is considered one of the most attractive in Central America. Originally designed, owned,

and managed by a Swiss hotelier named Tito Bassi, it perches over Lívingston harbor just off the main street. Distinguished by steeply pitched thatch roofs, mahogany interiors, and terraced balconies, the Tucán Dugú's architecture is a kind of Maya Modern. It offers fishing, river trips, bird and animal watching, sailing, and diving trips to Belize's barrier reef. The excellent (but relatively expensive) bar and restaurant offer the best views in Lívingston.

La Casa Rosada (tel. 0171-121) consists of 5 moderately priced seaside cottages on a pathway outside of town, near the water. Breakfast is included, and other meals are available. Children are not allowed, and the minimum stay is 2 nights. The owner is helpful in arranging tours. Hotel Garifuna (no phone) is located on a quiet, nameless side street in a residential part of Lívingston. The modern two-story structure is owned and operated by a local Garifuna family and is moderately priced, with private baths and ceiling fans. Recommended, though a bit away from the action. Hospedaje Doña Alida (tel. 481-567) is a moderately priced, 6-room lodge east of the main dock, overlooking the water and with its own private beach. Highly recommended.

The African Place (El Lugar Africano) has several rooms, some with shared bath, above the popular restaurant of the same name. Located on the main street, this budget-priced establishment attracts many young travelers, particularly Europeans, and may be too noisy for those less interested in socializing. No phone or services but great food. El Parador Flamingo (no phone) is a low-priced and justly popular 8-room hotel on the beach near the Catholic church, surrounded by a protective wall. The German-speaking owner can arrange trips around the area.

Typical Garifuna dishes include *tapado* (an exotic stew of shrimp, lobster, clams, fish, coconut, sweet potato, and coriander), *enchiladas* (baked stuffed tortillas), *pan de coco* (sweet coconut muffin), cassava bread, and drinks such as *horchata* and *rosa de Jamaica*. Local specialties include boiled fish in coconut sauce (known as "fish sere") and *caldo de mariscos* (fish soup).

The African Place and Margoth, which both serve Garifuna dishes, are particularly recommended. The latter is 1 block off the main street: turn left at the Happy Corner Store. Restaurant Raymundo, on Main Street just up from the dock, also serves good, low-priced regional specialties such as seafood soup and garlic shrimp. For a splurge, try the Tucán Dugú dining room. Several comedores on the main street serve tasty breakfasts and snacks. Do not be alarmed if the shrimp you are served in Lívingston still have their heads and tails: locals prefer them that way, discarding the inedible portions as they proceed with their meal.

Up the Río Dulce

A boat trip inland from the Caribbean first takes the visitor across the broad mouth of the Río Dulce, the sky full of fish-loving birds of all descriptions: gulls, pelicans, cormorants, frigatebirds, ospreys, herons, kingfishers, and egrets. Here, where the nutrient-rich fresh water of the mainland jungle meets the salty Caribbean, there is an unusually high concentration of marine life. Despite the close proximity of Lívingston, the ecosystem is fairly healthy, and as a result there is plenty to occupy the bird-watcher or sportfisherman.

Only a few hundred yards from the mouth of the Río Dulce, the river abruptly funnels into a 50-yard-wide gorge enclosed on either side by sheer rock cliffs up to 300 feet high. It is an incredible sight, especially in the early morning hours when large water birds congregate in the huge trees that loom over this slow-moving jungle stream. The rain forest is unusually thick along this stretch and virtually impenetrable, draped with vines and clogged with shrubbery.

Eventually the Río Dulce widens slightly and a few thatch huts are visible along the embankments, home to the Kekchí Indians seen spearfishing or hauling produce in their dugout cayucos. There are also a handful of riverside cottages with powerboat moorings, used by Guatemalans on holiday outings. At one point the Río Dulce is warmed on its north bank by an underwater hot spring, where you can take a soothing swim—while holding your nose against the noxious sulfur fumes. Then, several miles from the sea, the river opens into a broad lagoon called El Golfete.

This 4-mile-wide body of water and much of the land bordering it is a nature reserve protecting the manatee, or freshwater sea cow.

Small boats called "cayucos" are used to explore the shallow waters of the Chocón Machacas Manatee Reserve near Lívingston (Photo by Richard Mahler)

Enormous walruslike mammals that nurse their young and use lungs to breathe, the sighting of manatees is said to have given rise to the mermaid myth. According to legend, sailors who saw the vaguely human face of the creatures peering out of the water speculated that what they were seeing was half woman, half fish. Local people have never suffered such delusions, however, and the manatee are still hunted (illegally) throughout their range in Guatemala. A full-grown adult can weigh a ton or more, and its meat is considered a mouthwatering delicacy by some local residents.

The Manatee Reserve (officially called Biotopo Chocón Machacas) is jointly overseen by the Center for Conservation Studies of the University of San Carlos and INGUAT, with financial support from the World Wildlife Fund. The biosphere encompasses all of the water area of El Golfete and a large tract of nearly 18,000 acres on its northern bank. There is no admission fee for visitors, although donations are gladly accepted.

The manatee reserve is about 10 miles by water southwest of Lívingston and 16 miles northeast of the Río Dulce Bridge (a link in Route CA-13).

There are aquatic trails that nonmotorized, shallow-draft boats can navigate through various rivers and lagoons. The reserve also has several land trails into dense tropical rain forest frequented by monkeys, boa constrictors, tapirs, jaguars, and many other animals. Bird-watchers especially will be rewarded by the many local and migratory species in evidence. In fact, this area is believed to have the greatest variety of plants and animals anywhere in Guatemala.

Before setting out on foot, remember that this lowland jungle is also relentlessly hot (averaging 80° F) and rainy (more than 220 inches in a typical year). Also, bring plenty of insect repellent, and keep an eye out for snakes. If you camp, take precautions against vampire bats.

Manatees are notoriously shy, and the best way to catch a glimpse of these endangered mammals is to approach their grassy shoreline domain very slowly in a nonmotorized boat. The manatees surface regularly to breathe and seem to favor certain "blowholes" and feeding grounds known to local guides. Try the Escondida, Negra, Calix, or Salvador lagoons west of the visitor center (where maps are available). Early morning hours seem to be the best time to observe these magnificent creatures, but do not be surprised if you come away without seeing one.

There is a dock at the headquarters where boats can tie up (there are no roads in the park). This is also a good spot for snorkeling or a refreshing swim, although the water is rather shallow and full of grasses. Camping and hiking is permitted in the compound just beyond the pier. The main trail takes about 20 or 30 minutes to complete. Along it you can see mahogany, cohune palm, orchids, and bromeliads, as well as tropical birds and other wildlife. There are no vendors or services at the reserve, only a small open-air museum and rudimentary rest rooms, so bring your own food and drink. A guard is sometimes on duty with his mischievous pet spider monkey, Panchito, who will steal your hat if you are not careful. Guides can usually be hired at this location.

At the western end of El Golfete the Río Dulce narrows again and passes through a picturesque area that has long been a favorite for vacationing Guatemalans, many of whom have built second homes here. Some of these are quite lavish, with extensive yacht moorings and wide verandas that overlook the water. There are also a few hotels along the way, catering primarily to boating enthusiasts heading up the Río Dulce from the Caribbean. In 1992, the Guatemalan government announced plans to include much of this area in a new Río Dulce National Park, and new trails, campgrounds, and other facilities may be available by the time you visit.

Río Dulce Services and El Castillo de San Felipe

The river forms again about a dozen miles beyond the Manatee Reserve at the narrow point where a modern bridge crosses overhead, replacing the ferry that operated here for many years. This is the main artery in and out of the Petén, and you can catch buses at El Relleno (on the north side of the bridge) to Flores, Puerto Barrios, Guatemala City, and other destinations.

If you are heading for Flores, be sure to arrive before 11:00 a.m., as there is only one afternoon bus heading north, and it may be as many as 5 hours late. It is about 170 miles (4 to 5 hours) to Guatemala City from here, and a comparable distance (but 7 to 8 hours) to Flores. The buses are usually full by the time they reach the Río Dulce junction, and you will probably have to stand up inside or sit on the roof for the rest of the journey if you board here. One option is to overnight in Poptún, about halfway to Flores.

There are many cheap hotels and restaurants at El Relleno, but it is not a savory place to spend the night. Try the budget-priced Hotel Marilu, next to the bus stop, if you get stranded.

A short distance past the bridge is the old Spanish fort of San Felipe de Lara, overlooking the entrance of Lago Izabal, Guatemala's largest lake. This medieval-looking structure, more commonly called El Castillo de San Felipe, was built in 1652 to discourage the many British and Scottish pirates who plundered this area throughout the seventeenth century, raiding mule trains and stealing provisions. The raids persisted even after the fort's construction, however, and San Felipe was burned by buccaneers in 1686. After it was rebuilt, the Spanish went so far as to stretch an iron chain across the river to discourage unauthorized ships from entering the lake, but even this imaginative ploy was unsuccessful. A series of treaties between Spain and England ultimately put an end to the piracy problem, so San Felipe was converted into a prison, then abandoned.

Now a national monument cared for by INGUAT, San Felipe has been fully restored and is worth a tour. The fort is the only one of its kind in Guatemala and can be reached either by boat (about $2 and 10 minutes from El Relleno) or via a short unpaved access road off the main highway. The area around the fort, maintained as a park, is an excellent spot for swimming, kayaking, waterskiing, windsurfing, boating, and fishing.

There are several hotels and restaurants along the banks of the Río Dulce, most of them rather high priced. One exception is the 11-room Pensión Don Humberto (no phone), within walking distance of the fort. This little hotel has its own boat dock and an open-air restaurant. More expensive alternatives include the Restaurant El Galeón, with a pool and tennis court, and the nearby 10-room Hotel Izabal Tropical (478-401, or 680-746 in Guatemala City), which has a pool, marina, bar, and restaurant. The Izabal Tropical is located at the point where the Río Dulce flows out of Lake Izabal.

Water recreation gear can also be rented at these and other lodges. Local boatmen can be also hired here for fishing and nature trips or onward journeys to El Estor or Lívingston. The Mañana Marina, Mary's Restaurant, and Reed's Store, all near the Río Dulce Bridge,

The restored 17th-century fort of San Felipe defended the Río Dulce against incursions by English pirates (Photo by INGUAT)

are good sources of information about docking facilities and boat rentals. Turicentro Marimonte (344-964), a 16-room hotel and boat ramp east of the bridge on the south side of the river, is another place to inquire. As always, be prepared to bargain on prices.

Catamaran Island Hotel (7a. Calle 2-39, Zone 10, Guatemala City, tel. 324-829) is located on the tiny island of Punto del Chorizo and is especially popular among American sailors from Texas and Florida. Eight rooms of the hotel are in bungalows on stilts over the river. There are also 12 rooms on land, plus a swimming pool, tennis court, and dining room. Owned and operated by a retired American pilot and his Guatemalan wife, who built it in the 1970s, the moderately priced Catamaran is a good base for trips along the Río Dulce or around Lake Izabal.

Hotel del Río is a relatively expensive 14-room resort located just across the river from the Catamaran near El Relleno. Contact the hotel in care of Travel International, Avenida de la Reforma 6-30, Zone 9, Guatemala City, tel. 310-016.

Beyond Río Dulce to the Petén and Lake Izabal

The main road north into the Petén passes through El Relleno and several daily buses head north to Flores and south to Puerto Barrios or Guatemala City, usually via Morales.

El Estor, located on the northwest shore of Lake Izabal, was once a source of provisions for British ships and more recently the site of a large foreign-owned nickel mine whose operations were suspended in 1982. Izabal is a favorite weekend and vacation playground for Guatemalans from the capital, many of whom own shoreline property. The lake covers 228 square miles and reaches a maximum depth of 60 feet. Unfortunately, overhunting and overfishing have taken their toll; an April-June moratorium on fishing is virtually ignored. Most of the indigenous alligators and caymans have been killed for their hides, manatees and turtles for their meat, and iguanas for their eggs and skins. Parrots, toucans, and other exotic birds are captured for illegal export to stores and collectors. There are still perch, tarpon, snook, catfish, and large-mouth bass in Lake Izabal, however, and an experienced fishing guide can advise you of the best times and places to catch them. The wetland estuary of the Río Polochic at the west end of the lake is a protected area with a tremendous amount of bird life, plus some monkeys, caymans, and manatees.

Accommodations in El Estor include the moderately priced Vista del Lago right on the lake and the less expensive Hospedaje Santa Clara around the corner. The best restaurant in town is Hugo's, on the plaza. Hugo, the friendly owner, is a native of southern Guatemala who learned fluent English while taking premed courses in Canada some years ago. He is a wonderful source of information about Lake Izabal and the surrounding mountains. Unless you are interesting in sportfishing or bird-watching, there is not much to do in El Estor except swat mosquitoes and wait for a bus or boat. A fiesta is held every June 29.

There are about three buses early each morning that leave El Estor for Cobán, a journey of 6 or 7 hours that includes innumerable stops at Kekchí Indian villages along the way.

A ferry leaves El Estor every day at 6:00 a.m. for Mariscos, on the southern lakeshore, where there are bus connections to the rest of the country. The crossing takes about an hour and costs $1.50. Bird-watchers sometimes use these two towns as a base for boat trips up the Río Polochic, which for many years was the principal transportation link between Alta Verapaz and the outside world. Today there is little river traffic in the area, and what exists mostly consists of whitewater rafters and kayakers who float down the smaller Río Cahabón, over-nighting at El Estor. Accommodations in Mariscos are limited to a few basic hospedajes. There are several good restaurants near the ferry depot that serve local fish.

11
The Petén and Tikal

The Petén

Guatemala's 14,000-square-mile department of El Petén is the setting for one of the world's largest remaining subtropical forests, teeming with wildlife and lush with vegetation. Scientists have inventoried over 4,000 plant species in the Petén (including 700 trees and 500 orchids), plus more than 350 different resident birds and nearly 100 migrants.

Occupying fully one-third of Guatemala, the Petén is one of the fastest-growing regions in all of Central America, jumping from a population of 21,000 in 1960 to 120,000 in 1980 and an estimated 325,000 in 1992. New immigrants are arriving at the rate of three hundred or more a week. Many residents are farmers, loggers, and cattle ranchers, who have been cutting down the jungle at a cumulative rate of up to 100,000 acres a year. The Guatemalan government has belatedly taken action to curb this destruction, recognizing that if strong measures are not taken, the Petén could look like a subtropical Kansas within the next twenty years.

Experts now believe that a million or more Maya lived in the Petén during the height of that civilization's influence here, some 1,200 years ago. Sprinkled throughout the region are hundreds of archaeological sites, many unexcavated, plus vast sacred cave systems and waterways used by the Maya as trade routes.

This area was so cut off from the rest of Guatemala during the Spanish conquest that the colonizers did not get around to subduing local inhabitants until 1697, more than 150 years after the Europeans

The Petén and Tikal

settled into the western highlands. Even after Spain staked its claim to the Petén, its hostile climate, limited transportation, and lack of easily exploitable resources discouraged the Europeans from developing the area. Forest products such as chicle, rubber, balsam, and mahogany have been commercially exploited here only during the last century. As recently as 1940, the population was less than one person per square mile. It was twenty-one times that figure in 1992. Bear in mind that until 1970, the Petén was virtually inaccessible by road.

Set in the midst of this vast green sea, the ancient Mayan city of Tikal is a fascinating must-see destination, with 1,000-year-old limestone skyscrapers towering above the thick jungle. "Discovered" by the outside world in 1848, this is perhaps the largest city of the Classic era and arguably its most spectacular. Even if archaeology and anthropology have never turned you on, the sheer drama and majesty of this sprawling national park are calculated to amaze and inspire. UNESCO, the United Nations education agency, has officially declared Tikal a Cultural Treasure of Humanity. The park is also a nature lover's paradise: more than 250 species of birds have been sighted here, along with jaguars, monkeys, deer, and coatimundi. Accommodations at Tikal are limited and simple, the food is fair to lousy, and the weather is usually hot and rainy—with the inevitable flies and mosquitoes—but a trip to Tikal is well worth the effort.

Be forewarned: it takes some effort to take in the other amazing sights of Petén, which include scores of Mayan ruins, caves, lakes, wetlands, national parks, and nature preserves, as well as numerous jungle rivers. Physical endurance and patience are demanded of the visitor who strays off the beaten path, but, as in Tikal, the hardships are generously rewarded.

When to Go

Consider visiting the Petén early in your trip to Guatemala, unless you are exiting the country through this department en route to Belize or Mexico. Many travelers put off their excursion to Tikal and other Petén attractions until the end of their journey, which often results in a hasty visit that may of necessity take place during bad weather or involve poor accommodations. Remember that planes to and from Flores-Santa Elena, the area's only commercial airport, fill up quickly, and reservations should be made as far in advance as possible.

Because of the Petén's perpetually hot, humid climate, the best times of day to see and enjoy its attractions are early morning and evening, when the air is cool and the birds and other animals are most active. Therefore, it is worthwhile to plan on spending at least 2 full days in the area. Waking up to the exotic bird sounds of a crisp dawn at Tikal, for example, is very different from trudging through the oppressively hot and deadly silent ruins in the afternoon.

The high season for Petén visitors is mid-November through mid-April. Mornings from December through February can be cold enough to warrant a light sweater or jacket. March and April are the driest months, with cool nights and hot days. Heavy rains begin in May and continue at least through December. While a visit during

The scarlet macaw is indigenous to the thick forests of Guatemala's Petén (Photo by INGUAT)

the dry season may seem most appealing, it is also during this period that many trees of the forest turn brown and shed their leaves. By June, the lush tropical foliage has come back to life, full of multi-colored flowers and every shade of green imaginable. In August there is often a dry spell that lasts up to 3 or 4 weeks. Months with the fewest visitors are May and September.

Getting to Flores-Santa Elena and Tikal

By plane—Flying is unquestionably the fastest and easiest way to get to this remote region. A trip that requires at least a dozen hours by car takes only 35 minutes by jet. As of late 1992, four airlines were flying daily between the Flores-Santa Elena airport and Guatemala City. More carriers may have been added by the time you read this. Aerovías, Tapsa, and Tikal Jet flights leave Aurora airport at about 7:00 a.m. and depart Flores around 4:00 p.m. Aviateca makes the round-trip twice a day, with morning and afternoon arrivals and departures. The planes are almost always full departing Guatemala City, but because many passengers continue from Tikal to Belize or Mexico, there are usually empty seats on return flights from Flores. Round-trip airfare in 1992 was about $120; one-way, $70 (substantially less for Guatemalan citizens). From Flores, it is another 37 miles over a smooth paved road (the only one in the Petén) to Tikal National Park. There is an airstrip at the ruins, but it is no longer in use. Air connections can also be made from Santa Elena to Belize City, Chetumal, Cancún, and Mérida. Charter flights are also possible to Copán, Honduras, and other destinations.

By bus—A number of Fuente del Norte and Maya Express buses leave Guatemala City each day for the twin cities of Santa Elena and Flores, most departing between 9:00 p.m. and 7:00 a.m. The trip is scheduled for 15 hours but often takes longer, due to flat tires, bridge closures, military or guerrilla blockades, and occasional holdups by *bandidos*. Try to buy your ticket a day ahead or you may be forced to stand up all the way or ride on the roof amid piles of luggage. Tickets are only a few dollars each way and can be purchased on board, but those who have already paid their fare are given first crack at seats. Buses advertised as "express" or pullman are slightly faster, give you an assigned seat, and cost about $10 each way.

An even more grueling ride is Guatemala City to Flores via either Cobán-Sebol-Sayaxché or Sebol-San Luis-Modesto Méndez. Allow at least 18 hours for these routes during the dry season. Travel is usually suspended during rainy months.

From Flores-Santa Elena it is about an hour by local public bus to the Tikal ruins, or 45 minutes by private vehicle or tourist van.

By car—It is about 300 miles from Guatemala City to Flores, and under ideal conditions the route can be driven in about 9 or 10 hours. Unfortunately, the second half of the trip is over narrow, potholed, winding, unpaved roads that may take twice the "normal" amount of time or be completely impassable during wet weather. Even in the dry season, only a four-wheel-drive vehicle with high clearance should attempt this trip; one rarely gets out of second gear. If you do decide to drive, be sure to bring at least one spare tire, tools, a stout tow rope, and extra water. Be advised that most Guatemala City rental agencies will not allow their vehicles to be driven in the Petén. Avoid driving at night if at all possible; other vehicles sometimes drive without lights, animals congregate on the roadway, and criminals or guerrillas sometimes accost travelers.

By tour—Packaged tours to Tikal can be arranged for as short a visit as 2 hours, but it is better to spend at least 2 or 3 days at the site if at all possible, preferably overnighting in the park itself. Some of the more reputable operators shuttling visitors to and from Tikal by air are Clark Tours, Ney's Viajes y Turismo, Expedición Panamundo, and Servicios Turísticos del Petén (see chapter 13 for addresses and phone numbers). Some of these companies offer regularly scheduled excursions to Ceibal National Park, the Yaxhá ruins, Lake Petén Itzá, Santa Elena caverns, Lake Petexbatún, and other worthwhile destinations in the region.

Getting Around the Petén

Public buses, invariably slow and crowded but dirt cheap, maintain regular schedules on the few main roads of the Petén. The most popular routes, each costing a few dollars, are between Flores-Santa Elena and the Belize border; Flores-El Naranjo (with boat connections to Mexico via the Río San Pedro); Flores-Sayaxché (with connections to Cobán via Sebol); and Flores-Guatemala City (via Poptún and Río Dulce-El Relleno). Express buses leave at 5:00 a.m. daily from the San Juan Hotel terminal in Santa Elena for Belize City, Belize, and Chetumal, Mexico.

Other alternatives to bus travel include the renting of a private vehicle or airplane charter (both expensive) and traveling with a tour group. The latter often makes the most pragmatic sense, especially when going to remote archaeological sites, rivers, or caves that are not served by public transportation. Some destinations, however, can be reached only on horseback, by boat, or on foot.

As of late 1992, four airlines were flying to Flores-Santa Elena from Guatemala City: Aviateca, Tapsa, Tikal Jet, and Aerovías. Regular flights were also scheduled between the Petén and Belize City (Tropic Air, Aerovías), Chetumal (Aerovías, AeroCaribe), Mérida (Aero-Caribe), and Cancún (Aviateca, AeroCaribe). Connections can be made to other Belizean and Mexican destinations from each of these cities.

Flores

The island city of Flores, called Tayasal by its Indian founders, was one of the first Mayan cities visited by the Spanish but the last to be conquered. Hernán Cortés marched through here in 1525 on his way to Honduras and reported that the Indians were friendly and welcoming. When Spanish priests arrived in 1618, they found the Maya worshiping the stone image of a wounded horse left by Cortés almost a century earlier. The appalled Franciscans ordered it destroyed, but several residents of Tayasal tried to carry it away on a small boat. The sculpture was lost in a sudden storm, and some local people insist that they can still see the blurry image of the carved horse beneath the waters of Lake Petén Itzá.

In 1697, soldiers from Spain returned to conquer Tayasal, aware that according to a 257-year "cleansing cycle" of the Mayan calendar, a major disaster was expected to occur during that year. The Itzá Maya, who had fled generations earlier from Campeche and the Yucatán, appeared almost fatalistic about the outcome of the brief but decisive battle in which the last outpost of the Mayan empire fell to European hands. (Exactly 257 years later, the Maya were again rocked by the successful coup against reform-minded President Jacobo Arbenz.) On the same day of their attack, the conquerors destroyed the ancient temple at the crown of the hill on the island and celebrated mass there that night. The occupiers subsequently built a large Catholic church on that same spot, which still stands. In 1700, the island of Tayasal, renamed Flores, was fortified and turned into a penal colony.

The ancient island city of Flores is reached by a causeway that crosses Lake Petén Itzá (Photo by Richard Mahler)

For most of its modern history, Flores has been an isolated frontier outpost. Until late in this century it could be reached only by air or over a rough road from Melchor de Mencos on the Petén's eastern border with Belize. Rubber and chicle, two of the area's three major products, were usually exported by plane. The third, timber, was shipped through Belize or Mexico on rivers during months of high water.

Flores is now the capital of the department of Petén. It is linked by a causeway to the neighboring "mainland" towns of Santa Elena and San Benito. San Andrés and San José, twin villages immediately north of Flores across a narrow neck of the lake, are reached by boat or car.

With its pastel-colored buildings, cobblestone streets, and densely packed houses, Flores more closely resembles a village of the Aegean than Central America. Its main street circumscribes the island in ever smaller spirals as it winds toward the top of the hill on which the town is built, crowned by a whitewashed colonial era Catholic church with a few weathered Mayan stelae nearby.

Boats can be hired at reasonable rates for trips to any of the several small islands in the lake (one, Petencito, has a small zoo and amusement park) or around the shoreline, which has been gradually rising over the years, subsequently flooding many buildings. Destinations include an old Mayan observation tower (affording a good view of the lake) and forested areas with much bird life and an occasional Morelet's crocodile. Fishing for peacock bass and other species is good throughout the lake, particularly away from inhabited areas.

Flores is about two miles north of the Santa Elena airport, a short and inexpensive ride by taxi or minibus. Some of the hotels provide free shuttle service. If arriving by public bus, you will be let off at the terminal in Santa Elena, a dusty 10-minute walk across the Lake Petén Itzá causeway from Flores.

A tourist information and ecology center (CINCAP) was planned for the old Flores city jail; it may be operating at the time of your visit.

Hotels and Restaurants in Flores and Vicinity

Hotel del Patio Tikal (tel. 501-229, or in Guatemala City 323-365, fax 374-313; in U.S. 800 327-3573) is near the shoreline in Santa Elena. Each of the 21 rooms has private bath and satellite TV, and there is a bar and restaurant on the premises. The Patio is at the high end of the price range for this area, as is the Villa Maya (tel. 501-276) located several miles outside of town on Laguna Petenchel, an arm of Lake Petén Itzá. It is a full-service resort complex with 281 rooms, making the Villa Maya one of the largest hotels in the region. The owners are involved in rehabilitating animals retrieved from poachers, including scarlet macaws, parrots, monkeys, and cats, and these creatures can often be seen patrolling the hotel's spacious grounds.

Another upscale hotel is the Maya International in Santa Elena (tel. 501-276), which has 20 bungalow-style rooms, a good restaurant, and is well located on the lake. Tours can be arranged here, as at the Villa Maya and other large hotels. In Flores, the Hotel Petén (tel. 500-692) is more moderately priced and has 14 rooms, hot water, and both courtyard and roof terrace gardens. Breakfast is available, and there is a travel agency on the premises that will change traveler's checks. In the same price range is Yum-Kax (Avenida Centro América, tel. 500-386), with 37 rooms, hot water, restaurant, bar, and other amenities. It is on the left as you enter Flores on the causeway.

Two recommended budget hotels in Flores are the clean, friendly, and phoneless Don Quixote (which also has a good café) and the Savannah (tel. 500-248), with large rooms and good service. Another good choice in Santa Elena is the Hotel Jaguar Inn (tel. 500-002), operated by the family that owns a hotel and restaurant complex of the same name in Tikal National Park. Personnel at either accommodation can make reservations for the other.

In Santa Elena, the moderately priced Hotel San Juan (tel. 500-726) has a travel agency and (noisy) bus terminal on the ground level. A better recommendation is Hotel Miraflores, with a friendly staff and private showers, or Hotel Jade, located by the causeway and offering similar services. Neither has telephones.

There are a few basic places to stay across the lake in the villages of San Andrés and San José, or you can sometimes make arrangements to stay in a private home in any of the area towns. On the road to the Santa Elena airport is Hotel Tziquin-Ha (tel. 501-359), a rather expensive and modern-looking accommodation with swimming pool, tennis court, restaurant, gift shop, and car rental agency.

Restaurants in the Petén are generally poor, although those located in hotels are somewhat better than others. Visitors to Santa Elena have recommended the Café Maya, La Canoa, Las Puertas, El Tucán, and Café Lago Azul.

Services

Money changing can be carried out at the Banco de Guatemala branch office in Flores. Both Flores and Santa Elena have post offices, and the latter town also has a Guatel office. There is an INGUAT desk at the airport, open every day except Monday. The INGUAT representative is happy to arrange local tours, transportation, and guide services. You can buy plane tickets at airport airline counters: the Hotel San Juan and Hotel El Petén also change money and sell tickets, but you can expect to pay extra when not buying directly from the airline. Those two hotels also have minivans running back and forth to Tikal, as do several other operators. Cars can be rented at the airport or Hotel Tziquinaha, on the outskirts of Santa Elena. Buses leave from the market in San Benito and, for some routes, from the Hotel San Juan in Santa Elena.

In addition to local travel agencies, a few adventure-oriented tour operators, such as Expedición Panamundo and Servicios Turísticos del Petén, maintain representatives in Flores and arrange trips to remote archaeological sites, caves, and rivers. Several conservation organizations also have offices in Flores. These include Compañeros de las Américas, which conducts seminars on tropical rain forest management, and Conservation International, which is helping the Guatemalan government devise strategies to preserve the Petén rain forest while simultaneously meeting the region's economic needs. The University of San Carlos has a branch campus in Santa Elena which reintroduces into the wild animals retrieved from poachers through a group called ARCAS (Asociación de Rescate y Conservación de la Vida Silvestre). Personnel from the University of Guatemala are also conducting studies of medicinal plants and edible wild plants here, relying heavily on local Maya shamans, *hierberos* (herb collectors), and *curanderos* (healers). Check the Appendix for a list of conservation contacts here and elsewhere in Guatemala.

The Actun Kan and Jobitzinaj Caves

An easy half-day trip from Flores, the Actun Kan cave system is the legendary home of a huge serpent and is sometimes called La Cueva de la Serpiente. It can be reached by car or on foot by following the causeway through Santa Elena, turning left when the road forks in front of a small hill, and then taking the first right to the well-marked cave entrance. The walk from Flores takes about an hour.

There is a nominal entrance fee to Actun Kan and a guard who will turn on the lights and answer your questions. Small boys will also serve as guides for a dollar or less. There is not a lot to see in the cave, however, except for some unusual rock formations shaped like animals, a marimba, and a waterfall. The usual bats, stalactites, and stalagmites are also in evidence.

The western outlet of the same underground network is called the Jobitzinaj Cave and can be reached by turning right instead of left at the above-mentioned fork in the road at Santa Elena. Proceed left around the low hill until you reach the marked entrance to Jobitzinaj.

There are no electric lights, so you will need to bring your own flashlight. The galleries of both caves are often very narrow, and you can expect to get muddy, if not completely wet.

The Poptún Highlands

Whether traveling by private vehicle or public bus, the unpaved road linking Flores and Guatemala City via Río Dulce is long and arduous. Many visitors wisely break the journey just south of the town of Poptún (65 miles and 3 hours southeast of Flores, about the same distance and 4 hours from Río Dulce), at a delightful hostelry called Finca Ixobel. The farm and nearby community are nestled in the relatively cool highlands of the Maya Mountains, which stretch into this part of the Petén from neighboring Belize. The elevation is not very high—about 1,500 feet—but enough to demonstrably change the climate and vegetation from the lowland jungle that lies along much of this route.

There are other places to stay along this stretch of highway, small pensiones in San Luis farther south or in Dolores to the north, but Finca Ixobel has much to recommend it. The air is relatively cool here, and thick stands of pine provide plenty of shade. There are places to swim and hike, and most of the food is organic and home grown. You can camp, hang a hammock, or sleep in one of several rustic bungalows or treehouses. Travelers from all over the world swap stories over the delicious family-style meals, paid for on an honor system at check-out time. Solar panels are used to heat water and make electricity.

Ixobel is a working farm started in 1971 by Americans Mike and Carol DeVine and Dennis and Luise Wheeler. Mike was brutally murdered in June 1990, and several members of the Guatemalan military were subsequently arrested and convicted for his killing. As of late 1992, Carol DeVine was pursuing a lawsuit against the government in connection with the incident. She and several friends now run Finca Ixobel as well as the Restaurante Ixobel in downtown Poptún across from the gas station. (The U.S. government is also pressuring Guatemala for a speedy resolution of the Mike DeVine case.)

If you decide to spend some time at Finca Ixobel, a trip to one of the local caverns is highly recommended. Several caves (including a river cave with an underground waterfall) are easy day trips from the farm, but the most impressive, Naj Tunich (''stone house''), is a journey of 2 or 3 days. The cave has been closed to casual visitors in an attempt to reduce vandalism.

Naj Tunich was discovered and explored by Mike DeVine and his companions in 1980. It is a treasure trove of ancient Mayan art, the largest underground collection yet found. The walls of Naj Tunich (also called Cueva de las Inscripciones) are covered with extensive charcoal drawings and hieroglyphic texts, some relating to characters described in the Popol Vuh, the holy history book of the Quiché Maya, who live in Guatemala's western highlands. Pottery and other artifacts have also been found in this cave, one of many sacred spaces believed by the Maya to be entrances to the feared underworld called Xibalda. Archaeologists date the objects found in Naj Tunich from A.D. 733 to 762.

In the past, Finca Ixobel has arranged overnight mule trips to Naj Tunich Cave for a modest fee that covered food and the services of a guide. The trips have been suspended indefinitely. Vandals have damaged 23 of the 90 known priceless drawings in the cave by smearing them with mud, scratching them with sticks, or rubbing them out. If you visit this or any other Mayan cave, do not touch the painted walls, artifacts, stalagmites, or stalactites. The naturally occurring oils on your fingertips can dramatically alter the chemistry of the sensitive surfaces.

A sign marks the entrance to Finca Ixobel on the main highway (about 2 miles south of Poptún), but it can be difficult to see at night. Tell the bus driver where you are going, and he will know where to stop. The farm is an easy walk from the road.

In addition to several simple hotels and restaurants, the town of Poptún has a gas station, a produce market, a bank, a Guatel telephone office, and several grocery stores.

About 12 miles north of Poptún there is a turnoff to Dolores, founded in 1708 by Catholic missionaries who built a beautiful church that is still standing. The village is about one-half mile off the main road, and a few miles beyond Dolores is the ancient Mayan city of Ixkún. This is a largely unrestored, small site consisting of 8 plazas, several stone monuments, and a temple mound.

From Dolores, it is another several hours of lousy road to the Flores bus terminal, which is actually located in Santa Elena. (Because of the town's small physical size and narrow roads, Flores cannot accommodate buses.)

Nine miles south of Poptún the highway passes through the village of San Luis, where there are a few small stores and restaurants. A road heads west here to Sebol and, eventually, Cobán and Guatemala City. It is poorly maintained and recommended only for adventurous drivers with four-wheel-drive vehicles, extra tires, and plenty of time. During dry months there are sometimes buses traveling this route as well as the equally rough road between Modesto Méndez and Sebol.

The Road to Belize

Flores is 70 miles west of the Guatemalan border town of Melchor de Mencos. Several buses run each day between the two communities, a trip that ordinarily takes about 3 or 4 hours. Melchor de Mencos is a nondescript town on the Guatemalan side of the frontier that has a few hotels, restaurants, and swimming holes (along the Mopán River). Just across the international boundary is Benque Viejo, which has little more to offer except a dozen buses a day to Belize City. Melchor de Mencos is named after a Guatemalan soldier who did battle with English pirates a few centuries ago. Its economy has shifted over the years from the production and shipping of chicle to corn and cattle. The annual fiesta is May 16.

Immigration and customs formalities are fairly straightforward, although bribery requests (implicit and explicit) can be expected, and you may be charged for a passport stamp, which is technically illegal. Visas and tourist cards will sometimes (but not always) be issued for visitors entering Guatemala from Belize. The best course is to obtain these documents before leaving your home country. Belize does not require visas for most nationalities, and tourist cards are cheerfully dispensed by immigration authorities at this and all other border crossings. (For more details see *Belize: A Natural Destination*, by Richard Mahler and Steele Wotkyns, also published by John Muir Publications.)

If you are driving a car, be sure to have your registration and insurance papers in order. Vehicles entering Guatemala must be fumigated to kill agricultural pests, a 5-minute procedure for which there is a small fee. Try to get rid of your quetzales before crossing into Belize, where they can usually be exchanged only at banks or among money changers on the street. There is a bank at the border, which is closed on weekends.

There are as many as 12 buses a day heading east from Benque Viejo to Belize City. The most reliable companies are Batty Bus Service and Novelo's Bus Service. Depending on which Guatemalan bus has transported you, you may have to walk or take a taxi the short distance across the border to the bus station. The trip from Benque Viejo to Belize City takes about 3 hours and costs only a few dollars. You can also take a 5:00 a.m. express bus from Santa Elena-Flores directly to Chetumal, Mexico, that will bypass Belize City entirely. Inquire at the Hotel San Juan. Coming from the opposite direction, there are usually several minivans each day which head for Tikal from the cottage-style hotels of Belize's western Cayo district.

The best place to stay is the Hotel Melchor Palace (tel. 505-196, or 28-452 in Guatemala City), which is located right on the river and has a restaurant, a travel agency, and rents vehicles. The friendly, English-speaking staff can arrange trips to Yaxhá, Naranjo, and other Mayan ruins in the Petén and Belize. A more moderately priced hotel in Melchor de Mencos is the Mayab (no phone), which has 22 rooms, a coffee shop, and secure parking. Like the town's restaurants, it is very basic. Inexpensive lodging is also available at the Maya and Zaculeu hotels.

The Road and River to Mexico

Travelers can take one of two daily buses from Flores to El Naranjo, a village on the Río San Pedro, and continue from there into Mexico by motorized river launch. The Pinita line bus ride takes about 5 or 6 hours over a rough unpaved road, with departures at 5:00 a.m. and 12:30 p.m. The onward (twice daily) boat trip to the Mexican border outpost of La Palma is another 5 or 6 hours, and the bus ride from there to Tenosique takes 3 or 4 hours. From Tenosique there is a passenger train to Palenque and Mérida, or you can make bus connections to those destinations or just about anywhere in Mexico. Be sure to have your passport stamped in La Palma.

El Naranjo has only the most basic services, including a few comedores and two hotels, the better of which is Lodge El Naranjo, operated by the well-regarded Guatemala City tour company, Servicios
Turísticos del Petén. The boats to La Palma are privately owned and
will not depart with fewer than four passengers, usually early in the
morning. A small customs and immigration office handles formalities, and, again, you may be asked to hand over a few extra dollars to
speed "processing."

The trip down the Río San Pedro goes through an extensive wetland habitat, and the channel narrows and widens dramatically en
route. A few stilt houses are perched on the riverbanks, and there is
a fair amount of boat traffic, as there has been here since the days of
the ancient Maya. There is good swimming and fishing near La
Palma, plus many colorful birds and other fauna along the way.

An alternate route from Mexico into the Petén involves taking a boat
up the Río Usumacinta from Frontera Corozal to Sayaxché via the Río
de la Pasión, an Usumacinta tributary. A road connects Sayaxché
with Flores and the rest of Guatemala. The journey can be made by
private motor launch in a day or two. You will need to bargain over
the fare and have your passport checked by Mexican officials in Frontera Corozal and Guatemalan authorities in Sayaxché or Betél.

Mosquito-borne malaria is endemic throughout the Petén but especially along such waterways as the San Pedro, Usumacinta, and Pasión.
Be sure to take preventive medication when traveling in these areas.

The Road to Sayaxché and Cobán

At least one bus company (La Pinita) regularly operates vehicles on
the rough road that runs southwest of Flores to Cobán via Sayaxché.
The trip to Guatemala City takes about 20 hours, longer when the
ground is muddy. It is recommended that travelers break the journey into two or three segments, overnighting in Sayaxché, Lanquín,
or Cobán.

Sayaxché is a small jungle town located on a bend in the Río de la
Pasión, across which there is an auto ferry. Located about 40 miles
south of Flores, Sayaxché is an important supply, storage, and shipping center for local farmers, cattle ranchers, and timber cutters. In

recent years it has also become the center for excursions to several nearby Mayan ruins as well as river trips down the Pasión to Lake Petexbatún and, eventually, the mighty Río Usumacinta, which can be navigated all the way to the Gulf of Mexico.

There is not much to do in Sayaxché besides make onward travel arrangements and rest up for your next adventure. The area immediately surrounding the town is rapidly becoming deforested and polluted. Tremendous numbers of mahogany, cedar, balsam, and other valuable trees have been harvested here and floated downriver.

If you have not done so prior to your arrival, you can inquire at local hotels and among boatmen on the Río de la Pasión about trips to the area's various attractions. As you would expect, it is often much cheaper to join a larger group than to head out on your own.

There are at least two buses a day leaving Flores for Sayaxché, a journey of 2 to 3 hours. The road passes through La Libertad, the nineteenth-century capital of the Petén, and El Subín, a military outpost where buses (and passengers) are sometimes searched. There is an airstrip at Sayaxché that is open to charter and private aircraft only.

One of the few choices for overnight accommodations in Sayaxché is the Guayacán Hotel, located right on the river next to the ferry terminal. It has 8 rooms (with or without bath), a small restaurant, and parking, but no phone. The Guayacán's friendly owner is a former hunting guide who is very knowledgeable about the area. The Mayapán just down the street is slightly cheaper and equally hospitable. Among the town's very basic restaurants is La Montaña, whose owner (Julian) arranges trips and transportation for interested travelers. A fiesta is held by the local Kekchí Maya every June 13.

South of Sayaxché road conditions deteriorate rapidly, although it is usually possible in the dry season to take a public bus or drive a four-wheel-drive vehicle all the way to Cobán (where the pavement resumes). Traffic along this route is sometimes suspended because of guerrilla activity, so be sure to inquire locally before heading into the area.

Under ideal conditions, it is a 4- or 5-hour journey from Sayaxché to Raxrujá, a village on the upper Río de la Pasión in the department of Alta Verapaz. There are some basic places to stay here and a few simple comedores. A poorly maintained road branches off at Raxrujá for Playa Grande, about 60 miles west. Bus service from Sebol to

Playa Grande is sometimes available.

About 15 miles west of Raxrujá is the village of Xuctzul, where a second road heads 50 miles south to Cobán, the departmental capital of Alta Verapaz. Although transportation in this area is poor, you may wish to take this route if you are keen on seeing the Candelaria Caves, located about 8 miles south of Xuctzul on a poorly maintained access road.

There are plans to eventually extend an overland highway from Playa Grande all the way to Barillas, making it possible to continue to Huehuetenango and the Mexican border. This is now an arduous and perilous journey across largely uninhabited wilderness. An alternative route for travel through the area in the past has involved navigating the Río Chixoy (called Negro on some maps), which is said to be passable for much of its length during months of high water. Construction of a large dam on the upper reaches of the Chixoy reportedly has made this means of transport less reliable, however.

Yet another option is to take the rough Mexican road that heads south and west of Frontera Corozal just above the Guatemalan border to the Pan American Highway, which it intersects about 10 miles south of the town of Comitán in the state of Chiapas.

Be forewarned that these remote parts of the Petén, Alta Verapaz, and sometimes Chiapas are areas of occasionally intense guerrilla activity, in part because much of the land has been claimed by past and present members of the Guatemalan military and their cronies, who see this frontier as an excellent place to consolidate their economic and political power. Some oil development has been going on here, as well as equally controversial peasant resettlement projects. Both have been the target of guerrilla sabotage.

Continuing south toward Sebol on the main road from Raxrujá, the terrain changes from jungle lowlands to the subtropical foothills of the rugged Sierra de Chamá. There is no place to stay in tiny Sebol, although there are several inexpensive hospedajes a few miles away in the larger village of Fray Bartolomé de las Casas (inexplicably missing from most maps), from where it is another 8 or so hours to Cobán through gorgeous mountain forests decorated with orchids and flowering vines.

If you are lucky, you can travel from Sayaxché to Guatemala City in 18 bone-jarring hours, although you will almost certainly want to break the trip up into two or three segments. It is also possible to travel between Sebol and Sayaxché by boat on the Río de la Pasión and its tributaries, via the hamlet of El Pato, but arrangements need to be made locally.

The Road from Sebol to San Luis and Río Dulce

There is a very rough road heading east from Sebol that eventually splits and connects (separately) with the Flores-Guatemala City highway at the village of San Luis, south of Poptún, and at Modesto Méndez, 22 miles north of the Río Dulce. Neither road is in good condition, although the Sebol-Modesto Méndez route is somewhat more reliable. These routes should not be attempted without a good four-wheel-drive vehicle, preferably during dry weather. Depending on the time of year and the political situation, scheduled bus service is also available on these roads.

The Road to Tikal

Heading east from Flores, the paved and well-maintained road to Tikal passes through savannas and cultivated farmland until the turn-off to Belize at El Cruce, after which it follows the edge of Lake Petén Itzá, one of Guatemala's largest and most scenic bodies of water. The village of El Remate clings to the shoreline, a number of its low-lying houses inundated by the rising waters of the lake.

Near the small resort complex of Gringo Perdido a dirt road heads to the left, along the embankment. About a mile down this track is the only real first-class hotel in the Petén, opened in early 1991 by Biltmore International. Hotel Camino Real Tikal is located in a jungle compound with a spectacular view of Lake Petén Itzá and is immediately adjacent to Cerro Cahuí Biotope (see detailed description of the park and nearby hotels later in this chapter). In fact, the hotel's owners provided some of the funds for acquiring and developing the park, which is jointly administered by INGUAT and the University of San Carlos.

The coastal road continues along the north side of the lake but does not make a complete circuit. At the village of San Andrés, opposite

Flores, the road heads north for about 40 miles to the jungle outpost of Carmelita, where horses and guides can be hired for trips to El Mirador, Nakbe, and other remote Mayan sites. Check road conditions, as flooding is a problem beyond the Hotel Camino Real, and a four-wheel-drive vehicle is usually required.

Tikal National Park and Ruins

Artifacts of the mysterious Maya civilization are found throughout almost all of Guatemala, but nowhere is the documented concentration of ancient buildings greater than in the Petén. Of these, the most important excavated site by far is Tikal.

The massive ruins of Tikal are among the largest in all the Mayan world, covering some 10 square miles and encompassing thousands of individual constructions, including temples, plazas, ball courts, ceremonial platforms, residences, shrines, palaces, causeways, and reservoirs. There are over two hundred stone monuments, such as altars and plain or sculptured stelae. The latter served an important role in the religious Mayan political system, documenting important historical events and deifying autocratic rulers.

Excavation and restoration activities are almost continuously under way at the site, and it is believed that thousands of structures, monuments, and artifacts still lie below the shallow jungle topsoil.

The ruins are located on a low ridge at approximately the center of Tikal National Park and are surrounded by forest that has not been cut or significantly tampered with since the lowland Mayan empire collapsed around A.D. 850. Because of the special character of this primary broadleaf forest, Tikal has attracted many scientific researchers as well as amateur bird-watchers and other lovers of exotic plants, insects, and wildlife.

The variety and abundance of flora and fauna found here are truly mind boggling. As they have enjoyed protection from hunters since the mid-1950s, many of the resident creatures show little fear of people and thus can be easily approached and photographed, much as is the case on Ecuador's Galápagos Islands. (Some of Tikal's animals, including its scarlet macaws, have been confiscated elsewhere from poachers and released here after becoming locally extinct.)

Nearly 300 bird species have been identified in Tikal National Park, including unusually large concentrations of crested guans, ocellated turkeys, king vultures, and great curassows. Among the diverse mammal species found here are jaguar, puma, ocelot, margay, jaguarundi, white-lipped peccary, brocket deer, agouti, paca, and kinkajou. Spider monkeys and black howlers (nearly wiped out in a 1958 yellow fever epidemic) swing through the treetops. Sixteen species of bats have been recorded in Tikal and over 350 kinds of butterflies.

Few of these creatures pose any serious threat to visitors. Notable exceptions include several species of coral snake and the very deadly *barba amarilla*. Campers should be on the alert for vampire bats.

Besides the famous ruins, Tikal National Park has several nature trails extending for some distance into the thick jungle. One of the best of these begins on the grounds of the Tikal Inn and takes visitors past a tall treehouse platform built by scientists to study insect populations at various levels of the forest habitat. If you climb to the uppermost point, you will penetrate the canopy and have an unusual panoramic view of the *selva* (undisturbed jungle). Do not continue beyond the observation platform without a knowledgeable companion. One European tourist who kept on going with an uninformed guide was lost for two days in 1992 before being rescued through a chance encounter with some chicle tappers.

Orientation

At the park boundary several miles west of the ruins themselves, all vehicles must stop so that each visitor can register and pay the entrance fee. Tickets cost about $6 and are good for the date of purchase only. If you wish to visit the ruins at sunrise or sunset, be sure that special hours are indicated on your ticket. Normal visiting hours are 6:00 a.m. to 6:00 p.m., and the guards are aggressive in their enforcement. If you stay overnight at Tikal, you will have to buy a new, full-price ticket each day to reenter the ruins.

As you approach the compound south of the ruins, where Tikal's hotels and services are located, you will first notice a string of come-dores along the right side of the road. These open-air restaurants provide simple and relatively inexpensive meals. They also sell cigarettes, matches, postcards, and souvenirs.

On the left as you continue driving into the main compound is a small telegram and post office (there are no telephones in Tikal), next to which is an enormous modern building that serves as the park's visitor center. It is worth stopping here first to see the impressive scale model replica of the ruins in the lobby and a large collection of stelae and other sculpture housed in the central part of the building. At the opposite end of the center are rest rooms, a gift shop, and Tikal's most expensive restaurant (although not necessarily serving its best food).

The entrance road dead-ends beyond the visitor center in a parking lot that is actually part of the asphalt airstrip that was used for many years to ferry archaeologists and tourists in and out of Tikal. A decision was made in the late 1970s to discontinue flights because of vibrational damage to the Mayan structures and disruption of wildlife.

Along one side of the abandoned airstrip are the park's three bungalow-style hotels and their respective restaurants. On the northern end of the compound is the small but worthwhile Sylvanus G. Morley Museum of Archaeology, History and Nature (open daily 9:00 a.m. to 5:00 p.m., for a small admission fee) and a gift shop selling Guatemalan típica. On the opposite (east) side of the airstrip is a grassy area that serves as a public campground, complete with hammock hangers, rest rooms, and showers.

If you enter Tikal on a tour bus, your driver will probably head up the short access road that passes between the Jungle Lodge and the Inspector's Checkpoint, where you must show your ticket. Passengers are discharged at the gated entrance to the archaeological site, from where it is a walk of several hundred yards to the ruins themselves.

If you come by private car or are on foot, simply walk the short distance from the parking lot up the access road to the entrance gate to the ruins. On the right side of this road, through the trees, you may glimpse the encampment that houses several hundred employees of the park, most of whom return to their home villages 8 days each month. They also have Sundays off.

No matter what time of year you visit, it is likely to be hot during the afternoon. During the dry months of March and April daytime temperatures at Tikal often exceed 100 degrees Fahrenheit. For this reason, you are strongly advised to visit the ruins during morning and evening hours if at all possible. In the early morning it may be very damp and misty, but this usually burns off by 9:00 or 10:00 a.m. Remember to wear a hat and apply sunscreen. Carry a map (the ruins are vast and maps are widely available) and bring water (only a few soft drink vendors operate in the park).

There are plenty of shade trees among the ruins, and it is helpful to have a guide point out the most important species: ceiba (sacred to the ancient Maya and modern Guatemala's national tree, also called the kapok or silk cotton), mahogany, Spanish cedar, chicozapote (from which chicle is tapped and ironwood is cut), *ramón* (whose breadnuts are a favorite food of spider monkeys), and xate palm (its ornamental leaf is an important Petén export). You will also see flowering orchids and bromeliads clinging to the highest branches of many of these trees. Monkeys, coatimundi, deer, cats, and other mammals freely roam through the ruins, and scores of parrots, red-crested woodpeckers, oropendolas, and other colorful birds fly overhead.

Overview of the Archaeological Site

Tikal is dominated by five enormous temples—tall stone-block pyramids that rise as much as 212 feet above the jungle floor. Several of these magnificent structures are clustered around a Great Plaza, decorated with tall limestone stelae and other delicately carved monuments. The nearby North and Central Acropolis complexes have also been partially excavated amd restored. Other structures are scattered for many acres among the tall trees that have taken over the site. These include ancient mansions, storehouses, ball courts, and sacrificial platforms. All told, more than 4,000 structures have been mapped in Tikal, about half of them in the excavated core area. A complex network of causeways, aqueducts, and reservoirs—remnants of which are still visible—provided this ancient city with water for drinking, construction, and irrigation during the long annual dry season.

Because of Tikal's immense size and the rather confusing maze of trails linking various clusters of buildings, you are strongly urged to hire a guide or join an on-site tour group, at least for your first foray into the ruins. There are also several helpful books that describe the attractions, and they can be purchased at stores and hotels throughout Guatemala, including those at the park. The best of these is *Tikal, A Handbook of the Ancient Maya Ruins*, by the University of Pennsylvania's William R. Coe, director of archaeology here from 1962 to 1969. For birders, Frank B. Smythe's *The Birds of Tikal*, available in Spanish and English versions, is an indispensable guide to the hundreds of species observed within the park's boundaries. The same volume is useful throughout the rest of Petén and, for that matter, Guatemala proper. Roger Tory Peterson's *Field Guide to Mexican Birds* also identifies many of the varieties found here and in the rest of the country. Good background on Mayan history is found in Eric Thompson's *Rise and Fall of Maya Civilization* and the more recent *Maya* by Charles Gallenkamp.

A Brief History of Tikal

Tikal first became known to the non-Maya world in 1848, after two officials of the Petén's regional government, Modesto Méndez and Ambrosio Tut, toured the vast overgrown site. Their findings were published in a European archaeological magazine and inspired a Swiss adventurer to visit—and cart off a load of beautifully carved temple doorway lintels to Switzerland, where they remain in a Basel museum.

British archaeologist Alfred Maudslay began scientific exploration here in 1881, clearing mounds from the jungle and taking the first photographs of Tikal. The published pictures stirred worldwide interest and brought the head of the Carnegie Institute's archaeology program to the site as head of a large research team. This respected investigator, Sylvanus G. Morley, is credited with deciphering many of the hieroglyphic inscriptions on the stelae found here. His group remained in Tikal through most of the 1920s and 1930s, followed in the 1950s and 1960s by experts from the University of Pennsylvania, who worked under contract with the Guatemalan government's Institute of Anthropology and History, which continues to oversee the complex of excavated ruins, covering about 6 square miles. Tikal National Park was created in 1955 and occupies a square measuring about 16 miles on each of its four sides. It was the first fully protected archaeological preserve in Central America.

Based on archaeological evidence uncovered here, scientists believe Tikal was founded around 700 B.C., although habitation in the area may have begun as much as 1,800 years earlier. Because there is no consistent source of water in the area, the Maya were forced to develop an intricate system for gathering, storing, and distributing rainwater before Tikal could develop into a sizable city. This technology, developed about five hundred years before Christ, probably saved much of the nearby jungle from destruction at least through the Classic era, since Tikal's irrigated farmlands were able to produce enough food to feed the local population.

During this early period thousands of workers were used to build and flatten the large stone platforms on which large structures were constructed out of cut limestone blocks. The architectural achievements of the Maya are particularly impressive considering that they had no pack animals, wheels, metal tools, or pulleys. Their builders never mastered the formal arch; it was therefore impossible for them to create rooms wider than 8 feet.

By approximately A.D. 250, the beginning of the Early Classic period, the Maya were ready to build the largest of their temples and other monuments. Many of these commemorate the life and death of an individual ruler, who was often buried in a chamber beneath the pyramid. Curiously, no cemeteries have been found at Tikal, and it is believed that peasants were buried under their modest houses on the fringe of the city.

During the Early Classic era commissioned artists were kept busy carving stone stelae with inscriptions telling the history of the Maya and the accomplishments of their specific leaders. Friezes were carved as ornaments on buildings in the shape of animals real and imagined. Particular care was given to the sculpting of wooden lintels made from the chicozapote tree (also called ironwood). Many of these have been stolen or unrecognizably eroded, although a few are visible after more than a dozen centuries of exposure to the elements. During the mid-Classic period, from around A.D. 550 to 650, Tikal became the wealthy center of a vast trading network that extended throughout Central America and Mexico, perhaps even as far as South America and the southwestern United States. The discovery of large amounts of jade, obsidian, copper, coral, and other non-native materials suggests the Maya had developed a sophisticated system for exchanging precious goods.

The population of Tikal probably peaked at roughly 70,000 residents during the Late Classic era, which began around A.D. 550. With the city's infrastructure and largest ceremonial structures virtually complete, more attention could be paid to metaphysical pursuits, such as religion, mathematics, and astronomy.

Because the Maya had a habit of frequently tearing buildings down to construct new edifices on top of them—and smashing the carved images of Mayan rulers after their deaths—most of what we now see at Tikal is believed to date from between A.D. 700 and 750, during the Late Classic era. What we do not know is why the city suddenly became depopulated around the end of the eighth century, after perhaps 1,500 years of continuous occupation. Some buildings were even abandoned in the middle of construction. Theorists have sought to explain this abrupt decline, citing drought, land exhaustion, disease, social disorder, and internecine warfare as possibilities. There is evidence that, late in Tikal's history, Mexico's Teotihuacán people occupied the region for as long as 60 years. Perhaps the great city's demise was due to a combination of several factors. We will likely never know the truth with any degree of certainty.

A few Maya probably continued to inhabit Tikal during the centuries immediately preceding the Spanish conquest. Eventually, however, the site was swallowed by the jungle and apparently forgotten by all but a handful of local hunters and farmers until the mid-nineteenth century. Today it truly lives up to its Mayan name, "the place where spirit voices are heard." In fact, visiting these ruins and the surrounding forest provokes a depth of feeling akin to experiencing the great medieval cathedrals of Europe.

A Brief Tour of the Tikal Ruins

The Great Plaza

The Great Plaza (or Plaza Mayor) was the glorious center of the great city of Tikal and, for perhaps hundreds of years, the entire Maya civilization. It encompasses almost 3 acres of artificially flattened land surrounded by stone monuments, temples, and other constructions. Along each side of the plaza are about 70 carved stelae and sacrificial altars, some restored and all now protected by thatch-roof shelters. Most of the stelae date from the Post-Classic era and were originally painted red. They are believed to have told the dynastic history of Tikal through its various cultural epochs.

The Great Plaza Ball Court

This area is between Temple I and the Central Acropolis. It was built during the Late Classic era and has only been partially excavated. It can be identified by the two walls that run parallel to both sides of a grassy area, where the Mayan ball games were played before royal audiences who sat on the stairways at the ends of the field. The sport was a cross between basketball and soccer: rubber balls were thrown toward a hoop by members of opposing teams of four men, but their hands could never touch the sphere. Losing participants were sometimes sacrificed to the gods at the end of the game.

The North and Central Acropolis

These are palacelike structures situated north and south of the Great Plaza. The mortal remains of some of the ruling families of Tikal have been found beneath these buildings, which are believed to have served a combination of residential, administrative, and ceremonial functions, although no one is sure.

The North Acropolis, once painted bright red, contains some interesting mask carvings and stone monuments believed to pay homage to the Maya's ancient ancestors. The Central Acropolis, a warren of windowless rooms, narrow passageways, raised courtyards, and fragmented stairways, is bordered on its southern boundary by the Palace Reservoir. These structures were built over a 500-year period beginning about A.D. 200.

It is difficult to imagine what the view from the plaza might have been like 1,300 years ago, when the temples surrounding it were brightly painted and decorated with colorful plaster masks, hieroglyphic murals, and stucco relief friezes. Yet even today, with only a few eroded masks amd friezes remaining, the grandeur is spellbinding.

The East Plaza
The Méndez and Maler causeways (ancient pathways that once directed rainwater to reservoirs) lead to this conglomeration, north of the Great Plaza, where Temple 5D-38 and the sloping terraces of Structure 5D-43 can be found. There is also a market area and a ball court, neither restored. In fact, much of this area is now overgrown with tall trees and thick shrubbery.

The West Plaza
This grassy plaza contains several stelae and smooth altar stones but no restored buildings. A rest room and a refreshment stand, however, can be found here under tall shade trees.

Temple I
This famous pyramid rises to 145 feet above the east end of the Great Plaza and faces Temple II directly to the west. Also called the Temple of the Giant Jaguar, it is capped by an ornamental roof comb that sits atop a three-room structure, which in turn rests on an immense nine-level limestone base. At the very top of the temple is the badly eroded image of a seated priest-king, surrounded by ornate carved scrolls and snakes. This statue was originally painted vivid red and white. Deep inside the bottom of the temple is a burial tomb, from which archaeologists extracted the remains of the royal ruler Ah Cacau (Lord Cacao), adorned with precious jewels and other artifacts. Some of these are on display at the park's museum, which has re-created the tomb as it was originally discovered. Experts believe this and the facing temple were built around A.D. 700.

If you look at the doorway to the middle chamber of the temple, you will see one of only two ornately carved lintels at Tikal that has survived looters, archaeologists, and the elements. (The other is atop Temple III.)

Temple II looms above stone stelae along the Great Plaza of Tikal (Photo by Richard Mahler)

In the past it has been possible to climb the steep stairway to the sacred altar on top of Temple I, and this may still be the case. At the time of my last visit, in April 1992, access to the structure was prohibited because extensive reinforcement work was under way. In any event, you climb the temple at your own risk. A chain was once set in the steps as a handgrip, but it was removed in 1988 after experts determined that it was damaging the underlying stone.

The acoustics between the temples of the Great Plaza are uncanny. When the plaza is quiet, two people speaking in a normal voice can easily converse between Temples I and II, across several hundred yards of open space. This design was deliberate, so that Mayan priests could easily be heard by the masses gathered below.

Temple II

Directly opposite Temple I on the Great Plaza, this is perhaps the most photographed of Tikal's buildings. The Temple of the Masks, as it is otherwise known, is 125 feet tall and is believed to be a burial monument to the wife of Ah Cacau, the ruler found beneath Temple I. No tomb has yet been discovered beneath Temple II, however. The temple takes its name from the two large masks on either side of the stairway at the third terrace, believed to have been a royal reviewing stand.

There is a ceremonial structure on top of the three-level pyramid, and at one time the very top of the temple was crowned with a roof comb, now mostly eroded. The interior walls of the small ceremonial building were originally covered with friezes, but these have been chipped away or covered with graffiti.

This pyramid is much easier to climb than Temple I, which originally had a similarly broad stairway that has almost disappeared over the centuries. Temple II's wide block steps were used by Mayan dignitaries as they ascended the temple to perform sacrifices and other sacred rituals, while lesser mortals watched from far below.

Temple III

Located some distance from Temples I and II, this 180-foot pyramid is across the Tozzer Causeway from the West Plaza. The steep base of the Temple of the Jaguar Priest has not been fully excavated or restored, and you will need to grab onto tree roots and hanging vines to pull yourself up to the high platform that supports a two-room ceremonial building. Your reward is not only a splendid view of the surrounding jungle but a look at one of the two carved lintels at Tikal that remains relatively intact and in its original position. The carving shows a rotund holy man (probably an unidentified ruler) dressed in a jaguar skin: thus the temple's name. Temple III was built around A.D. 810, the last great pyramid constructed at Tikal.

Temple IV

The highest human-built structure in the Tikal ruins is the 212-foot Temple of the Double-Headed Serpent. This pyramid is located several hundred yards north of the Great Plaza and, like Temple III, is unexcavated at its base. Fortunately, there is a sturdy wooden ladder built into the sides of the steep, soil-covered platform beneath the monument itself, which rests on an amazing 250,000 cubic yards of building material.

There is a partly restored ceremonial building at the top of the platform, which overlooks an uninterrupted sea of green forest. The rock walls of these three rooms are up to 40 feet thick. Tests have pinpointed the time of their construction to A.D. 741, under the reign of Yaxkin Caan Chac.

An even better view—in fact, the best in Tikal—is obtained by climbing a narrow vertical metal ladder up one side of the structure to the base of the large roof comb crowning the temple. Its namesake, the double-headed serpent, is not in evidence, however; the carved lintel containing this image and a similar one on Temple I were removed in 1877 and are now on display in Switzerland's Basel Archaeology Museum, along with four other Tikal lintels. This was the highest known man-made point in the Western Hemisphere until the first skyscrapers went up in Manhattan in the nineteenth century. (Archaeologists recently determined that a temple at the El Mirador site, northwest of Tikal, is about 10 feet taller than Temple IV.)

You can drive to the base of Temple IV by way of an access road. There is a parking lot and a rest room. The strenuous climb to the top of the temple is not recommended for those with a fear of heights, a heart condition, or a poor sense of balance. The best times of day to climb Temple IV are at sunrise, when the din of bird calls and insects can be almost deafening, and at sunset, when the eerie grunts and groans of howler monkeys fill the air.

Temple V

Located adjacent to the South Acropolis and El Mundo Perdido along the Palace Reservoir, this pyramid is 172 feet high and was built around A.D. 750. It has been seriously eroded by weather and vegetation and appears more like a steep hillside than a temple. There are no ladders or stairways, but the many trees and roots available to hold on to make this a fairly easy climb.

Temple VI

Located at the southern end of the Méndez Causeway, this structure takes its nickname, Temple of Inscriptions, from a long hieroglyphic text found here, which refers to the date A.D. 766 and mentions rulers dating back to Olmec times. It is believed that the temple was built by Yaxkin Caan Chac and that the glyph inscription, the longest in Tikal, was added by a ruler named Chitam. There is also a fine stela and altar in front of this building which relate to blood sacrifices.

The South Acropolis

This pyramidlike cluster of ceremonial buildings is located between Temple V and the plaza of El Mundo Perdido. It has not yet been fully investigated and to the casual observer seems to be nothing more than a hill in the jungle—a sort of mezzanine of trees.

Palace of the Windows

Also known as the Bat Palace, this is a group of structures west of Temple III. The partially restored building that gives its name to the group has many interconnecting rooms and passageways, some of them very dark and inhabited by bats and spiders. The function of this complex is unknown, but the common assumption is that priests and royal family members lived here and/or performed certain ceremonies in some of the rooms.

One of the old temples of Mundo Perdido has been partially excavated. The tree in the foreground is a ceiba, sacred to the Maya and prized for its cottony blossoms. Note the orchids and bromeliads in its branches. (Photo by Richard Mahler)

El Mundo Perdido

Also known as the Plaza of the Great Pyramid, El Mundo Perdido is located about 300 yards southwest of the Great Plaza. Its name—Spanish for "the lost world"—refers to a 116-foot temple here (Structure 5C-54) which is believed to be the oldest of Tikal's excavated buildings, built some time before A.D. 300. This pyramid, with its surrounding ceremonial structures, forms part of an astronomical observatory. A short distance to the north is Temple 5C-49, a pyramid that collapsed after a series of rainstorms in 1980.

Plaza of the Seven Temples

East of El Mundo Perdido, this serene plaza is surrounded by several ceremonial buildings from the Late Classic period, as well as a triple ball court and an Early Classic era palace that dates from before the birth of Christ. Rising majestically from the thick jungle are two enormous pyramids, one with four staircases framed by remnants of huge masks.

Palace Reservoir

Located just south of the Central Acropolis, this reservoir was created by damming a ravine and lining the underlying limestone bedrock

This doorway arch of chicozapote wood has been exposed to the elements for more than a thousand years. The Maya chose this timber for its resistence to rotting and insects. (Photo by Richard Mahler)

with impervious clay. Causeways were built along adjacent slopes to funnel rainwater into the impoundment area.

Because most of the ground beneath the Petén is very porous, there are no year-round underground rivers, springs, or *cenotes* (limestone sinkholes filled with water), as in the Yucatán and Belize. The Maya were forced to build reservoirs to have enough water to survive the four or five months of dry weather each year. Wells drilled in Tikal during the 1950s failed to provide a reliable source of water, and experts decided to refurbish ancient Mayan catchment basins, which are now in use a dozen centuries after their construction.

Hotels and Restaurants in and around Tikal

The three hotels in Tikal National Park have no telephone or telex, these services having been denied by government officials in an apparent effort to direct business to fancier accommodations elsewhere. You can make bookings through travel agents in Guatemala City, however, or send a letter with a one-night deposit to the hotel in care of Tikal National Park, El Petén, Guatemala. Early reservations are advised during the high season, mid-November through mid-April. In 1992, rates for the hotels ranged from $20 to $40 a night, double occupancy.

The Jaguar Inn is owned and operated by Mundo Solis, formerly Tikal's Aviateca ticket agent, with his British wife, Patricia, and their children, all of whom speak English and are well informed about local attractions. Accommodations consist of several rustic bungalows, some private and others dormitory style (a few also have their own baths). There is a restaurant and a campsite on the premises; you can rent a tent. The food is mediocre, as it is every place in Tikal, but the staff is very friendly and eager to please (telephone the Jaguar Inn's booking agent at 760-294 in Guatemala City for reservations, or contact the Hotel y Restaurante Jaguar Inn in Flores, operated by the same family).

The Jungle Lodge (La Posada de la Selva) is a recently upgraded bungalow-style hotel with about 35 rooms. Accommodations are basic, although some rooms have private baths. Hot water and electricity are intermittent. A restaurant, open to the public, prepares hot meals and picnic lunches. There is a separate bar and gift shop. This rather dreary complex, operated by a Guatemalan family, was originally built in the 1950s to provide shelter for the archaeologists and other scientists working at the nearby ruins. Some travelers have complained about poor service here. The Tikal Inn is a favorite of conservationists and scientists visiting Tikal. This pleasant lodge has 3 bungalows and about a dozen standard rooms, plus a dining room that serves three meals a day. There is also a swimming pool that is open to nonguests for a small fee. The Ortíz family, which has run the Tikal Inn for many years, is extremely knowledgeable about attractions in and around the park. Mike Ortíz speaks fluent English and can arrange nature and archaeology tours, sometimes conducted by his brother and sister, who, like Miguel, are environmental activitists. Highly recommended, although most of the rooms are only semiprivate; open ceilings mean loud conversations and lovemaking may be shared experiences.

Tikal Campground is opposite the old airstrip from the Tikal Inn. The park's only official campground, it is clean and well maintained, with about a dozen tent sites and hammock spaces. There is also a rest room and shower block, although water is sometimes unavailable. There is a daily fee of $6 per person for use of this facility, restricted to campers only. Recreation vehicles are allowed to park overnight in the main parking lot near the campground.

The Hotel Camino Real, located about 15 miles from the park at El Remate, is arguably the most luxurious hotel in the Petén (tel. 500-207, fax 500-222; in the U.S. 800-373-3573). Each of the 120 rooms in this expensive lakeside facility has cable TV, radio, air conditioning, telephone, private bath, and mini-bar. Hotel Camino Real has three restaurants, a full bar, gift shop, beauty parlor, and room service. Car rentals and tours, as well as canoeing, windsurfing, diving, fishing, and bird-watching excursions, can be arranged from here to Tikal and other archaeological sites. A recycling and water purification system has been put in place to process wastes from the hotel. For example, only pure water is discharged into Lake Petén Itzá, one of the last habitats of the cayman in Guatemala. Credit cards are accepted.

Gringo Perdido (tel. 520-605, in Guatemala City 370-674) is a restaurant, campground, and 40-bed lodge near the intersection of the paved road to Tikal and the dirt road to El Remate and Cerro Cahuí Biotope. Gringo Perdido has rustic bungalows, hammocks, and a campsite. Its name, "the lost Gringo," refers to the American, David Kuhn, who built a campground here after becoming confused about which of the routes led to Tikal. The restaurant serves good food and is recommended. There are campsites and dormitory-style accommodations.

Tikal Services
Besides the dining rooms of the three hotels, there is one expensive restaurant at Tikal (beneath the overhanging shell of the visitors center) and several moderately priced comedores. Comedor Imperio Maya is your best bet, with friendly people, decent fried chicken, sweet plantains, and cold beer. Remember that most restaurants are closed Sundays.

A tiny post office operates limited hours in a small house next to the visitor center. You can also send telegrams from this location. Snack foods, cold drinks, guidebooks to the ruins, postcards, and other souvenir items are sold by vendors throughout the park and by Tikal's restaurants.

Tour guides charge about $30 for a 4-hour tour. There are usually plenty of English-speaking guides looking for customers near the parking lot. If not, inquire at the inspector's hut or any of the hotels.

Vans and minibuses ply the highway between Tikal and Flores frequently during the morning hours, charging about $4 each way. Afternoon buses return to Flores and the Santa Elena airport at noon, 2:00 p.m., and 4:00 p.m. The trip takes 45 minutes to an hour.

The Maya Biosphere Reserve

In theory, all of Guatemala lying north of the 17th parallel is under the protective jurisdiction of the Maya Biosphere Reserve, created by the government in 1990 as part of a master plan for studying and conserving the area's phenomenal natural resources. In actual practice, however, only a fraction of these 4.3 million acres enjoy any measure of enforced protection from overzealous chicleros, xateros, hunters, drug lords, farmers, and timber harvesters. Much of the reserve is explicitly intended for controlled extraction.

The problem is a complex one and should be familiar to anyone who has spent time in Central America or other "developing" parts of the subtropics. Those interested in saving Guatemala's forest ecosystems and archaeological sites are competing with a much larger number of powerful individuals, companies, and institutions with an economic interest in exploiting its timber, wildlife, ancient artifacts, and raw land. Widespread corruption, violent crime, drug trafficking, military abuses, and poverty exacerbate these conflicting interests in the Petén.

Officials in Guatemala City are therefore taking a cautious approach in their implementation of conservation policies north of the 17th parallel. Their strategy is a pragmatic one whereby about a dozen specific areas, including Tikal, are targeted for the most strict rules regarding usage, while the protection of other areas is more relaxed. Buffer zones have been set up around the most restricted regions to smooth the transition to densely inhabited or cultivated areas. Sadly, in much (perhaps most) of the biosphere it appears that an "anything goes" approach is the accepted norm.

On the positive side, Guatemala's National Protected Areas Council is working closely with local and overseas conservationists on preservation designs and management plans for protection of the Maya Biosphere. With support funds from the U.S. government's Agency for International Development, the nonprofit Conservation International has undertaken extensive training of local Guatemalans in park management techniques and sustainable harvesting of wild trees and plants. Other conservation groups are conducting an exhaustive (and overdue) inventory of the region's flora and fauna.

The several distinct ecologically and/or archaeologically sensitive areas falling within the boundaries of the Maya Biosphere that currently enjoy a special measure of protection (at least on paper) include Tikal National Park, Cerro Cahuí Biotope, Naachtún-Río Azul-Dos Lagunas Biotope, Uaxactún Park, El Zotz-San Miguel La Palotada Biotope, Río Azul-Dos Lagunas Biotope, Laguna del Tigre-Río Escondido Biotope, Lacandón National Park, and the Yaxhá-Nakum-Naranjo Triangle.

Cerro Cahuí Biotope

Cerro Cahuí Biotope is a nature reserve set up to specifically protect the Petén (or ocellated) turkey, the howler monkey, and several species of waterfowl. It is located near the village of El Remate on the road between Flores and Tikal at the eastern tip of Lake Petén Itzá. It is accessible by private car, taxi, or the Jobompiche-El Remate microbus, which departs from the Santa Elena market each day at about 11:00 a.m.

The protected area encompasses about 1,600 acres of hot and rainy subtropical forest. Preservation of this broadleaf jungle is partly calculated to maintain the quality of water entering Lake Petén Itzá. Elimination of trees around other parts of the lake have accelerated erosion, which threatens to change the aquatic ecosystem. The varied plant life in the reserve includes many species of orchids and bromeliads, along with mahogany, cedar, and marmalade fruit trees. Several trees cultivated by the ancient Maya, including the sacred ramón and the multipurpose sapodilla, are also found here.

Besides the threatened howler monkey, dozens of mammals have been recorded at Cerro Cahuí, including ocelot, jaguar, raccoon, armadillo, and white-tailed deer. Several kinds of primates, snakes, and reptiles are also found here, plus 24 species of fish in the waters of Lake Petén Itzá.

Wild ocellated turkey in Tikal, also called the Peten turkey (Photo by Richard Mahler)

The Petén turkey is fully protected in the park, one of the few places where the once-common bird still thrives, although it is now in greater evidence in Tikal National Park. Sharp-eyed visitors can also expect to see parrots, toucans, hook-beaked hawks, kingfishers, grey herons, purple herons, ducks, woodpeckers, and, during winter months, many migratory birds. More than 50 varieties of butterflies also make Cerro Cahuí their home.

The park has several footpaths, a spectacular lookout point above the lake, and a camping area. Guards and other personnel are on duty during most daylight hours. Two hotels, Gringo Perdido and Hotel Camino Real, are located near the reserve (see list of Tikal hotels for information). The nearest villages, El Remate and Jobompiche, also provide basic services to the visitor.

Uaxactún Park

Directly north of Tikal, reached by 14 miles of recently improved road, is the largely unrestored ruin of Uaxactún, built and rebuilt during roughly the same era as its famous and larger neighbor.

A tour of the site can be disappointing after a visit to Tikal, which Uaxactún resembles on a much smaller scale. The tallest temple pyramid here rises to only 27 feet, for example, and most of the stelae have either been removed or eroded almost beyond recognition.

The site is best known for its massive astronomical "observatory." A set of three temples known as Group E are oriented so that when viewed from the middle structure (with its two large stucco faces flanking the stairway), the sun passes directly over the northernmost pyramid on the summer solstice and over the southernmost pyramid on the winter solstice. This distinctive Mayan architectural pattern was first discovered here and later turned up at similar observatories at other ancient sites.

As in many places, archaeological fieldwork at Uaxactún was clumsy in its earliest phase. Dynamite was reportedly used to remove some of the friezes, stelae were carted off to overseas collections, and buildings were crudely cut open to look for burial tombs. The explorations turned up some interesting painted murals, however, and evidence that portions of the temple pyramids may have been originally covered with wooden, thatch-roof shelters. A copy of a magnificent

Uaxactún fresco is displayed at the National Museum of Archaeology and Ethnography in Guatemala City.

The ruins are in eight groups of structures, bisected by an abandoned airstrip. Once used to transport balls of rubber and chicle, the runway now serves as a combination soccer field, plaza, and pasture for the village of Uaxactún, home to about 200 people, mostly Kekchí Maya. The largest cluster of buildings is on the west side of the airport and includes a wooden observation platform that provides a good view of the area.

The name *Uaxactún* means "eight stone" and is derived from a stelae found here with an inscription that begins with that number, apparently an early date on the Mayan historical time line. Uaxactún appears to have been occupied longer than any other known Mayan city. This may well be, therefore, the place where the culture was consolidated, the writing system perfected, and the calendar started. Artifacts found here provide an unusual record of how Mayan ceramics evolved over the centuries. A number of exquisite jade pieces have also been recovered at Uaxactún, and beneath one temple is a building dating back to 2000 B.C., one of the oldest structures found in the Petén.

An examination of local soil history found evidence of extreme erosion here toward the end of the Classic era, apparently due to overuse of the land. Much of the forest was denuded and topsoil was washed away, bolstering one theory about the cause of the Maya's decline. Skeletons found at nearby Tikal show signs of malnutrition among the lower classes during the same period.

After checking in at the park's security office, you can camp in the archaeological park or spend the night with a local family. Inquire at the Tienda La Ceiba, where drinks and snacks are sold. There are no restaurants or other services, although beans, rice, and tortillas can be purchased from residents.

Most of the men of Uaxactún roam the jungle collecting chicle, allspice, or xate palm leaves for export. Many area residents are *Cobaneros*, Indians from Alta Verapaz who, driven by their desperate poverty, moved to this relatively empty land in search of a better life.

Representatives of Conservation International and the Guatema-

Three Kekchí Indians pause on a wooden bridge after a morning spent cutting xate palm leaves, used as floral decorations in Europe and the United States (Photo by Richard Mahler)

lan government have been working successfully with local people here (and elsewhere) to set up a system of "sustainable development" whereby natural resources are not overexploited. It is particularly important to work with newcomers who may be unfamiliar with the delicate process involved in harvesting wild crops from the forest. A xate palm cut too often or too severely by inexperienced hands, for example, may become overstressed and die.

The environmental educators are also trying to get area woodcutters to shift their emphasis away from prized—and increasingly scarce—hardwoods such as cedar and mahogany toward faster growing and more common "secondary" trees, such as rosewood, breadnut, and Santa María. Selective cutting of the latter is much less damaging to the jungle ecosystem, while still yielding marketable timber.

The road to Uaxactún begins at the inspection station for the Tikal ruins. The route takes about 30 minutes by car, or you can walk the distance in about 6 hours each way. Be sure to wear a hat and carry plenty of water. Public buses have run to Uaxactún from Tikal in the past and may have resumed by the time you visit. Tour guide Lorenzo de León is a recommended guide to Uaxactún. He is based in Tikal and has his own four-wheel-drive van. An ecotourism lodge being planned here may be open by the time of your visit.

The small unrestored ruin of Xultún is located at the end of a very poor track that branches off the Uaxactún road about 9 miles north of Tikal. There is not much to see here, and the road is not recommended except for four-wheel-drive vehicles traveling in dry weather.

El Zotz-San Miguel La Palotada Biotope
This tract of forest and savanna runs the exact length of Tikal National Park's 16-mile western border and continues west for about 10 miles. It serves as a buffer zone where limited exploitation of the forest is allowed without jeopardizing the integrity of its ecosystems or those of neighboring Tikal.

The small Mayan ruin of El Zotz is located within the borders of this reserve on a dirt road that runs between the village of San Miguel (13 miles north of Lake Petén Itzá) and Uaxactún. The site consists of four unrestored temple pyramids and several other structures, plus a cluster of unexcavated mounds. Camping is permitted, but there are no services of any kind.

El Zotz is 12 miles (1 hour) northeast of San Miguel and 20 miles (2 hours) southwest of Uaxactún. The road may be impassable during the wet season.

Naachtún-Dos Lagunas Biotope and Río Azul National Park

A large rectangle of land extending directly south of Guatemala's northern border with Mexico, contiguous with Mexico's 1.8-million acre Calakmul Biosphere Reserve, the Naachtún-Dos Lagunas Biotope, and Río Azul National Park encompass a rugged and mostly unpopulated tract of primary forest and wetland.

The dirt road that heads north from the Uaxactún airstrip deteriorates rapidly and is recommended for dry-season travel by rugged four-wheel-drive vehicles only. It is about 35 miles to the village of Dos Lagunas and another 20-odd miles to the archaeological site of Río Azul, just below the Mexican frontier. The small and largely unexcavated Mayan ruins of Naachtún and La Muralla are even more remote—some 28 miles northwest of Dos Lagunas by a nearly impassable track.

Dos Lagunas is named after two small lakes located near a minor ruin. Some chicleros and xateros live at this remote jungle intersection, but there are no services for travelers beyond a biological research station.

From Dos Lagunas, the dirt road veers east through dense jungle. Expect to stop often to clear trees and other debris from the road, which seems to go from unimaginably bad to even worse. Your reward at the end of this track is a large collection of Classic era ruins spread over about 750 acres. A good overview can be obtained by climbing to the top of Río Azul's 155-foot temple. Scattered in the distance are the remains of an intricate network of dams, aqueducts, and causeways, as well as the usual pyramids, ball courts, residential buildings, and monuments. It is believed that Río Azul served as a kind of frontier buffer for Tikal, fending off would-be invaders from the north. There is also evidence of Mexican influence at the site, probably late in Río Azul's pre-Columbian history.

Although much of this remote site has been badly looted since its 1962 discovery by Shell Oil Company geologists, archaeologist R. E. W. Adams managed to uncover a pristine, brightly painted burial chamber dating from about A.D. 400. Another discovery was a one-of-a-kind ceramic pot with an ancient screw-top lid. Río Azul is also noted for the high quality of the brightly painted murals and hieroglyphics in many of its sacred burial tombs.

Experts believe that the Río Azul area had a peak population of 5,000 and may have been founded by Stormy Sky, one of Tikal's most powerful rulers, in order to consolidate his influence in the region. One of the emperor's sons was found buried here. (See the April 1986 *National Geographic* for a fascinating article on discoveries at the site.)

It is recommended that trips to Río Azul be arranged with the help of a local guide or tour operator. Advance permission may be necessary from local authorities and Guatemala's Department of Archaeology. The round-trip journey from Tikal usually demands a minimum of 4 days, camping out each night. There are resident guards at the site and occasional researchers but no services, food, or water. Contact the Flores-Santa Elena INGUAT office or travel specialists listed in chapters 12 and 13 for assistance. The army sometimes restricts travel north of Dos Lagunas because of guerrilla activity, so inquire locally before heading into the area. One of the more reliable tour operators for Río Azul is Manuel Zotz in Flores.

South of Río Azul and just west of the Belize frontier are the minor Mayan ruins of Kinal, La Honradez, Xmakabatún, and Holmul, none accessible by road. Visitors who wish to proceed to these sites by mule or helicopter must first obtain permission from local authorities.

Laguna del Tigre-Río Escondido Biotope and National Park

A vast wetland area north of the Río San Pedro, near the Mexican border, the Laguna del Tigre-Río Escondido Biotope and National Park encompasses about a third of the Maya Biosphere's acreage. Laguna del Tigre theoretically enjoys strict environmental protection by the Guatemalan government, but the reality of the current situation is more sobering. Representatives of U.S. and Guatemalan conservation agencies established a scientific research station on the Laguna del Tigre in the early 1990s only to be burned out by disgruntled locals who felt the presence of outsiders inhibited their own activities. It seems that this biologically sensitive area is also the domain of a motley assortment of guerrillas, timber rustlers, drug dealers, and wild-life poachers. Environmentalists, who have received death threats here, are keeping a low profile in this part of the Petén until things settle down. So should you.

During their limited forays into the Laguna del Tigre wetlands, scientists concluded that they are a globally significant wintering and feeding ground for many migratory North American songbirds. There are some unusual nonmigrants as well, including the rare jabiru stork (largest bird north of the Andes) and the secretive gray-necked wood rail. The presence of crocodiles, jaguars, and other predators at the top of the food chain suggests that this ecosystem is still in fairly healthy condition.

Access to the wetlands involves a 6-hour boat trip up the Río San Pedro, past the small Mayan ruin of Mactún, one of several archaeo-logical sites in this part of the Maya Biosphere Reserve. Mactún was an important trading center where macaw feathers, medicinal plants, and wood products were exchanged for salt, copper, and other goods brought in from downriver. A 4-foot waterfall near the ruin marks the end of easily navigable water, and a shell midden (trash heap) below the Mactún site attests to the Maya's fondness for aquatic delicacies.

Sierra del Lacandón National Park

This park preserves a vast, little-explored wilderness area in the remote Lacandón Mountains. Its boundaries extend along the east side of the Usumacinta River for about 50 miles, starting a few miles north of Frontera Corozal, Mexico. The park has no services or roads and is primarily being protected as an important watershed, nature preserve, and wildlife habitat.

The Yaxhá-Nakum-Naranjo Triangle

This triangular chunk of the eastern Petén wilderness butts against Tikal National Park on the west, Río Azul National Park on the north, and the Belize frontier on the east. Besides relatively undis-turbed wetlands and subtropical forest, the reserve protects several major and many minor archaeological sites.

Located on the shoreline of a lake of the same name, the Mayan ruin of Yaxhá is about 20 miles southeast of Tikal, from which there is a horse trail through thick jungle. The recommended route for visitors, however, is via a rough dirt road that cuts north from the Belize Highway west of Melchor de Mencos. The trip from Flores takes about 2 hours (dry season only). The 8 miles from the highway can be covered in about 30 minutes by four-wheel-drive vehicle, or you can walk there in 2 or 3 hours.

Yaxhá, discovered by Europeans in 1904, is believed to be the third largest Classic era Maya ceremonial center in Guatemala. Unlike other communities from that period, two sectors of Yaxhá adopted a grid system much like modern cities. You can still see how the streets were lined with buildings in blocklike quadrangles of high density. Archaeologists suspect that since the site shows Teotihuacán influence in its stelae and architecture, this contemporary urban layout was adopted from the Mexican migrants. There is an interpretive center and bird release/observation tower at the site.

Topoxte, a small, separate site, is located on an island in Yaxhá Lagoon and can be reached only by boat. Little excavation work has been done at Topoxte, a city unusual among Mayan sites because it

The view from the top of Tikal's Temple IV is a sea of green as far as the eye can behold (Photo by Richard Mahler)

flourished between the twelfth and fourteenth centuries, long after most other Mayan communities of the Petén had been abandoned. Several smaller Mayan ruins have been found along the lagoon's western shoreline and on La Naya island in nearby Macanche Lagoon. There is a small but highly recommended lodge near the Yaxhá ruin, whose Petenero owners, Juan and Gabriela Bergamo, are very knowledgeable about the area and will arrange horseback tours or treks to Tikal, Nakum, and some of the more remote jungle attractions. The Bergamos also provide windsurfing, fishing, and boating services at their lakeside hotel, which has complete meal service. Camping is also permitted along the lake near the ruins. Tikal tour operator Juan de la Oz also arranges horseback trips in this area.

Nakum is an ancient Mayan city about 12 miles (1 hour) north of Yaxhá. It is noted more for its size than its buildings and monuments, although several structures are still standing. It is believed that Nakum was founded shortly before the end of the Classic era and occupied through at least A.D. 850. It was an important trading center, and fifteen well-preserved stelae have been found here.

The site can be reached by a very poor road, either on foot or on horseback, or by four-wheel-drive vehicle during the dry season. You may have to walk the last few miles to the site. You will pass a small Mayan site, La Ponchitoca, on the right side of the road about 4 miles south of Nakum. Camping is allowed at either location, but there are no services. The road was being improved in 1992.

Not to be confused with the ruin and village of El Naranjo much farther west, Naranjo is an unexcavated site 14 miles (3 hours of poor road) northwest of the Guatemalan border town of Melchor de Mencos. Camping is permitted, but there is little to see here beyond mounds, an overgrown plaza, and some structural artifacts. There is also a Mayan ball court with an intact stone ring, one of the few such artifacts found in Guatemala.

Naranjo is believed to have been a satellite city of Tikal that flourished during the Classic and Late Classic eras, although it also may have had its own priest-king for a time. You can get there by private vehicle (four-wheel-drive recommended) or chartered plane (check airstrip conditions before heading out).

Other Mayan Sites in the Petén

El Naranjo (West)

The small Mayan ruin of El Naranjo is on the banks of the Río San Pedro downstream from the village of the same name. The archaeological site itself is not very important, but its beautiful location in lush jungle and wetlands makes it worth a visit. In fact, El Naranjo is on the same transportation route used by the ancient Maya, who traveled up and down the Río San Pedro from Palenque to this and other ceremonial centers. You can make the same trip today; it takes about 4 or 5 hours to reach the Mexican border post of La Palma from El Naranjo and another half day to reach the much larger town of Tenosique, from which there are buses to the Mayan ruins of Palenque and trains to Mérida.

The village of El Naranjo is about 100 miles (5 hours or more) west of Flores at the end of a poorly maintained dirt road. You can also charter a plane between the two communities.

El Mirador

Only a few miles south of the Mexican border, smack in the middle of the Petén wilderness, El Mirador ("the vantage point") is currently being excavated. Archaeologists have already determined that the site (part of the much larger El Mirador National Park) contains some of the most massive constructions in the Mayan world, found in unusually concentrated numbers and built beginning around 200 B.C., before Tikal. Unfortunately, many of the structures are overgrown and the painted murals are in a degraded condition, partly because of the swampy environment.

First explored by Westerners in 1926, El Mirador is best known for its massive pyramid structures, which rise in a series of platforms as high as 220 feet above the jungle floor, now considered to be the most massive known Mayan structure. There are five temples that rise beyond the forest canopy, a half-dozen smaller pyramids, and over 200 other buildings.

While probably not as large in area as several other Maya cities, it appears that El Mirador was nevertheless a very important ceremonial site during the pre-Classic era, reaching its zenith several centuries

Mayan Sites

before Tikal. Not much is yet known about the history of this city pending further archaeological work. It is apparent, however, that village populations that had been stable for hundreds of years were moved to this central location to drain swamps and erect huge structures. Somehow the Mayan elite were able to create a social system whereby such mammoth architectural projects became possible.

The remoteness of the locale makes it difficult to visit El Mirador except by helicopter or a 2-day mule trek (each way) from Carmelita, 22 miles southwest by a barely passable track. Carmelita is a tiny chicle and xate center about 40 miles north of Flores that can be reached via public bus or private vehicle in 5 or 6 hours. Guides with pack horses or mules can be hired in Carmelita for the 4- to 6-day

round-trip to the ruins. As in the rest of the Petén, this route is likely
to be impassable during the rainy season. Along the way you will pass
near the minor ruin of Tintal. There are guards (and sometimes
researchers) at the El Mirador site who will let you camp there. Bring
your own food, mosquito net, and other gear. A guide recommended
by several travelers is Victor "Chepe" Krasborn, based in Carmelita.

Nakbe

This hard-to-reach site, also called Zacatal, is located about 14 miles
southeast of El Mirador. Nakbe made headlines in 1992 after the
oldest and largest Mayan religious sculpture was discovered here by
archaeologist Richard Hansen of the University of California at Los
Angeles. Finding the massive head of the bird god Itzam Ye was considered particularly significant because it suggests religion was the
final major catalyst that pushed the ancient Mayan culture into blos-
soming as a full-blown civilization. The stone sculpture, 34 feet wide
by 16 feet high, dates from 300 B.C., about two centuries earlier than
most known examples of similar sculpture, an era scientists previously believed was dominated by very simple village life. The stucco-
covered carving was placed on the outside of one of Nakbe's oldest
pyramids, then inexplicably covered over with rocks and earth.

"We may be looking at the beginning of a great tradition of religious architecture," archaeologist David Friedel of Southern Meth-
odist University told the *Los Angeles Times* soon after the Itzam Ye
finding was made public. "The discovery at Nakbe confirms the
early importance of this royal capital in Mayan civilization."

Nakbe was identified in an aerial survey of the region in 1930, but
because of its isolated location, excavations did not begin until 1989.
It was quickly determined that construction had begun here in about
630 B.C., making it possibly the oldest-known Mayan city. Archaeologists Hansen and Friedel suspect that the harsh jungle environment
is largely what prompted the early Maya to build organized communities like Nakbe. By working together, the people were able to build
causeways and reservoirs for the collection and storage of rainwater,
then drain swamps and create irrigated terraced gardens that could
feed large numbers of people. Hansen believes that the emergence of
powerful religious images such as Itzam Ye reflects the apparently

successful attempt by Mayan leaders to use religion to consolidate their own power and to force hundreds of peasant workers to build massive religious-themed structures. Urbanization may have also been undertaken to facilitate commerce: thousands of sea shells, pieces of obsidian, and other valued trade items have been uncovered here. Besides the massive Itzam Ye sculpture, archaeologists have found evidence of at least one hundred pyramid-shaped temples and other buildings at Nakbe (some as tall as 150 feet). Other excavations revealed a large number of tombs and stone monuments, including an intricately carved limestone frieze that depicts a mysterious historical event. Remnants of an even older community beneath the pre-Classic ruins were found beneath Nakbe.

Nakbe is a 3-day trek (each way) by mule or horse from Carmelita, the nearest roadhead (see El Mirador above). There are no services, and the nearest potable water is 3 hours away. Because the site is currently being studied, permission to visit must be obtained from the Petén government. Some Guatemala City adventure tour operators, including Expedición Panamundo and Monkey Eco Tours, arrange mule treks and helicopter trips to Nakbe and El Mirador. Current information should be available at CINCAP, the nature and culture tourism center in the old Flores jail.

Ceibal

Sometimes referred to as "the Mayan art gallery" because of the fine, well-preserved Late Classic sculpture found here, Ceibal is located 12 miles east of the town of Sayaxchá (roughly 60 miles southwest of Flores), in a forest with many ceiba trees—thus the name, which is occasionally spelled Seibal. After Tikal, this is the most accessible Mayan ruin of any size in the Petén. Ceibal is now believed to be one of at least seven ancient cities that formed an interlocking society around Lake Petexbatún and Río de la Pasión, once a major Maya trade route for the shipment of quetzal feathers, chert tools, jaguar skins, jade cobbles, and fine pottery. Internecine warfare between factional leaders is thought to have led to a breakdown of these alliances during the Late Classic era.

Much of the ruin is still unexcavated, but a couple of plazas and several buildings are visible, along with some unusually fine stelae.

The basic culture sequence of the site is illustrated by its ceramics, particularly the male and female figurines that are remarkably similar to those made by highland Maya during the same period. Ceibal's original residents are thought to have come from either Guatemala's western mountains or Mexico's Olmec lowlands of present-day Tabasco around 900 B.C., but the community did not really grow until about A.D. 830, when it is believed to have had a population of 10,000 or more.

Investigations have been carried out here periodically by Harvard University and the Peabody Museum. One of their most interesting findings was a stairway in Complex A that is decorated with many glyphs and stelae, some with Mexican-looking faces, clothing, and designs. This suggests that Ceibal may have been dominated during its decline by people from the north. Some archaeologists speculate that members of the Toltec and Maya civilizations lived in harmony here and elsewhere in the Petén for several generations. The glyphs also confirm that one of Ceibal's rulers was captured by the priest-king of Dos Pilas, then sacrificed.

For unknown reasons, the corbeled arch found at so many other early Mayan cities is not present here, and the use of round platforms recalls Mexico's Quetzalcoatl cult, whose adherents apparently moved into the region after the lowland Maya's sudden decline. Seibal seems to have peaked between A.D. 830 and 890.

The low ruins of Complex A include some unusually well-preserved and finely carved stelae depicting in sharp relief various warriors, gods, ball players, priests, and other important figures. Some are still pastel colored, others are snow white. Many bear resemblance to sculptures found in the Yucatán and Campeche, Mexico, dating from the mid-eighth century. Pieces of stucco found here indicate that Ceibal's ceremonial platforms were originally decorated with brilliantly painted friezes, of which only a few fragments remain.

The site can be reached in about 45 minutes by four-wheel-drive vehicle via a dirt road from Sayaxché. This route may be impassable during the wet season, however. A boat trip up the Río de la Pasión takes 2 hours, followed by a half-hour trek through the jungle. Many miles farther upstream is the unexcavated Mayan site of Cancuen, believed to have been an outlier community of the same Petexbatún complex that Ceibal was once a part of. Private boat transportation upriver can be arranged at Sayaxché, with air charters from Flores via Avcom.

There are guards stationed at Ceibal who will allow you to camp there. You must be sure to bring your own food, water, mosquito nets, and other supplies (beware of biting ants). Next to the caretaker's hut is a small museum.

Aguateca and Lake Petexbatún

The fortresslike ruins of Aguateca, discovered in 1957, are about 15 miles south of Sayaxché, up a small stream that runs into Lake Petexbatún (also referred to as a *laguna*, or lagoon) and then across a natural bridge over a deep chasm. The site is accessible only by boat, unless water levels are low, in which case part of the distance must be walked. Allow 90 minutes of trekking time in each direction.

There are no towering temples at this relatively minor site, but several of the finely carved Late Classic stelae here are magnificent, particularly Stela 2. A main plaza, pyramid, and royal stairway are discernible, and you can visit an underground passageway (the only one known in the Mayan world) that connects Aguateca with the nearby lake. Excavation is currently in progress at these otherwise unprotected ruins, and archaeologists may be present during the dry season. They believe Aguateca became the capital of the transplanted rulers of Dos Pilas, 14 miles to the northwest.

From the top of the hill where Aguateca is located you can look down over Lake Petexbatún. On the shoreline nearby are some natural springs that make a soothing warm bath for weary hikers.

Expedición Panamundo maintains the Mahogany Lodge on the lagoon for overnight visitors to Aguateca, Dos Pilas, and other nearby attractions. Contact the tour company's Guatemala City office for information (see chapter 13 for address and phone number). The lodge provides boat transportation to nearby ruins and arranges birdwatching, swimming, and fishing excursions around the lake. Large snook, tarpon, and other game fish have been taken in these rich waters.

An alternative to the Mahogany Lodge on Lake Petexbatún is the inexpensive Posada del Mundo Maya, which rents basic rooms, hammock spaces, and campsites. Meals, boats, and jungle guides are also available.

Tamarindito and Arroyo de Piedra

There is not much to see at these small Mayan sites, both of which can be reached on foot or by horse or mule from the banks of Lake Petexbatún. The tree-covered ruins are about a mile west of the lake on a rocky outcrop bisected by several streams. Do not attempt to reach these sites without the help of a guide: the trail is inevitably overgrown.

Vanderbilt University is overseeing excavation of several temple pyramids and other structures at Arroyo de Piedra. A number of stelae have also been found here, dating from A.D. 715. Other unexcavated minor ruins in the general vicinity include Punta de Chimino, a compact fortress city, and Itzán, discovered in 1968. It is believed that all these cities were under the control of Dos Pilas, although Tarandito rebelled (unsuccessfully) at least once.

Dos Pilas

First reported to the outside world by geologist G. L. Vinson in 1960, Dos Pilas (Two Sinks) gets its name from a pair of ponds found at the site. Extensive excavations here and inside nearby sacred Mayan caves are currently being supervised by Vanderbilt University archaeologist Arthur Demarest using sophisticated computer-based technology. Dos Pilas was an important and powerful Lowland Maya city-state, and for centuries its leaders apparently waged wars against neighboring cities in an attempt to create a single regional "superstate."

Significant findings here include several huge, well-preserved stelae, along with royal palaces, temples, and ceremonial structures. A well-preserved, carved hieroglyphic triumphal staircase was found buried in the ceremonial plaza here in 1990, and the following year Demarest's team discovered the burial crypt of an eighth-century ruler. Ruler 2's skeleton was adorned with a jade necklace, headdress of cut shell, and the skin of a jaguar, the Maya symbol of royal power.

The ruins are approached first by boat, then by a 3-hour journey on foot, mule, or horseback through dense vegetation where you may see toucans, parrots, macaws, howler monkeys, and an occasional jaguar or ocelot.

With the help of Kekchí Indian villagers from nearby Nacimiento, archaeologists on Demarest's team have discovered more than a half dozen previously unexplored caves, including the spectacular Cueva de Sangre, where the discovery of a skeleton-filled underground lake has fueled speculation about human sacrifice rituals. None of these sacred caves, which still hold priceless Mayan artifacts, is open to the public.

Altar de los Sacrificios

This Classic era site was named in 1895 by its discoverer, pioneering archaeologist Teobert Maler, to commemorate its enormous stone sacrificial altars. Altar de los Sacrificios is located at the strategic confluence of the Río de la Pasión and Río Chixoy (also called Salinas), opposite the Mexican border, about 30 miles west of Sayaxché. An unusual aspect of construction here, as at El Ceibal, is the absence of the Mayan-style arch. Other research here suggests a full-scale occupation of Altar de los Sacrificios by a Mayan group much more influenced by ancient Mexico than Guatemala. Much of the site has been looted (it remains unprotected to this day), and only a few stelae remain scattered on the ground. The last stela was erected here in A.D. 771, about the time foreign sculptures appeared at El Ceibal. If your visit coincides with the dry season, you may see bits of orange pottery and other ancient artifacts strewn on the sand beneath the ruins, which are slowly being undermined by the nearby river.

Altar de los Sacrificios is best reached by boat from Sayaxché. The trip takes a minimum of 6 hours (unless you hire a high-speed motorboat). Camping is permitted. Try the river beaches during the dry season, or the Río de la Pasión weather station in the event of high water. The clear waters of the Río Pucté, which flows into the Pasión along this stretch, are ideal for fishing and diving.

Two more hours downstream the Pasión becomes part of the Usumacinta River. There are good campsites at the junction. A few miles farther down the Usumacinta is the village of Benemerito, Mexico. From Benemerito it is a 9-hour (or more) bus ride to the magnificent Mayan ruins at Palenque. Road connections can also be made here for the smaller sites of Bonampak and Yaxchilán (reachable by boat via Frontera Corozal or by chartered plane).

If you stay on the Río Usumacinta beyond Benemerito, you will soon pass the Mayan site of Planchon de Figuras, located on the Mexican bank near the confluence of Mexico's Río Lacandón (also spelled

Lacantún). Very little is known about this large slab of limestone, which has been inscribed with glyphs, animal drawings, and architectural designs. A short distance beyond Planchon de Figuras is the cascading Chorro waterfall, from which it is another 20-odd miles to Frontera Corozal, a Mexican village with an immigration post and other basic services. Bus service is sometimes available from El Subín to the villages of Betél and La Técnica, across the river from Frontera Corozal.

Piedras Negras

These ruins are located on the hilly Guatemalan side of the Río Usumacinta, in the remote northwest corner of El Petén. Marxist guerrillas have established permanent bases in the area but are reportedly friendly and nonthreatening to foreign tourists. If you do encounter guerrillas here or elsewhere, be respectful and avoid taking photographs of them or their encampments.

Piedras Negras (Black Rocks) has been only partially excavated since its discovery in 1935, and many of its pyramidal mounds have been reclaimed by the jungle. What has survived, besides one room with a vaulted roof and a few eroded zoomorphs, is a complete set of "period markers" erected by the Maya to document the end of 22 successive 1,800-day time periods called *hotuns*. The carving of these dated stelae began some time after the Maya settled here. This ceremonial practice was followed more consistently here than at any other known Mayan site. Twenty-two successive hotun monuments were found at Piedras Negras, marking each of the appropriate epochs between A.D. 608 and 810. These stelae, originally excavated by the University of Pennsylvania, have proven invaluable in helping reconstruct Mayan history of the lowlands. Piedras Negras collapsed, along with much of the lowland Maya empire, around A.D. 830. (Excellent documentation of the art of Piedras Negras and Yaxchilán is found in Linda Schele's beautifully illustrated books, *The Blood of Kings* and *The Forest of Kings*.)

Evidence has also been found in these ruins of considerable human sacrifice. Blood spilled from the arms, legs, tongues, ears, and genitalia of specially chosen individuals, apparently in return for favors from the Mayan gods. Animals, fish, food, and jade were also offered for sacrifice at this location, according to anthropologists. Based on an examination of brightly colored masonry and ornamented stucco found here, the inhabitants of Piedras Negras were some of the best artists in all of ancient Guatemala. Unfortunately, they and their comrades seem to have come to a sudden end long before the Spanish Conquest.

Many of the stone monuments here are totally overgrown, but you can still make out a large carved monkey face next to the ancient ball court. Not far away, visitors will notice a network of hot-water channels used by the Mayan elite to fill their bathtubs.

Piedras Negras can be reached only by river boat. An airstrip a few miles away in the village of Lacandón, Guatemala, has fallen into disuse.

Navigable Rivers of the Petén

Río de la Pasión
A southeast tributary of the Usumacinta, this river has long been an important transportation link between the southern Petén and the outside world. Boats regularly travel up the Pasión as far as Raxrujá and Sebol in Alta Verapaz and south via the Río Usumacinta into Mexico. A number of adventure-oriented tour operators in the United States, Canada, and Guatemala arrange trips along the Río de la Pasión that combine archaeology, natural history, camping, trekking, fishing, and other activities.

Río Usumacinta
The Río Usumacinta forms about one-third of the border between Guatemala and Mexico, along more than 100 miles of the Petén's western frontier, through some of the most unspoiled tropical forest in the northern hemisphere.

Although the region has few inhabitants today, it was at one time a major population center for the ancient Maya, who flourished along the Usumacinta from around A.D. 200 to A.D. 1300. The ruins of several important Classic era ceremonial sites, including remote Yaxchilán and Piedras Negras, are along the river and very much worth visiting.

Boat trips typically cover 80 miles in 6 days, beginning at Frontera Corozal (called Echeverría on some maps) and ending at Boca del Cerro, near Tenosique, all on the Mexican side of the border. The inflatable rafts are pulled up at various riverside campsites each evening. A 9-day trip can take you all the way to Palenque, or up the Río San Pedro to El Naranjo and by vehicle to Flores. Outfitters arranging such trips include Ceiba Adventures of Durango, Colo.; Mountain Travel-Sobek Expeditions, based in El Cerrito, Calif.; and Far Flung Adventures, located in Terlingua, Texas. The best local operators are Izabal Adventure Tours and Maya Expeditions in Guatemala City. See chapter 13 for addresses and phone numbers.

The downstream trip is along a generally wide and slow-moving river, fringed by limestone banks and shadowed by a dense forest canopy. Spider and howler monkeys are common along the route, and jaguars, ocelots, coatimundi, and other mammals are occasionally seen. Among the many bird species you are likely to encounter are scarlet macaws, toucans, parrots, parakeets, egrets, herons, hawks, and swallows. In fact, there are as many varieties of birds found along the Usumacinta as in the United States and Canada combined. Wild papaya, cacao, mahogany, mango, banana, Spanish cedar, palm, and ceiba trees make up part of the dense jungle.

Only a few hours south of Frontera Corozal, at an enormous bend in the river, Yaxchilán comes into view on the Mexican bank. These Mayan ruins are made up of imposing palaces, pyramids, and temples, clustered around an immense plaza dotted by tall stone stelae.

There is one massive waterfall on a tributary of the Río Usumacinta, called Budsilha (Smoking Water) by the Maya, located several miles downstream from the largely unexcavated Piedras Negras ruins. Powerful rapids are encountered farther north at the scenic Cañon Grande del San José, where the narrowed river swirls (with whitewater and whirlpools) between thousand-foot walls of limestone.

Unfortunately, the Río Usumacinta is threatened by plans made by the Mexican government to dam the river below Cañon Grande and flood much of the surrounding forest, as well as the Piedras Negras archaeological site. Although the project has been under discussion for more than twenty years, there were mixed signals from Mexico's president in 1992 that construction was either imminent or cancelled. Timber cutting, farming, and oil development are other ongoing threats to the area, so it is prudent to visit the relatively unspoiled Usumacinta while you can.

Frontera Corozal, where river trips usually begin, can be reached by road from the Mexican city of Villahermosa or by private plane from either that city, Tuxtla Gutiérrez, or Flores. River travelers heading to or from Guatemala are required to clear Mexican immigration and customs in Corozal. In 1992 there were no Guatemalan border officials on the opposite side of the river, although facilities were being planned.

12

Special Interests

Indigenous Crafts and Dance

Crafts

The native craftwork of Guatemala, referred to locally as artesanía or típica, is among the most varied and interesting in the world, a natural result of the country's rich pre-Columbian and Spanish colonial traditions. Few of the artisans producing these objects have any formal training, relying instead on techniques and designs passed down to them through many generations. The materials used in their creations, such as vegetable dyes and natural fibers, often are obtained locally. Much of the thread used in Guatemalan textiles (*tejidos*) is still spun and colored by hand, and ceramics are frequently produced with local clays and wood-burning kilns.

Marketplaces dot the countryside: almost every village sets aside at least one day each week for the buying and selling of a dizzying array of handicrafts and foodstuffs. These markets are the gathering places where Indians not only bargain for, trade, and purchase the daily necessities of life but also gossip, strengthen family ties, and reaffirm social traditions that date back centuries.

Many stores, galleries, and workshops sell handcrafted items directly to the public. Look for signs containing the words *artesanía* or *confecciónes típicas*. Other hints: a *taller artesanál* is an artist's studio, and a *cooperativa de tejidos* is a textile cooperative.

Traditional fiestas, filed with dancing, drinking, music, and merry-making, commemorate the patron saints of each town and major events of historical or religious significance. On any given day, a fiesta is being held somewhere in one of Guatemala's more than 4,000 towns and villages.

A good place to get an overview of Guatemalan crafts is the Mercado de Artesanías (Artisans Market) located near the national museum complex on Calzada del Aeropuerto in Guatemala City's La Aurora Park, across from the international airport terminal in Zone 13. The market is dedicated exclusively to handcrafted típica that reflects the country's traditions and cultural heritage. It is open daily from 9:30 a.m. to 6:00 p.m. except on Sunday, when the *mercado* closes at 2:00 p.m.

Those interested in buying products directly from indigenous people may wish to contact Mayan Crafts (845 N. Lincoln St., Arlington, VA 22201, tel. 703-527-5067), Shawcross Aid Programme (R.D. #4, Box 10, 4043 State Route 39, Shelby, OH 44875, tel. 419-347-2937), Pueblo to People (P.O. Box 2545, Houston, TX 77252, tel. 800-843-5257), or Trade Wind (P.O. Box 380, Summertown, TN 38483, tel. 800-445-1991). These progressive organizations work with Guatemalan Indians on craft projects as well as human rights, economic development, and literacy programs. An excellent source of information about these and similar projects around the world is nonprofit Cultural Survival and its quarterly magazine of the same name (53-A Church Street, Cambridge, MA 02138, tel. 617-495-2562). There are retail outlets for some Guatemalan artisans' cooperatives in Antigua, Quetzaltenango, and Guatemala City.

Textiles and Clothing

The traditional traje, or dress, of the indigenous Guatemalan people is admired around the world for its high quality and colorful embroidery. The intricate designs, which vary dramatically from one village to the next, are carefully made using pre-Columbian techniques on back-strap or stick looms or, less commonly, foot-powered treadle looms introduced by the Spanish. Textiles are mostly woven with wool, silk, or cotton thread, depending on the region.

It is estimated that there are at least 325 major patterns reflected in the traditional dress still worn by the Indian residents of about two thousand Guatemalan villages. Each costume reflects some aspect of

A North American visitor bargains for handwoven clothing in a Guatemalan market (Photo by Richard Mahler)

its own geography, family structure, patron saint, or history, in some cases even incorporating Spanish colonial dress. Dress may also be altered depending on the wearer's sex, age, tribal affiliation, and social rank.

A woman often has a minimum of four different ceremonial costumes, their designs and symbols varying for each occasion. Men, who have been less loyal to the customs of traditional dress, usually have only one or two costumes.

Despite the many ceremonial and regional differences, the typical dress of Guatemalan Indian women usually includes a *huipil* (untailored smock-style blouse), *corte* or *refajo* (skirt), *faja* (belt), *tzute* (scarf or headdress), and *rebozo* (shawl). The word *huipil*, incidentally, is derived from an Aztec phrase meaning "my covering" (in Spanish, *mi tapado*).

Traditional men's attire includes *pantalones* (trousers), *cincho* (belt), *camisa* (shirt), *capixay* (tunic or vest), *cotón* or *chaqueta* (jacket), *banda* (sash), and a shoulder bag called a *morral*.

Some of the more popular markets for textiles are in Santiago Atitlán (noted for its animal and geometric designs), Panajachel (vibrant combinations of red and purple, along with animals), San Juan Chamelco (braided work), Chichicastenango (traditional-looking Indian clothes in North American sizes), San Francisco El Alto (huipiles), and San Antonio Aguas Calientes (high-quality designs and dyes). In many textile centers interested foreigners can easily obtain personalized weaving instruction from some of the most talented practitioners. See chapters 6 and 7 for a more detailed discussion of these communities, their weavers, and their markets.

Blankets

In the western mountains of Guatemala, the town of Momostenango is famous for its woolen *ponchos momostecos* ("blankets from Momo"). These are made on foot-operated looms by local Quiché Maya men and sold at the town's weekly market. The women are in charge of washing, carding, and spinning the wool, which is sheared from sheep grazed in nearby upland meadows. The finished blankets are washed in a local hot spring before being sold.

Leather

From traditional sandals to leather portfolios and cigarette cases, leather has always been a major resource for Guatemalan craftworkers. A *talabartería* sign indicates a saddlery, leather goods store, or studio (*taller*).

Jewelry

Since the Mayan epoch, Guatemalan jade has been one of the main elements used in jewelry making. The craft has been revived in Antigua over the past two decades with the production of traditional and modern designs of bracelets, earrings, necklaces, and other pieces of jewelry. High-quality jade quarried in ancient and recently rediscovered mines of the Sierra de las Minas range of southeast Guatemala is used. (See chapter 6 for a discussion of this subject.)

The town of Tactic, in Alta Verapaz, is known for its silver jewelry, and filigree is the specialty of craftsmen in nearby San Pedro Carchá. There are gold and silver workers in other parts of the country who specialize in religious artifacts for churches and homes. Tin is also crafted in various Guatemalan communities into cages, candlesticks, and other decorative objects. If you are interested in these kinds of craftwork, be on the lookout for stores marked *joyería* (jewelry).

In Lívingston, on the Caribbean coast, seeds of the wild *guiscoyol* plant are used to make rings and earrings. You can also see jewelry made out of black coral and turtle shells, although it is now illegal for visitors to take these items out of the country. The government believes that commercial use of these items threatens their continuing presence in the marine ecosystem.

Cane and Palm

Woven palm hats are popular throughout Guatemala. Some of the most attractive and colorful are made in Todos Santos Cuchumatán and Santa Cruz del Quiché. It is not accurate to call these Panama hats, since the slender reeds used to make Panamas are found exclusively in Ecuador.

From San Raimundo, Iztapa, and San Juan Sacatepéquez come the large variety of mats and baskets made with different types of cane and reed as well as fibers from the maguey cactus. Small straw baskets are mostly made in Tecpán, near Chimaltenango.

Wood

Wood-crafted Guatemalan products (*productos de madera*) include vivid folkloric masks (*máscaras*), delicately carved squash gourds, brightly colored chests (*cajas*), colonial doors and furniture, rattan chairs, musical instruments, wooden fruit, and bent-wood boxes. The villages of the wooded area of southwestern Totonicapán are particularly noted for their carved toys (*juguetes*), varnished fruit, and furniture (*muebles*). The town of Palin is noted for its fine masks, and Antigua is a major producer of colonial-style doors and furniture, much of it exported to the United States. In Antigua, Francisco Márquez and the Juárez brothers are famous for their woodwork, and their studios are open to the public.

Mask makers sitting in front of their stand on the main street of Panajachel (Photo by Richard Mahler)

Ceramics

There are a great variety of ceramic (*cerámica*) objects produced in Guatemala, reflecting two primary traditions—pre-Columbian and Spanish colonial. Examples range from the glazed pottery of Jalapa, Huehuetenango, and Totonicapán (made with techniques introduced in the colonial era) to the unglazed animal-shaped clay creations of Chiantla and San Luis Jilotepeque. The latter are produced using open-air bonfires rather than kilns just as they were in prehistoric times by the Pokomán Maya. Rabinal, in Baja Verapaz, is one of the few places where a combination of Indian and European techniques is applied to figures, toys, and other objects, using nij, an unusual dye derived from insects.

Some artists, such as the brothers Federico and Andrés Tuymax of Totonicapán, have established national reputations for the quality of their ceramic work. As with weavers, Indian potters often use designs and materials whose origins are lost in Mayan antiquity. In Santa Apolonia, for example, the red ceramic ware draws heavily on Cakchiquel Indian techniques, yielding balloon-shaped bowls and flat cooking pans called *comales*.

It is primarily the women who have carried on the pre-Columbian ceramic traditions, molding clay by hand and using natural clays and dyes. Their products are mainly utilitarian, and decorative motifs are simple: plants, animals, and human forms, such as the *mengalas* (maidservants) and *chichiguas* (nursemaids) of the nineteenth century.

The Spanish introduced potters' wheels, oxide glazes, mineral enamels, and painted crockery to Guatemala. The main producer of colonial-style white earthenware (*majólica*) is Antigua, where Francisco Montiel and his family are recognized as perhaps the foremost practitioners (Subidita a San Felipe 20). Other renowned craftsmen in Antigua include Cruz and Guillermo España (Calle Real de San Felipe 83), for his ceramic pigeons and other birds, and members of the Rodenas family (Calle de Chajón 24), for their painted miniatures, including tiny dishware, butterflies, and nacimientos (Nativity scenes). In nearby Jocotenango, the Familia Barrios (Camino a San Felipe 3-26) and José Gerardo López Pérez (Colonia Clarita 6) are famous for their wood, ceramic, and bronze work.

Other centers of European-type ceramics are Jalapa, Totonicapán, and San Cristóbal. The many workshops of Totonicapán, located between Quetzaltenango and Santa Cruz del Quiché, are especially worth visiting during the annual fiesta of the Archangel (September 14-30), Holy Week, and the village's Tuesday and Saturday markets.

Dance

The traditional *danzas* (dances) of Guatemala are often a kind of musical play re-creating a specific historic event through the use of unvarying ritualized scripts and masks. Some danzas are performed in only one community, while others, like the dance of the Spanish Conquest, are part of the annual fiesta in many towns and villages. Rabinal presents portions of its extended dance drama, the ancient Rabinal Achí, during its January 25-29 fiesta, along with an elaborate ceremony calling for a bountiful harvest. In Lívingston, the unique traditions of the Garifuna people are celebrated in dance celebrations several times a year, particularly during the May 13-15 commemoration of the arrival of their ancestors from Puerto Barrios and Belize (see chapter 10).

The most dependable times of year to see dances are during a town's patron saint celebration, the Christmas season (December 7 through January 6), and Semana Santa. Typically, dances are only one small part of a communitywide fiesta that includes much drinking and carousing. This is why many dancers are often so drunk that they can barely stand up, particularly if the danza is scheduled toward the end of the day. Besides aguardiente (sugarcane liquor) and atol (a hot corn beverage), large quantities of food are consumed, including such special-occasion treats as *buñuelos* (honey-coated fried pastries), *jocón* (a chicken dish), *torrejas* (similar to French toast), stuffed peppers, and *plátanos en gloria* (plantains fried in sweet sauce).

An excellent resource for those interested in seeing Guatemalan dances is the *Directory of Fiestas* (Directorio de Fiestas) published and distributed free of charge by INGUAT. It contains a detailed description of festivals throughout the country, indexed by date and location.

Flora and Fauna

For such a small country, Guatemala is richly endowed with an amazing array of plants and wildlife. Within its 50,900 square miles are distinct ecological zones ranging from frigid mountain peaks to sweltering lowland rain forests, from shallow coral reefs to deep freshwater lakes. As the northernmost link in the isthmus bridge between North and South America, Guatemala is a place of incredible biodiversity. Its habitats support an estimated 1,533 species of vertebrate animals and several thousand invertebrates. Some botanists believe the country is home to the most diverse flora in Central America, hosting an estimated 8,000 species of vascular plants and over 700 kinds of trees.

In proportion to its size, Guatemala has a particularly large variety of birds. Nearly 700 species have been recorded within its borders, including about 200 migratories that visit (mostly from the north) during winter months. See the Appendix for a suggested reading list of books about Guatemalan birds and other flora and fauna.

One of the unusual indigenous birds is the Petén turkey (*pavo*

This basilisk lizard is one of 124 reptile species found in Guatemala (Photo by Kevin Schafer and Martha Hill)

dorado), also known as the ocellated or golden turkey, found only in the northeast Petén. Another large native fowl is the horned guan (*pavo de cacho*), extant on the slopes of the Tajumulco, Tolimán, Tecpán, Fuego, and Zunil volcanoes. Known locally as the *pavón*, this surprisingly graceful bird is distinguished by its black-and-white plumage and a 2-inch scarlet horn on the top of its head. The guan prefers dense vegetation, where it survives on a diet of green leaves, fruit, and insects. It is more frequently heard than seen, muttering a low mooing sound and clacking its yellow beak when alarmed. The biggest threat to the horned guan is the market for its delicious meat, considered a local delicacy despite the fact that fewer than a thousand birds remain in the wild.

One of the world's rarest birds, the flightless Atitlán grebe (locally called the poc), inhabits the reeds along the south and west shorelines of Lake Atitlán. This grebe has been pushed to the brink of extinction through habitat destruction, poaching, and the killing of hatchlings by nonnative bass.

Although somewhat less endangered, the quetzal has become increasingly scarce in Guatemala and could become locally extinct within the next ten or fifteen years. In pre-Columbian times, the regal plumage of this bird was used in the headdresses of Mayan royalty, and its elegant feathers were traded like currency. The markings of a quetzal are unmistakable: brilliant green and blue wings, iridescent red breast, and a 2- to 4-foot tail that curls up at the end like an inverted question mark. Although it has long been illegal to capture or kill the quetzal, live specimens are rarely seen—mostly in the highest cloud forests of the departments of Verapaz. Attempts to breed the bird in captivity have never been successful.

Another winged creature of special significance to the ancient Maya was the *azacuán*, a species of falcon. These birds fly as far as Canada during April and May, returning after the rainy season in November. From this migratory pattern, the Maya concluded that the gods had given the azacuán the responsibility for opening and closing the celestial springs from which rain is derived.

Guatemala has its share of endangered mammals, too. The freshwater manatee, for example, was once common in Lake Izabal and along the Río Dulce. This enormous, gentle vegetarian, also called a sea cow, is still hunted throughout its diminishing range, although the animals are now protected within the Chocón Machacas Preserve near Lívingston.

The manatee is one of at least 30 animal species in Guatemala listed as endangered. The jaguar, regarded as the most sacred of all beasts by the lowland Maya, is fighting for its survival in the country's forests and wetlands, where it is often regarded as a destructive predator by cattle ranchers. Along the Pacific slope cattlemen pay bounties of $600 or more for jaguar carcasses—equivalent to a peasant's entire annual salary. Thankfully, enough undisturbed habitat remains to sustain healthy populations of 4 other species of cat in the jungles of the Petén and Verapaz: the puma, ocelot, margay, and jaguarundi.

Monkeys are another family of large mammals that has been hard hit by poaching and habitat destruction in addition to infectious diseases. Spider and howler monkeys have become locally extinct in much of their former range and are still killed by rural Indians for food. However, successful reintroduction of monkeys has been achieved in some areas, including Tikal National Park.

The Morelet's crocodile is another top-of-the-food-chain species whose presence in patches of Guatemalan wilderness is a healthy ecological sign. Like its smaller relative, the cayman, the crocodile is often poached for its meat and skin.

Guatemala's national flower is the *monja blanca* or white nun (*Lycaste virginalis alba*), which grows wild in Alta Verapaz and is now seldom seen anywhere else. This rare, beautiful flower, believed to be the only immaculately white orchid in the world, derives its name from its six large white petals and stamen, which are shaped like a tiny nun's habit.

A good nature-oriented travel specialist is Leif Ness at Green Trail Tours in Guatemala City (tel. 323-540).

Water Recreation

Guatemala is one of the least known destinations in Central America for water sports. While most people are familiar with the country's archaeological ruins and indigenous cultures, few potential visitors think much about Guatemala's whitewater rivers, freshwater lakes, and long stretches of Caribbean and Pacific coastline when planning a trip.

Several local tour operators specializing in water recreation and adventure travel are excellent resources for those interested in this kind of recreation. They provide regularly scheduled package tours and can arrange customized trips as well. Only a handful of U.S.-based travel companies organize trips to Guatemala that are specifically based around rafting or other kinds of water sports. See chapter 13 for details.

Sailing and Boating
Sailboats and other small craft can be chartered (with or without a skipper and crew) at many locations. There are also a number of marinas where private boats entering Guatemalan waters can be berthed for brief or extended periods of time, mainly on the Río Dulce and at the Pacific port of San José. Inquire locally for suggestions.

The main destinations for sailboat and power boat recreation in Guatemala are, in descending order of popularity, Lake Atitlán, Lake Amatitlán, Lake Izabal, Lake Petén Itzá, and Lake Petexbatún. The Pacific and Caribbean coasts offer ocean boating opportunities, and the Caribbean coast is particularly well suited for sailors and yachtsmen. The Río Dulce and Lake Izabal make safe and attractive anchorages during hurricanes and tropical storms. For more details, see chapters relating to them geographically, or inquire at local travel agencies, such as Guatemalan Adventures in Antigua (4a. Calle Oriente 12A).

Kayaking and Canoeing

Kayaking and canoeing are increasingly popular in Guatemala, but so far neither sport is very accessible to the foreign visitor due to a lack of local services and equipment. Your best bet for rentals is at the major hotels and marinas of Lake Atitlán in the western highlands and Lake Amatitlán south of Guatemala City. You may also be able to rent a kayak or canoe along the Chiquimulilla Canal parallel to the Pacific, at the Monterrico nature reserve near San José, or the marinas of the Río Dulce. Several local operators, such as Izabal Adventure Tours and Excursiónes Spross, will arrange sea kayaking expeditions through the southern cayes of Belize. English-language newspapers in Antigua and Guatemala City also sometimes carry advertisements for sailboats available for charter on the country's lakes and coastlines.

Water levels fluctuate dramatically, depending on local rainfall. For this reason, the waterways are often unpredictable and sometimes downright dangerous. Best bets include the Río Cahabón, Río San Pedro, and Río de la Pasión, as well as the country's various lakes and wetlands.

Whitewater Rafting

Since the late 1980s, Maya Expeditions (374-666 in Guatemala City) and members of the Guatemala Kayaking Club have explored the country's principal rivers to determine their suitability for whitewater rafting, kayaking, and canoe trips. Maya's knowledgeable American

Running the rapids of the Río Cahabón (Photo by Richard Mahler)

owner Tammy Ridenour and her experienced Guatemalan guides use only topnotch equipment for their many float trips down the Cahabón, Usumacinta, Pasión, Mopán, Chiquibul, Naranjo, and upper Motagua rivers. Her services, which also include excursions to remote archaeological sites and volcanic peaks, are highly recommended.

Izabal Adventure Tours, Servicios Turísticos del Petén, Aventuras sin Límites, and Expedición Panamundo also offer river trips on the Río Usumacinta, which forms the middle third of Guatemala's northwestern border with Mexico, as well as its Guatemalan tributary, the Río de la Pasión. Similar excursions are booked by outfitters serving the United States and Canada: Far Flung Adventures (Terlingua, Texas), Ceiba Adventures (Durango, Colo.), and Mountain Travel-Sobek Expeditions (El Cerrito, Calif., and Unionville, Ont.). See chapter 13 for the addresses and phone numbers.

The Usumacinta, known as "the river of the sacred monkey," was (and still is) an important Maya trade route, linking the lowlands of Mexico and the Petén with the Guatemalan highlands through such navigable tributaries as the Río Chixoy and Río de la Pasión. This river system is the best way of seeing the region, particularly such remote archaeological sites as Yaxchilán, El Cayo, and Piedras Negras. Wildlife is also abundant, particularly near the campsites of Desempeño (Cayo Island) and Piedras Negras.

The Usumacinta is a large and fairly slow-moving jungle river, with only a few Class I and II rapids. Archaeology and nature are its main attractions. The upper reaches of the Pasión are narrower, with more whitewater. Trips from Sayaxché to Palenque usually take 9 days and 8 nights but can be broken up into segments as short as one day each. Separate boat trips can be arranged to the several Mayan ruins along the shoreline of Lake Petexbatún.

Guatemala's best whitewater river (Classes III and IV) is the Cahabón, which is a 1- to 5-day trip from the Sierra de Chamá of Alta Verapaz to a pull-out point near Lake Izabal at Cahaboncito. Attractions along the way include a natural thermal hot spring (El Paraiso), several large waterfalls, and large, seldom-visited caves. There is abundant bird and animal life along the lower reaches of this river, which are inhabited only by a handful of Kekchí Maya.

Class II and III rapids are run on the Río Naranjo, along the Pacific slope, during the wet season, with side trips to nearby ancient Olmec and Mayan sites, plus natural hot springs. This is a 1- to 5-day trip.

The upper Río Motagua, northwest of Guatemala City, combines a day of Class II and III rapids with a visit to the Mixco Viejo ruins and geologically rich side streams.

Perhaps Guatemala's most unusual river trip involves the Río Candelaria, north of Cobán in Alta Verapaz. On a 3- or 4-day excursion, visitors can explore much of the Candelaria Cave network on an underground rafting expedition. The river eventually flows outside the cavern network and continues through dense jungle to join the Río Chixoy.

There are several slow and nonthreatening jungle rivers in Guatemala that also can be navigated, such as the Sarstoon along the southern Belize border and the upper Mopán in the Petén. Inquire locally about access and guides.

Discussed at length in chapter 10 is the Río Dulce, the slow but scenic jungle river that connects Lake Izabal and El Golfete with the Caribbean. Visitors can book passage on the twice weekly mail boat along the river or hire a motorized private launch for a trip that includes stops at a hot spring and a manatee reserve.

If you are planning to take a trip on a Guatemalan river, be sure to ask your tour company or guide in advance what you should bring. Some operators provide tents and sleeping gear; others do not. Your personal effects should always include strong sunscreen, sunglasses (with all-important safety cord), hat, insect repellent, swimming suit, tight-fitting shoes that can get wet, and personal identification. A flashlight is also helpful. Waterproof boxes and duffel bags are usually provided to stow your gear. Children under 12 are sometimes barred from river trips for safety and insurance reasons.

Windsurfing
Windsurfing is an increasingly popular sport on Guatemala's Lake Atitlán, Lake Izabal, and Río Dulce. The ideal season is October through May, with strongest winds prevailing from October through early January. Lake Atitlán's average wind speed throughout the year is 15 knots per hour, increasing to 25 knots during November and December. Conditions are similar on Izabal and the Río Dulce, with the highest average wind speeds (20 to 25 knots) between November and January. About 300 local windsurfers belong to La Ráfaga (Gust of Wind), Guatemala's national windsurfing club, which hosts regattas and excursions at various times of the year. There are several stores and tour operators in Guatemala City catering to windsurfers; inquire locally as to names, addresses, and phone numbers.

Bicycling

Guatemala is a very good place to ride a bicycle. The distances between villages and towns, particularly in the highlands, are short, and there is a fairly comprehensive road network. Drivers are used to people on bicycles and generally treat them with courtesy. Because of the hot climate and more limited services, few cyclists attempt major trips in the Petén or coastal lowlands.

Mountain bikes will have an easier time of it in rural areas, where roads are unpaved and full of potholes. Racing and street bicycles are very popular among urban Guatemalans, many of whom can be seen on the Pan American Highway and other paved thoroughfares every dry weekend. The twisting mountain road between Antigua and the capital seems to be a perennial favorite.

Guatemala City has several large bicycle clubs and some very well-equipped specialty stores. In fact, almost any town in the country has at least one place where you can change a tire, fix a gearshift, or buy spare parts. As anywhere, it is prudent to carry a spare tire and emergency tools with you at all times. If your problem cannot be repaired on the spot (or you cannot face another steep hill), second-class buses will carry bikes on their roofs.

There are many places to rent bicycles in Guatemala City, Quetzaltenango, Antigua, and Panajachel. Rates are quoted for hourly, daily, weekly, or monthly rentals. The widest selection seems to be in Antigua, where many Spanish students use bicycles while attending language school there. This is also the home of perhaps Guatemala's best bike-based tour company, Antigua Mountain Bike (El Rosario #9, 5a. Avenida Sur Final). Arturo Rosales and his American wife, Susan, have fifteen bicycles available for rent, some equipped with child carriers. The couple can be hired as guides for tours lasting up to 5 days of such highland destinations as Lake Atitlán and the Agua volcano. Day trips are made to indigenous villages near Antigua, including the textile center of San Antonio Aguas Calientes, and nearby coffee, macadamia nut, and rose plantations. Antigua's Rent-A-Bike (5a. Avenida Norte 14) rents mountain bikes by the hour, day, or week.

In Panajachel, another ideal place for cycling, bicycles can be rented from Moto Servicio Quiché (which also has motorbikes) and from Bicicletas Gaby, near the beach off Avenida Santander. You can also check availability at the larger hotels and at Los Geranios Turicentro on Avenida Rancho Grande.

Always be sure to thoroughly inspect and road test your bicycle before completing the rental transaction.

Chapter 12

Spanish-Language Schools

Teaching Spanish is a booming industry in Guatemala and an important source of income for the many people who now rent rooms or teach classes. Those who run the restaurants and other businesses frequented by foreign visitors also benefit from the scores of private schools in Guatemala offering various levels of instruction in the speaking, reading, and writing of Spanish. Some of these are very specialized, catering exclusively to a Japanese-speaking or Christian clientele, for example. Some are designed for entry-level students, while others can help the mid-level Spanish speaker become more fluent.

As of mid-1992, more than eighty language schools were registered in Antigua alone, enrolling up to a thousand students each month. Quetzaltenango is also emerging as a center for instruction, and there are Spanish schools in Huehuetenango, Panajachel, San Andrés, and Guatemala City as well. The government of Guatemala occasionally updates its list of school names, addresses, and phone numbers. This roster can be obtained free of charge by writing your nearest Guatemalan embassy, consulate, or tourism office. Besides academic excellence, one factor in choosing a school may be the distribution of its profits. Some institutions now devote a certain percentage of their income to charitable causes, such as orphanages and Indian development programs. If this is an important criterion to you, be sure to make inquiries.

Fees charged by the schools vary substantially, although all are quite reasonable by North American standards. You can expect to pay about $150 a week for room and board plus 5 hours of daily instruction.

13

Practical Extras

Transportation

Airlines

Note: Airline service to and from Guatemala is subject to frequent change. The following carriers were serving Guatemala to and from the following destinations as of late 1992. All phone numbers are in Guatemala City unless otherwise indicated.

AeroCaribe
Flores, Chetumal, Cancún, Mérida, Tuxtla Gutierrez, Oaxaca. Tel. 336-001.

Aeronica
Mexico City, Managua, San José, Panama City, Toronto. Tel. 325-541 or 316-759.

Aerovías
Flores, Belize City, Chetumal, Cancún. Tel. 537-885 or 81-463.

American Airlines
Miami, Dallas. Tel. 346-915, in U.S. (800) 433-7300.

Aviateca
Flores, Miami, New Orleans, Los Angeles, Mexico City, Cancún, Managua, San José. Tel. 318-222 in Guatemala City; 501-337 in Flores; (800) 327-9832 in U.S.

Continental
Houston. Tel. 312-051, in U.S. (800) 525-0280.

COPA
San Salvador, Managua, San José, Panama City. Tel. 316-813 or 318-443.

Iberia
Santo Domingo, Madrid, Panama City, Miami. Tel. 373-911; in U.S. (800) 772-4642.

KLM
Curaçao, Lisbon, Amsterdam. Tel. 370-222; in U.S. (800) 777-5553.

LACSA
Los Angeles, New York, Mexico City, San José, San Salvador. Tel. 373-905; in U.S. (800) 225-2272.

Mexicana
Los Angeles, Mexico City, San José, Flores; from Cancún. Tel. 518-824; in U.S. (800) 531-7921.

Sahsa
Tegucigalpa, San Salvador. Tel. 321-071; in U.S. (800) 327-1225.

SAM
San José, San Andrés, Bogotá. Tel. 316-311.

TACA
Los Angeles, Washington, Houston, New York, Miami, New Orleans, Belize City, San Salvador. Tel. 316-979; in U.S. (800) 535-8780, in Canada (800) 387-6209.

Tapsa
Flores. Tel. 314-860 or 319-180.

Tikal Jet
Flores. Tel. 325-070 or 345-631.

Tropic Air
Flores; from Belize City and Ambergris Caye. Tel. in U.S. (800) 422-3435, except Texas (713) 440-1867.

United
San Francisco, Los Angeles, Miami, San José. Tel. in U.S. (800) 722-5243.

Boats

To and from Punta Gorda, Belize to Puerto Barrios, Guatemala *(twice a week)*
To and from Tiradero, Tenosique, and La Palma, Mexico, to El Naranjo, Guatemala *(daily)*
Puerto Quetzal on the Pacific coast and Puerto Santo Tomás on the Caribbean are served by about a dozen (mostly European) cruise ships per year. Lines serving the region include:

American Canadian Caribbean Cruise Line
(800) 556-7450

Clipper Adventure Cruise Line
(800) 325-0010

Dolphin Cruise Line
(800) 222-1003

Royal Caribbean Cruise Line
(800) 327-6700

Special Expeditions
(800) 762-0003

Sun Line Cruises
(800) 872-6400

Buses

Check with local hotels or travel agencies for the various international bus companies serving the Guatemalan land border crossings at Talismán and Tecún Umán, Mexico; Benque Viejo, Belize; El Florido and Agua Caliente, Honduras; Ciudad Pedro de Alvarado and San Cristóbal Frontera, El Salvador. Major domestic bus companies include the following.

PAN Shuttle (first-class)
Calle Los Arboles
Panajachel
Tel. 621-474 or 621-516 in Panajachel
Guatemala City/Antigua/Chichicastenango/
Panajachel Shuttle

Galgos (first-class)
7a. Avenida 19-44, Zone 1
Guatemala City
Tel. 23-661
Guatemala City/Coatepeque/Quetzaltenango

Líneas América (first-class)
2a. Avenida 18-47, Zone 1
Guatemala City
Tel. 21-432
Guatemala City/Quetzaltenango

Litegua (first-class)
15a. Calle 10-40, Zone 1
Guatemala City
Tel. 27-578
Guatemala City/Puerto Barrios

Maya Express (express)
17a. Calle 9-36, Zone 1
Guatemala City
Tel. 21-914
Guatemala City/Petén

Fuente del Norte (second-class)
17a. Calle 8-46, Zone 1
Guatemala City
Tel. 83-894
Guatemala City/Petén-Puerto Barrios

San Juan Travel (first-class)
Hotel San Juan
Santa Elena, Petén
Tel. 500-041
Flores/Sayaxché/Belize City/Chetumal

Transportes Esmeralda (second-class)
El Trébol Terminal
Guatemala City
(no telephone)
Guatemala City/Escuintla

Rápidos del Sur (second-class)
Estaciín Central
20a. Calle 8-55, Zone 1
Guatemala City
Tel. 27-025
Guatemala City/Mexican border via Pacific coast

Transportes Melva/Transportes Pezzarossi
4a. Avenida 1-20, Zone 9
Guatemala City
(no telephone)
Guatemala City/San Salvador

Trains

Passenger rail service on the government-operated FEGUA line connects with Mexican trains at Tecún Umán and continues to Guatemala City with connections as far as Puerto Barrios. The line to El Salvador no longer accepts passengers.

The Puerto Barrios train leaves Guatemala City on Tuesday, Thursday, and Saturday at 7:00 a.m., returning the following day. The Tecún Umán train leaves the capital on Tuesday, Thursday, and Saturday at 7:15 a.m. and returns the next day.

The main station is at 9a. Avenida 18-03, Zone 1, in Guatemala City, tel. 83-030.

Auto Rental
All in Guatemala City except as noted.

Aventuras sin Límites
Hotel Melchor Palace
Melchor de Mencos
Tel. 505-196
Specialists in Petén and Belize car rentals

Avis
12a. Calle 2-73, Zone 9
Tel. 316-990, fax 321-263

Avis
5a. Avenida Norte No. 22
Antigua
Tel. 320-387

Budget
Avenida de la Reforma 15-00, Zone 9
Tel. 322-591, fax 312-807

Budget
Hotel Ramada Antigua
Antigua
Tel. 320-011

Dollar
Avenida de la Reforma 6-14, Zone 9
Tel. 348-285, fax 326-745

Hertz
7a. Avenida 14-76, Zone 9
Tel. 322-242, fax 317-924

National
14a. Calle 1-42, Zone 10
Tel. 680-175, fax 370-221

National
Hotel Ramada Antigua
Antigua
Tel. 320-015

San Juan Auto Rental and Travel Agency
Hotel San Juan
Santa Elena, Petén
Tel. 500-042, fax 500-041
Specialist in Petén car rentals

Tabarini
2a. Calle A 7-30, Zone 10
Guatemala City
Tel. 316-108, fax 341-925

Tikal Rent A Car
2a. Calle 6-56, Zone 10
Guatemala City
Tel. 367-832
Arranges for cars to be picked up in Flores and Santa Elena, Petén.

Travel Information

U.S. State Department Travelers' Advisory Service
(202) 647-5225
(Washington, D.C.)

Center for Disease Control Travelers' Advisory Service
(404) 332-4559
(Atlanta, Ga.)

Institución Guatemalteco de Turismo (INGUAT)
7a. Avenida 1-17, Centro Cívico, Zona 4
Guatemala City, Guatemala
Tel. 311-333, fax 314-416

Guatemala Tourist Commission (INGUAT)
P.O. Box 144351
299 Alhambra Circle, Suite 510
Coral Gables, FL 33134
Tel. (305) 442-0651, fax 442-1013

Institut für Touristik Guatemala
Bienenstrasse 63
P.O. Box 447 CH-4104
Oberwil/Basle, Switzerland
Tel. 401-5032, fax 401-5151

Institut Guatemalteque du Tourisme
Ecrit-11, Rue de Cronstadt
75015 Paris, France
Tel. 4530-1866, fax 4250-1878

Instituto del Turismo del Guatemala
Viale Rassilia 152
00124 Rome, Italy
Tel. 609-2740, fax 505-3406

Instituto Guatemalteco de Turismo
Paseo de la Reforma #64
Colonia Juárez
Mexico, D.F. 06600 Mexico
Tel. 705-4911

Chapter 13

Important Telephone Numbers

Guatemala City
Police (general) 20-221
Police (emergencies) 120
Volunteer Fire Department 122
City Fire Department 123
Red Cross Ambulance 125
Public Hospital (San Juan) 300-716
Private Hospital (Bella Aurora) 681-951
International Long Distance 171
Direct Dial Prefix for U.S. 190 AT&T,
195 Sprint
Domestic Long Distance 121
Domestic Information 124
Phone Telegrams 127

Antigua
Fire & Rescue 320-234 or 320-309
Hospital 320-301
Police 320-251

Panajachel
Fire & Rescue 621-123
Police 621-120

Quetzaltenango
Hospital 612-746
Police 612-120

Chichicastenango
Fire 561-066
Police 561-365

Flores
Hospital 811-333
Police 811-365

Huehuetenango
Fire 641-553
Hospital 641-414
Police 641-284

Puerto Barrios
Fire & Rescue 480-122
Hospital 480-351
Police 480-385

Tour Guides and Travel Agencies

GUATEMALA CITY

Clark Tours/Guatemala Travel Advisors
(Mark Rogers)
Edificio El Triangulo, Nivel 2
7a. Avenida 6-53, Zone 4
Tel. 310-213, fax 315-919
Traditional tours of highlands, cities, and Tikal.

Exclusive Travel (Olga Pokorny)
16a. Calle 7-29, Zone 9
Tel. 343-854 or 316-667, fax 343-901
Traditional tours of highlands, major cities, and Tikal.

Excursiones Spross
(Edwin Francisco Spross)
2a. Avenida 3-25, Zone 9
Tel. 366-594
Tours of Lake Izabal, Río Dulce, and Belize cayes.

Maya Tours (Carlo Cardente)
6a. Avenida 1-36, Zone 10
Tel. 313-575
Traditional circuit plus adventure and archaeology tours.

RIDE (Luis V. Vásquez)
Edificio La Galera, Planta Baja, Local 11
7a. Avenida 14-44, Zone 9
Tel. 340-318, fax 340-322
Traditional tours of western highlands, cities, and Tikal.

Sun Travel (Anabella Staebler)
8a. Calle 7-01, Zone 9
Tel. 312-043, fax 348-369
Traditional circuit plus cultural tours.

Turansa (Yolanda de Cruz)
Centro Comercial El Molino
Km 15, Carretera Roosevelt
Tel. 953-574, fax 954-688
Traditional circuit including Tikal and other Mayan sites.

Turismo Kim'Arrin (María Esther Zaldivar)
Edificio Maya
5 Via 4-20, Zone 4
Tel. 324-931, fax 322-791
Traditional circuit plus archaeological tours and trips to Mario Dary Quetzal Preserve, Lake Izabal, and Copán.

Unitours (Rony Liang)
7a. Avenida 7-91, Zone 4
Tel. 365-065, fax 342-001
Traditional circuit plus archaeology, adventure and nature-oriented tours.

ANTIGUA

Guatemalan Adventures
4a. Calle Oriente 12A
Tel. 322-613, fax 322-755
Adventure travel specialists, including scuba, sailing, and raft trips as well as camping and volcano climbing. Provides tourist information, shipping services, and international money transfers, as well as visa extensions and document translations.

Turansa
Ramada Antigua Hotel
9a. Calle Final
Tel. 322-928
5a Avenida Norte 22
Tel. 322-664, fax 322-928
Traditional tours of Antigua and the highlands, as well as Tikal, Copán, and other Mayan ruins.

Viajes Tivoli
5a. Avenida Norte 10A
Tel. 322-041 or 320-892
Traditional tours of Antigua and the highlands.

QUETZALTENANGO

SAB de Guatemala
1a. Calle 12-35, Zone 1
Tel. 616-402, fax 618-878
Traditional tours of Quetzaltenango and the western highlands.

PETÉN

Aventuras sin Límites
Hotel Melchor Palace
Melchor de Mencos
4a. Calle 8-15
Santa Elena
Tel. 505-196
Mayan sites, river trips, auto rental, hotel, and restaurant.

Hotel San Juan
Santa Elena
Tel. 500-041, fax 500-041
Mayan sites, including Tikal. Auto rental, hotel, bus service, plane tickets.

UNITED STATES

Ladatco
Tel. in Miami, FL
(305) 854-8422 or (800) 327-6162
Tour packages to popular destinations throughout Guatemala.

Mexico Travel Advisors
Tel. in Los Angeles, CA
(213) 462-6444 or (800) 876-6824
Books various package trips to popular destinations throughout Guatemala, often in conjunction with American Airlines.

Saga Holidays
Tel. (800) 343-0273
Package tours to such popular destinations as Lake Átitlán, Chichicastenango, Antigua, and Tikal, in conjunction with American Airlines.

Sanborn Tours
Tel. (800) 531-5440
Package tours of traditional sights.

Tara Tours
Tel. in Miami, FL
(305) 871-1246 or (800) 327-0080
Package tours of traditional circuit.

Unique Adventures
Tel. in San Francisco, CA
(415) 986-5876 or (800) 227-3026
Package tours of traditional circuit.

Adventure and Nature-based Travel

IN GUATEMALA

Aventuras sin Límites
11a. Avenida 9-30, Zone 1
Guatemala City
Tel. 28-452, fax 947-293
4a. Calle 8-15
Santa Elena
Tel. 505-196
Emphasis on archaeology, bird-watching, photography, canoeing, trekking, whitewater rafting, and fishing. Petén specialists.

Caribbean Internacional de Viajes
(Miguel Angel Morláes)
9a. Avenida 13-58, Zone 1
Guatemala City
Tel. 514-952
Adventure travel in the Petén, Alta Verapaz, Caribbean coast, and Lake Izabal areas.

Expedición Panamundo (Roger Brenner)
6a. Avenida 14-75, Zone 9
Guatemala City
Tel. 317-621 or 317-588, fax 317-565
Specializes in archaeology, nature, volcano climbing, trekking, rafting, bird-watching, and botany trips, with particular emphasis on remote Mayan sites in the Petén, Belize, Mexico, and Honduras. Highly recommended.

Green Trails Cultural and Ecological Tours
(Leif Ness)
9a. Calle 4-10, Zone 10
Guatemala City
Tel. 323-540
Emphasis on natural history and Mayan sites, particularly in Alta Verapaz and the Petén.

Izabal Adventure Tours (Alfredo Toriello)
Edificio Galería, Local 35
7a. Avenida 14-44, Zone 9
Guatemala City
Tel. 340-323, fax 340-341
Specializes in boating, natural history, archaeology and fishing trips, plus volcano climbing, cave exploration, whitewater rafting, and other adventures. Specialized study groups escorted to flower, sugar, and coffee plantations. Customized work-study trips of remote archaeological sites. Highly recommended.

Jungle Tours (Richard Callaway)
Hangar #15, Aeropuerto La Aurora
Avenida Hincapié y 28a. Calle, Zone 3
Guatemala City
Tel. 314-495 or 367-946, fax 347-205
Nature, archaeology, and cultural tours, including overnight camping expeditions and trips by private charter aircraft. Also offers boat trips on Lake Petén Itzá and Río de la Pasión.

Maya Expeditions (Tammy Ridenour)
15a. Calle 1-91, Zone 10
Guatemala City
Tel. 374-666, fax 562-551 or 321-836
Specializes in whitewater rafting, volcano climbing, and treks to remote archaeological sites, caves, and other "natural" destinations. Custom trips by boat, foot, or horseback. Highly recommended.

Monkey Eco Tours
(María Esther Zaldivar, Bernal Mittlestadt)
Local 5, Planta Alta
7a. Avenida 14-44, Zone 9
Guatemala City
Tel. 344-651 or 324-931, fax 322-791
Specializes in nature and archaeology, especially remote Mayan sites of the Petén, as well as other ruins in Mexico, Belize and Honduras. Recommended.

Outdoors Life/Excursiones Calypso
3a. Calle 7-15, Zone 9
Guatemala City
(no telephone)
Wilderness treks in Guatemala and beach camping trips to Belize cayes. Retail store at this location also sells camping and mountaineering equipment.

Servicios Turísticos del Petén
(Rafael Sagastume Ortíz)
2a. Avenida 7-78, Zona 10
Guatemala City
Tel. 346-235 or 347-887, fax 346-237
Specializes in archaeology, nature, rafting, and trekking, with special emphasis on Mayan sites of the Petén.

Travel International
Avenida de la Reforma 6-30, Zone 4
Guatemala City
Tel. 310-016
Río Dulce, Belize, and Lake Izabal fishing and boating trips; booking agent for Catamaran Island Hotel.

Viva Tours (Carmen María Fernández)
Avenida de la Reforma 12-81, Zona 10
Guatemala City
Tel. 680-677 and 372-987
Specializes in volcano and fishing tours as well as the traditional circuit of popular destinations.

IN THE UNITED STATES AND CANADA

Above the Clouds Trekking
P.O. Box 398
Worcester, MA 01062
Tel. (800) 233-4499
Adventure travel.

Adventure Center
1311 63rd Street, Suite 200
Emeryville, CA 94608
Tel. (800) 227-8747, in California
(510) 654-1879
Adventure travel with small groups and expert guides. Send for current catalog.

Big Five Expeditions Ltd.
2151 E. Dublin-Granville Road, Suite 215
Columbus, OH 43229
(614) 898-0036 or (800) 541-2790
Adventure travel.

Castle Rock Center for Environmental Adventures
412 Road 6NS
Cody, WY 82414
Tel. (800) 356-9965
Whitewater rafting, mountain biking, sea kayaking, sailing, mountain climbing, and windsurfing.

Ceiba Adventures (Scott Davis, Don Usner)
P.O. Box 3075
Durango, CO 81302
Tel. (303) 247-1174
River trips on the Usumacinta, excursions to Mayan sites in the Petén and Chiapas, as well as Lacandón Indian villages. Highly recommended.

Far Flung Adventures
P.O. Box 377
Terlingua, TX 79852
Tel. (915) 371-2489
Boat trips on the Río Usumacinta, emphasizing nature and archaeology.

Fourth Dimension Tours
1150 NW 72nd Avenue, Suite 250
Miami, FL 33126
Tel. (800) 343-0020; in Florida
(305) 477-1525, fax (305) 477-0731
Nature, adventure, and cultural tours.

Gallivanting Inc.
515 East 79 Street, Suite 20
New York, NY 10021
Tel. (800) 933-9699; in New York
(212) 988-0617, fax (212) 988-0144
Outdoor and cultural discovery tours for singles ages 28 to 48.

Global Adventures
P.O. Box 1897
Boulder, CO 80306
Tel. (303) 440-6911 or (800) 322-6911
Adventure travel.

Global Fitness Adventures
P.O. Box 1390
Aspen, CO 81612
Tel. (303) 920-1780, fax (303) 925-7085
Combining adventure travel "with healthy eating, extensive daily exercise, and weight loss."

Guatemala Travel Representatives
720 Worthshire
Houston, TX 77008
(800) 451-8017; in Texas (713) 688-1985, fax (713) 869-2540
Individual and group travel to highlands, Petén, and Guatemala City, specializing in culture, history, nature, and archaeology.

International Expeditions
One Environs Park
Helena, AL 35080
Tel. (800) 633-4734; or (205) 428-1700, fax 428-1714 in Alabama
Natural history and archaeology-oriented soft adventure trips to Tikal, Copán, and Belize. Recommended.

Mountain Travel-Sobek Expeditions
(Richard Bangs)
6420 Fairmount Avenue
El Cerrito, CA 94530
Tel. (800) 227-2384, fax (510) 525-7710
In Canada:
159 Main Street
Unionville, ONT L3R 2G8
Tel. (416) 479-2600
Fiestas and markets in highlands. River trips on the Río Usumacinta, ecological adventures, and explorations of Mayan ruins.

Ocean Connection
16734 El Camino Real
Houston, TX 77062
Tel. (713) 486-6993
Adventure travel with emphasis on nature, Mayan sites, water recreation, birds, and extensions throughout Belize.

Voyagers International
P.O. Box 915
Ithaca, NY 14851
Tel. (607) 257-3091
Adventure travel.

Fishing, Bicycling, and Water Recreation Services

Caiman Expeditions
2901 East Speedway
Tucson, AZ 85716
Tel. (800) 365-2383; in Arizona
(602) 299-1047
Diving, rafting, sea kayaking, archaeology, climbing, and mountain biking.

ConoAndes Expeditions
37-12 75th Street
Queens, NY 11372
Tel. (800) 242-5554; in New York
(718) 446-8577
Canoe, kayak, and adventure trips.

Outback Expeditions
Box 16343
Seattle, WA 98116
Tel. (206) 932-7012, fax (206) 935-1213
Wildlife, hiking, photography, and kayaking tours, with options to Belize and Mexico.

Paradise Bicycle Tours
P.O. Box 1726
Evergreen, CO 80439
Tel. (800) 626-8271
Cycling for riders of all abilities, specializing in Belize, Guatemala, and Africa.

Salsa Cycle Tours
1-303 Bay Street
Ottawa, ONT KIR 527
Canada
Tel. (613) 237-3761
Bike tours of Mayan sites.

Slickrock Adventures
P.O. Box 1400
Moab, UT 84532
Tel. (801) 259-6996
Kayak and whitewater raft trips, including the Río Usumacinta in Guatemala.

Southeastern Aquatours of Guatemala
Tel. in Florida (813) 685-9545
Sailboat charters to Lake Izabal, Río Dulce, Guatemala Caribbean coast, and Belize cayes.

Tour de Caña
P.O. Box 7293
Philadelphia, PA 19101
Tel. (215) 222-1253
Bicycle tours throughout Guatemala and Central America.

Wilderness Alaska/Mexico
1231 Sundance Loop
Fairbanks, AK 99709
Tel. (907) 452-1821
Boat trips on the Río Usumacinta, emphasizing archaeology and natural history. Low-impact camping, experienced guides.

Archaeological Tours and Expeditions

IN GUATEMALA

Maya Tours (Carlo Cardente)
Edificio Valsari, Nivel 3, Oficina 304
6a. Calle 1-36, Zone 10
Guatemala City
Tel. 403-712 or 313-575
Adventure, culture, and archaeology tours.

Ney's Viajes y Turismo (Erick Mencos)
13a. Calle 0-56, Zone 10
Tel. 680-959, fax 370-884
Traditional tours of highlands, cities, and Tikal, with emphasis on cultural sights and archaeology.

Tropical Tours (Anabella Porres)
4a. Calle 2-51, Zone 10
Guatemala City
Tel. 345-893, fax 323-748
Adventure and archaeological tours of Tikal and other Petén sites.

IN THE UNITED STATES AND CANADA

Earthwatch
680 Mt. Auburn Street
Watertown, MA 02272
Tel. (617) 926-8200
Work-study archaeological tours.

Far Horizons (Mary Dell Lucas)
16 Fern Lane
San Anselmo, CA 94960
Tel. (415) 457-4575, fax (415) 457-4608
"Cultural discovery" trips by guides trained in Mayan history and archaeology. Options include contemporary Mayan Indian festivals and Guatemalan natural history.

Foundation for Field Research
P.O. Box 2010
Alpine, CA 91903
Tel. (619) 445-9264
Archaeological (and nature) field research and study trips. Send for free copy of "Explorer News."

Foundation for Latin American Anthropological Research
6355 Green Valley Circle, #213
Culver City, CA 90230
(no telephone)
Trips to well-known and lesser-known Mayan sites in Guatemala and neighboring countries, as well as botany, bird, and zoology tours of the same region.

Maya Seminars
968 Corona Street
Denver, CO 80218
Tel. (303) 467-7112
History and archaeology of the Mayan world; will customize trips for groups of four or more.

The Mexico Connection
9400 Vicount
El Paso, TX 79925
Tel. (800) 521-4455, fax (915) 593-0330
Trip extensions to Guatemala's Mayan ruins are included as options on tours of Mayan sites in Mexico, Belize, El Salvador, and Honduras.

The Nature Conservancy
1800 North Kent Street
Arlington, VA 22209
Tel. (703) 841-5300
Trips to nature and archaeological sites of Tikal and Belize arranged through International Expeditions (see listing under Adventure Travel).

The Sierra Club
730 Polk Street
San Francisco, CA 94109
Tel. (415) 776-2211
Education and study trips to Mayan sites and nature reserves of Central America.

Smithsonian Odyssey Tours & Research Expeditions
Smithsonian Institution
1100 Jefferson Drive SW
Washington, D.C. 20560
Tel. (202) 357-1350 or (800) 524-4125
Archaeology, anthropology, and nature-related study tours and fieldwork trips.

Weaving Schools and Craft Tours

Far Horizons
P.O. Box 1529
San Anselmo, CA 94960
Tel. (415) 457-4575, fax (415) 457-4608
Cultural tours of highlands that include weaving centers.

Panorama Guatemala Cultural
(Vilma de Sosa)
5a. Avenida 8-57, Zone 9
Tel. 314-174
Tours specializing in archaeology, textiles, crafts, history, and folklore.

Viajes Nuevo Mundo
Edificio Plaza Viva, Oficina 20-3
6a. Avenida y 10a. Calle, Zone 1
Guatemala City
Tel. 518-759
Cultural and religious tours. Check with language schools and on bulletin boards in Antigua, Panajachel, Quetzaltenango, Huehuetenango, and Guatemala City for other possibilities.

Appendix

Protected Areas

Archaeological Sites
Ceibal, Altar de los Sacrificios, and many other Mayan ruins throughout the country are protected as national monuments.

Atitlán National Park
Encompassing entire shoreline of Lake Atitlán in the western highlands.

Cerro Cahuí Biotope
Northeast shoreline of Lake Petén Itzá, Petén, and surrounding forest.

Chocón Machacas Manatee Preserve
Encompassing entire shoreline and northern bank of El Golfete, Río Dulce, in department of Izabal.

El Zotz-San Miguel La Palotada Nature Reserve
Jungle and archaeological sites north and west of Tikal National Park, Petén.

Sierra del Lacandón National Park
Mountain wilderness of Sierra del Lacandón, east of Usumacinta River in the Petén.

Laguna del Tigre-Río Escondido National Park and Nature Reserve
Wetlands in northwest Petén.

Laguna Lachuá National Park
Lachuá Lagoon and part of Río Chixoy watershed, department of Alta Verapaz.

Lanquín Cave National Park
Lanquín cavern system, Alta Verapaz.

Las Ninfas (The Nymphs) National Park
Encompasses part of the shoreline of Lake Amatitlán and nearby slope of Pacaya Volcano.

Mario Dary Quetzal Preserve
Cloud forest and quetzal habitat in Sierra de Chuacús, department of Baja Verapaz.

Maya Biosphere Reserve
Petén wilderness north of 17th parallel, encompassing Tikal National Park and other protected areas.

El Mirador National Park and Nature Reserve
Protecting Mayan site of the same name and surrounding forest in northeast Petén.

Montecristo-Trifinio Biosphere Reserve
Portion of Montecristo range on Honduran and Salvadoran border, department of Chiquimula, contiguous with international parks in Honduras and El Salvador.

Monterrico-Hawaii Biosphere Reserve
Wetlands and mangrove forest along Pacific Coast between villages of Monterrico and Hawaii.

Naachtún-Dos Lagunas Biosphere Reserve
Jungle, wetland, and archaeological sites in northeast Petén.

Petén Reserves
Includes nature and biological reserves at El Chorro, Río San Ramón, and several other locations in the Petén.

Pinos de Poptún Nature Reserve
Protecting pine forests of Maya Mountains near Poptún, east-central Petén.

Poc National Park
Lakeshore habitat of endangered flightless water bird known as Atitlán grebe or poc.

Proyecto Quetzal Sanctuary
c/o Roger Brenner, Expedición Panamundo
6a. Avenida 14-75, Zone 9
Guatemala City
Tel. 317-588, Fax 317-565
Private reserve protecting the quetzal located above the Río Polochic Valley in Alta Verapaz; may be visited by reservation only.

Punta Manabique Biosphere Reserve
Wetlands, shoreline, and forest of Punta Manabique on Caribbean coast.

Río Azul National Park
Wetlands, jungle, and archaeological sites in northeast corner of the Petén.

Sierra de las Minas Biosphere Reserve
Divided into two parts: Las Nubes (the cloud forests) and Los Cedros (the cedar forests), located in mountain range of same name, between Cobán and Puerto Barrios.

Tikal National Park
Encompasses archaeological site of Tikal and surrounding jungle.

United Nations Park
(Parque Naciones Unidas)
Portions of mountain slopes of Pacaya volcano, above Lake Amatitlán.

Volcanoes
The peaks and upper slopes of most of Guatemala's 33 volcanoes are federally protected.

Conservation Groups

Based in Guatemala

Josefina Chavarría, Executive Director
Asociación Amigos del Bosque
9a. Calle 2-23, Zone 1
Guatemala City
Tel. 83-486

Rafael Cuestas, President
Asociación de Amigos del Lago de Atitlán
Apartado Postal 170C
Guatemala City
Tel. 334-872

Asociación de Rescate y Conservación de la Vida Silvestre (Association for Rescue and Conservation of Wildlife)
Avenida de la Reforma 0-63, Zone 10
Guatemala City
Tel. 28-531 or 81-647

Ismael Ponciano
Centro de Estudios Conservacionistas (Center for Conservation Studies) and Compañeros de los Américas (Friends of the Americas)

University of San Carlos
Avenida de la Reforma 0-63, Zone 10
Guatemala City
Tel. 28-531 or 81-647

Antonio Ferrate Felice, Coordinator
Comisión Nacional del Medio Ambiente (CONAMA)
7a. Avenida 4-35, Zone 1
Guatemala City
Tel. 532-477 or 21-816, fax 535-109

Consejo Nacional de Areas Protegidas (CONAP)
2a. Avenida 0-69, Zone 3
Guatemala City
Tel. 322-671

Andreas Lehnhoff, Executive Director
Fundación Defensores de la Naturaleza
7a. Avenida y 13a. Calle, Zone 9
Guatemala City
Tel. 325-064

Paseo Pantera/Wildlife Conservation International
c/o Alfredo Toriello, Izabal Adventure Tours
Edificio Galería, No. 35
7a. Avenida 14-44, Zone 9
Guatemala City
Tel. 340-323, fax 340-341

Horacio Valle Dawson, Chuck Vielman
United Council of the Protected Areas of the Petén (UNEPET)
8a. Avenida 2-92, Zone 3
Flores, Petén
Tel. 500-196, fax 500-197

Based outside Guatemala

Audubon Society (Fran Webber, Karen Ziffer)
950 Third Avenue
New York, NY 10022
Tel. (212) 832-3200
Guatemala City office:
Federico Fahsen
10a. Avenida 2-44, Zone 14
Tel. 337-491

Central American Commission on Development and the Environment
Guatemala City office:
Jorge Cabrera Hidalgo, Executive Secretary
Tel. 343-876 or 320-684

Conservation International (Jim Nations, Conrad Reining)
1015 18th Street NW, Suite 1000
Washington, D.C. 20036
Tel. (202) 429-5660
Guatemala office:
ProPetén
Flores, Petén
Tel. 501-370

Greenpeace International
1436 U Street NW
Washington, D.C. 20009
Guatemala City Office:
Erwin Garzona
Tel. 534-206

The Nature Conservancy
Latin America Program
1815 N. Lynn Street
Arlington, VA 22209
Tel. (703) 841-5300, fax (703) 841-1283
Guatemala City office:
Margaret Kohring, In-Country Director

David Whitacre, Director, The Maya Project
The Peregrine Fund/World Center for
Birds of Prey
5666 West Flying Hawk Lane
Boise, ID 83709
Tel. (208) 362-3716, fax (208) 362-2376

Rainforest Alliance
270 Lafayette Street, Suite 512
New York, NY 10012
Tel. (212) 941-1900

U.S. Agency for International Development
Guatemala Conservation Project
(Alfredo Nakamatsu, María José González)
Guatemala City
Tel. 320-202 or 320-322

World Wildlife Fund (Lily Valle,
Steve Cornelius)
1250 24th Street NW
Washington, D.C. 20037
Tel. (202) 293-4800

Prohibitions

It is illegal to bring any products made from endangered species into the United States. Also banned are products made from coral, ivory, tortoise shell, crocodile, lizards, sea turtles, marine mammals, or wild cats.

For more information on prohibited products from Guatemala or other countries around the world, write: Traffic (USA), World Wildlife Fund, 1250 24th Street NW, Washington, D.C. 20037. Information about what the United States will allow to cross its borders can be obtained from the Division of Law Enforcement, U.S. Fish and Wildlife Service, P.O. Box 3247, Arlington, VA 22203-3247.

In Guatemalan parks, it is illegal to carry or use firearms or use sound amplification equipment. It is also against the law to injure or collect plants or animals without authorization.

Animals: English-Spanish / Mayan Names

agouti *guatusa*
Atitlán grebe *poc*
bat *murciélago*
bird *pájaro, ave*
brocket deer *cabra de monte*
butterfly *mariposa*
coati *pizote*
collared peccary *sano, coche de monte*
cougar, mountain lion *puma*
dolphinfish, mahi-mahi *dorado*
fox (sometimes opossum) *zorro*
frog *rana*
howler monkey *saraguate*
jaguar *jaguar, tigre*
jaguarundi *león breñero*
kinkajou *martilla, micoleón*
manatee *manatí*
margay *caucel, tigrillo*
mullet *lisa*
ocelot *tigrillo, ocelote*
oppossum *tecuazin*
oropendola *oriole*

owl *tecolote, búho*
paca *tepezcuintle*
parrot *loro*
raccoon *mapachín*
river otter *nutria, perro de agua*
scarlet macaw *guacamaya, lapa roja*
skunk *zorrillo*
snake *serpiente, culebra*
snapper *pargo*
snook *róbalo*
spider monkey *mico* or *mono araña, colorado*
squirrel *ardilla*
tapir *danta*
tarpon *sábalo*
toad *sapo*
toucan *tucán*
trout *trucha*
turtle *tortuga*
white-lipped peccary *cariblanco, jabali*
white-tailed deer *venado coliblanco*

Art Galleries and Museums

Antigua

Casa de la Cultura de la Antigua Guatemala
Parque Central
Daily 9 to noon and 2 to 6, except holidays

Casa K'ojom (Museo de la Música
Tradicional Indigena)
Calle de Recoletos 55
Daily 9:30 to noon and 2 to 6, except Sundays

Casa Popenoe
1a. Avenida Sur y 5 Calle Oriente
2 to 4 Monday-Saturday

Centro de Investigaciones Regionales de
Mesoamérica
5a. Calle Oriente 5 (at Avenida Norte)
Daily 9 to 5, 9 to noon Saturday

Museo de Arte Colonial
University of San Carlos
5a. Calle Oriente
Daily 9 to noon and 2 to 6

Museo del Libro Antiguo
Portal of City Hall (Ayuntamiento)
Daily 9 to noon and 2 to 6

Museo de Santiago
Portal of City Hall (Ayuntamiento)
Daily 9 to noon and 2 to 6

Chichicastenango

Museo de Rossbach
Plaza Central
Daily except Tuesday, 8 to noon and 2 to 5

Guatemala City

Biblioteca Nacional, Hemeroteca y Archivo
General de Centro América
Parque del Centenario, Zone 1
M-F 8:30 to 5:30

Centro Cultural Miguel Angel Asturias
Parque del Castillo de San José, Zone 1
(irregular hours)

Museo de Historia Natural (Jardín Botánica)
Calle Mariscal Cruz 1-56, Zone 10
Weekdays 9 to 4

Museo Fray Francisco Vásquez
6a. Avenida y 13a. Calle, Zone 1
Daily 9 to 4

Museo Ixchel (del Traje Indígena)
4a. Avenida 16-27, Zone 10
M-F 8:30 to 5:30, Sat. 9 to 1

Museo Militar
National Office, Zone 4
M-F, 8 to 6

Museo Nacional de Antropología y Etnología
Parque Aurora
T-F 9 to 4:30, Sat.-Sun. 9 to noon and
2 to 4:30

Museo Nacional de Arte Moderno
Parque Aurora, Zone 13
(same hours as above)

Museo Nacional de Artes e Industrias
Populares
10a. Avenida 10-72, Zone 1
(same as above)

Museo Nacional de Historia Natural
Parque Aurora, Zone 13
(same hours as above)

Museo Nacional de Historia
9a. Calle 9-79, Zone 1
Tu-Sun., 9 to noon and 2 to 4

Museo Popol Vuh
Avenida de la Reforma 8-16, top floor,
Zone 9
M-Sat. 9 to 5:30

Palacio Nacional (National Palace)
Parque Central, Zone 1
M-F 8:30 to 5:30

Quetzaltenango

Museo de Arqueología, Historia y Naturaleza
Casa de Cultura del Occidente, Parque
Central
M-F 8 to noon and 2 to 6

San Pedro Carchá

Museo Regional de la Verapaz
Parque Central
Sat.-Sun. 9 to noon and 3 to 5, or by
appointment

Tikal

Museo de Arqueología, Historia y
Naturaleza Sylvanus G. Morley
Tikal National Park
Daily 9 to 5

Zacapa (Estanzuela)

Museo de Paleontología, Arqueología y
Geología
Bryan Patterson
Estanzuela, Department of Zacapa
Daily except Monday, 8 to 5

Guatemalan Embassies and Consulates

Guatemalan Embassy
2220 R Street NW
Washington, D.C. 20008
(202) 745-4952

Guatemalan Consulate
57 Park Avenue
New York, NY 10016
(212) 686-3837

Guatemalan Consulate
548 S. Spring Street, Suite 1030
Los Angeles, CA 90013
(213) 489-1891

Guatemalan Consulate
9700 Raymond Avenue, Suite 218
Houston, TX 77042
(713) 953-9531

Guatemalan Consulate
300 Sevilla Avenue
Coral Gables, FL 33134
(305) 443-4828

Some Foreign Diplomatic Missions in Guatemala City

United States
Avenida de la Reforma 7-01, Zone 10
Tel. 311-541

Canada
Edificio Galerías España, Nivel 6
7a. Avenida 11-59, Zone 9
Tel. 321-411

Mexico
16a. Calle 1-45, Zone 10
Tel. 682-968

Honduras
16a. Calle 8-27, Zone 10
Tel. 373-919

El Salvador
12a. Calle 5-43, Zone 9
Tel. 326-421

Nicaragua
10a. Avenida 14-72, Zone 10
Tel. 680-785

Costa Rica
Avenida de la Reforma 8-60, Zone 9
Tel. 319-604

Germany
Edificio Plaza Martima
6a. Avenida 20-25, Zone 10
Tel. 370-028, fax 370-031

France
16a. Calle 4-53, Zone 10
Tel. 372-207

Great Britain
Centro Financiero Torre II, Nivel 7
7a. Avenida 5-10, Zone 4
Tel. 321-601

Italy
5a. Avenida 8-59, Zona 14
Tel. 374-578

Switzerland
Edificio Seguros Universales, Nivel 5
4a. Calle 7-72, Zone 9
Tel. 365-726

Austria
6a. Avenida 20-25, Zone 10
Tel. 682-324, fax 336-180

Netherlands
12a. Calle 7-56, Nivel 4, Zone 10
Tel. 313-505

Belgium
Avenida de la Reforma 13-70, Zone 9
Tel. 316-597

Japan
6 Ruta 8-19, Zone 4
Tel. 319-666

Suggested Reading

History

Galeano, Eduardo. *Guatemala: Occupied Country.* Translated by Cedric Belfrage. New York: Monthly Review Press, 1967.

Galeano, Eduardo. *Memory of Fire, I, II and III.* Translated by Cedric Belfrage. New York: Pantheon, 1987.

Handy, Jim. *Gift of the Devil: A History of Guatemala.* Toronto: Dumont/South End Press, 1984. *An excellent history of Guatemala from the colonial period through 1983, with an emphasis on economic conditions and peasant uprisings.*

Appendix

Moore, Richard E. *Historical Dictionary of Guatemala*. Metuchen, N.J.: Scarecrow Press, 1973.

Muñoz, Joaquin, and Anna Bell Ward. *Guatemala: Ancient and Modern*. New York: Pyramid Press, 1940.

Perez-Brignali, Hector. *A Brief History of Central America*. Berkeley: University of California Press, 1989.

Stephens, John Lloyd. *Incidents of Travel in Central America, Chiapas, and Yucatán*. 2 vols. New York: Dover, 1969.

Stewart, Gene and George. *The Mysterious Maya*. Washington: National Geographic Society, 1983.

U.S. Army. *Guatemala: A Country Study*. Washington: U.S. Government Printing Office, n.d.

Mayan Culture and Civilization

Bunch, Roland and Roger. *The Highland Maya: Patterns of Life and Clothing*. New York: Indigenous Publications, 1977.

Coe, Michael. *The Maya*. New York: Praeger, 1966.

Coe, William R. *Tikal: A Handbook of the Ancient Maya Ruins*. Philadelphia: University of Pennsylvania Press, 1967.
The best description and maps of Tikal, written by a supervising, on-scene archaeologist. Available in separate Spanish and English editions.

Colby, Benjamin N. *Ixil Country: A Plural Society in Highland Guatemala*. Berkeley: University of California Press, 1969.

Everton, Macduff. *The Modern Maya: A Culture in Tradition*. Albuquerque: University of New Mexico Press, 1991.
Excellent photos of the contemporary Maya, accompanied by anthropological essays. Ideally read in tandem with Ronald Wright's book listed below.

Gallenkamp, Charles. *Maya: The Riddle and Discovery of a Lost Civilization*. New York: McKay, 1976.

Graham, Ian. *Archaeological Explorations in El Petén*. New Orleans: Middle America Research Institute, 1967.

Hunter, C. Bruce. *Guide to Ancient Maya Ruins*. Norman: University of Oklahoma Press, 1986.

Kelly, Joyce. *The Complete Visitor's Guide to Mesoamerican Ruins*. Norman: University of Oklahoma Press, 1982.

Petterson, Carmen L. *Maya of Guatemala: Their Life and Dress*. Seattle: University of Washington Press, n.d.

Schele, Linda. *The Blood of Kings: Dynasty and Ritual in Maya Art*. Ft. Worth: Kimbell Art Museum, 1986.
An exquisite and comprehensive survey of ancient Mayan artwork.

Schele, Linda, and David Freidel. *The Forest of Kings: The Untold Story of the Ancient Maya*. New York: Morrow, 1990.

Smith, A. Ledyard. *Archaeological Renaissance in Central Guatemala*. Washington: The Carnegie Institution, 1955.
A detailed account of Carnegie-sponsored excavations near Salam.

Tedlock, Dennis, trans. *The Popol-Vuh: The Maya Book of Wise Council*. New York: Simon & Schuster, 1986.
Several other translations of this unique and sacred book of the Quiché Maya are available.

Thompson, Eric S. *The Rise and Fall of Maya Civilization*. Norman: University of Oklahoma Press, 1956.

Wright, Ronald. *Time Among the Maya*. New York: Weidenfield & Nicolson, 1989.
Entertaining and insightful contrasts between the ancient and modern Maya, including a good summary of post-Conquest history.

Human Rights and Politics

Americas Watch. *Guatemala: A Nation of Prisoners*. New York: Americas Watch, 1984.

Amnesty International. *Guatemala: Human Rights Violations Under the Civilian Government*. London: Amnesty International, 1990.

Barry, Tom. *Guatemala: A Country Guide*, 2nd ed., Albuquerque: Inter-Hemispheric Education Resource Center, 1990.

Black, George. *Garrison Guatemala*. New York: Monthly Review Press, 1984.

Calvert, Peter. *Guatemala: A Nation in Turmoil*. Boulder: Westview Press, 1985.

Clay, Jason, ed. *Voices of the Survivors*. Boston: Cultural Survival, Inc., and the Anthropology Research Center, 1983.
A series of firsthand reports on civil unrest and political violence in Guatemala during the early 1980s.

Daniels, Antony. *Sweet Waist of America: Journeys around Guatemala*. London: Random Century Press, 1990.

Davis, Shelton. *Witnesses to Political Violence in Guatemala*. Boston: Oxfam America, 1983.

Fauriol, Georges A. *Guatemala's Political Puzzle*. New Brunswick, N.J.: Transaction Books, 1988.

Fried, Jonathon, ed. *Guatemala in Rebellion*. New York: Grove Press, 1983.

Frundt, Harry J. *Refreshing Pauses: Coca-Cola and Human Rights in Guatemala*. New York: Praeger, 1987.

Lovell, W. George. *Conquest and Survival in Colonial Guatemala*. Toronto: University of Toronto Press, 1991.
Examination of the impact of Spanish rule on the Maya of Guatemala's Cuchumatanes Mountains from 1500 to 1821.

Schlesinger, Stephen, and Stephen Kinzer. *Bitter Fruit: The Untold Story of the American Coup in Guatemala*. New York: Doubleday, 1979.

Schwantes, V. David. *A Cry from the Heart*. N.p.: Health Institutes Press, 1990.

Sexton, James D., ed. *Son of Tecún Umán: A Maya Indian Tells His Story*. Tucson: University of Arizona Press, 1981.

Simon, Jean-Marie. *Guatemala: Eternal Spring/Eternal Tyranny*. New York: W.W. Norton, 1987.

Conservation and the Environment

Castner, James L. *Rainforests: A Guide to Research and Tourist Facilities*. Gainesville: Feline Press, 1990.

Chickering, Carol. *Flowers of Guatemala*. Norman: University of Oklahoma Press, 1973.

Correll, Donovan Stewart, and Oakes Ames. *Orchids of Guatemala & Belize*. New York: Dover, 1985.

Ferraté, Antonio, ed. *Situación Ambiental de la República de Guatemala*. Guatemala City: Comisión Nacional del Medio Ambiente, 1992.
The most comprehensive and up-to-date summary of Guatemala's environmental situation; prepared for the 1992 Rio de Janeiro world conference on the environment. Available in Spanish only.

Forsyth, Adrian. *Journey through a Tropical Jungle*. Toronto: Grey de Pencier Books, 1988.

Griscom, Ludlow. *Distribution of Bird Life in Guatemala*. New York: American Museum of Natural History, 1932.

Kricher, John C. *A Neotropical Companion: An Introduction to the Animals, Plants and Ecosystems of the New World Tropics*. Princeton: Princeton University Press, 1980.
Researched primarily in Central America, this book provides a good overview of nature in the subtropics.

Moser, Don. *The Jungles of Central America*. New York: Time-Life Books, 1975.
The photos and information on the Sierra de las Minas and Petén are especially good.

Peterson, Roger Tory, and Edward L. Chalif. *Field Guide to Mexican Birds*. Boston: Houghton Mifflin, 1973.

Skutch, Alexander Frank. *Birds of Tropical America*. Austin: University of Texas Press, 1976.

Appendix

Smythe, Frank B. *The Birds of Tikal*. Garden City, N.Y.: Natural History Press, 1966. *Available in separate Spanish and English editions.*

Travel Guides

Beresky, Andrew E., ed. *Fodor's Central America*. New York: Fodor's Travel Publications, 1991.

Box, Ben, ed. *Mexico and Central America Handbook*. New York: Prentice Hall, 1991.

Brosnahan, Tom. *La Ruta Maya: Yucatán, Guatemala & Belize*. Berkeley: Lonely Planet, 1991.

de Koose, Barbara Balchin. *Guatemala for You*. Guatemala City: Editorial Piedra Santa, 1989.

de Koose, Barbara Balchin. *Antigua For You*. Guatemala City: Watson Publications, 1992.

Glassman, Paul. *Guatemala Guide*. Champlain, N.Y.: Passport Press, 1990.

Greenberg, Arnold, and Diana K. Wells. *Guatemala Alive*. New York: Alive Publications, 1990.

Kelsey, Vera, and Lilly de Jongh Osborne. *Four Keys to Guatemala*. New York: Funk & Wagnalls, 1967.

Long, Trevor, and Elizabeth Bell. *Antigua, Guatemala: An Illustrated History of the City and Its Monuments*. Guatemala City: Filmtrek, 1991.

Muñoz, Joaquin. *Guatemala: From Where the Rainbow Takes Its Colors*. Guatemala City: Serviprensa Centroaméricana, 1975.

Samson, Karl. *Frommer's Costa Rica, Guatemala & Belize on $35 a Day*. New York: Prentice Hall, 1991.

Schreiber, Ari. *The Gringo's Guide to the Guatemalan Good Life*. Guatemala City: Self-published, February 1988.

Whatmore, Mark, and Peter Eltringham. *The Real Guide: Guatemala and Belize*. New York: Prentice Hall, 1990.

Travelogues and Travel Literature

Brigham, William T. *Guatemala: The Land of the Quetzal*. New York: Charles Scribner's Sons, 1887.

Canby, Peter. *The Heart of the Sky: Travels Among the Maya*. New York: Harper Collins, 1992.

Dodge, David. *How Lost Was My Weekend: A Greenhorn in Guatemala*. New York: Random House, 1948.

Fergusson, Erna. *Guatemala*. New York: Knopf, 1938.

Ford, Norman D. *Mexico & Guatemala by Car: How to See Them Without Being Rich*. Greenlawn, N.Y.: Harian Publications, 1962.

Franck, Harry A. *Tramping Through Mexico, Guatemala and Honduras*. London: T. Fisher Union, 1916.

Huxley, Aldous. *Beyond the Mexique Bay*. New York: Harper, 1934.

Lougheed, Vivian. *Central America by Chicken Bus*. Prince George, B.C.: Repository Press, 1981.

Montgomery, G.W. *Narrative of a Journey to Guatemala in 1838*. New York: Wiley & Putnam, 1839.

Rodman, Sheldon. *The Guatemala Traveler*. New York: Meredith Press, 1967.

Theroux, Paul. *The Old Patagonian Express*. Boston: Houghton Mifflin, 1979.

In Spanish Only

Prahl Redondo, Carlos E. *Guía de los Volcanes de Guatemala*. Guatamala City: Club Andino Guatemalteco, 1990.

In French Only

Gloaguen, Phillipe. *Le Guide de Routard: Mexique, Guatemala et Belize*. Paris: Hachette, 1992.

In Dutch Only

Van der Bijl, Yvonne. *Reishandboek Guatemala*. Rijswijki: Elmar Reishandboeken, 1992.

Appendix

In German Only

Honner, Barbara. *Guatemala Handbuch*. Frankfurt: Peter Rump Verlags, 1992.

Miscellaneous

Bowles, Paul. *Up Above the World*. New York: Simon & Schuster, 1966.

Drombowski, John, ed. *Area Handbook for Guatemala*. Washington: U.S. Government Printing Office, 1970.

Lavine, Harold, and the editors of *Life* magazine. *Central America*. New York: Stonehenge, 1964.

Marnham, Patrick. *So Far from God*. New York: Penguin, 1985.

Maslow, Jonathan Evan. *Bird of Life, Bird of Death: In Search of the Quetzal*. New York: Dell, 1980.

Perera, Victor. *Rites: A Guatemalan Boyhood*. New York: Harcourt Brace Jovanovich, 1986.

Sloan, Julie and Christine, eds. *People of the Tropical Rainforest*. Berkeley: University of California Press, 1988.

Newspapers and Magazines

Amnesty Bulletin
Amnesty International
322 Eighth Avenue
New York, NY 10001
Tel. (212) 807-8400
Bulletins and updates on human rights issues in Guatemala.

Cultural Survival
53A Church Street
Cambridge, MA 02138
Tel. (617) 495-2562
Nonprofit organization devoted to survival of indigenous peoples, publishes quarterly magazine of the same name ($45 a year).

El Rescate
2675 W. Olympic Boulevard
Los Angeles, CA 90006
Tel. (213) 387-3284
Nonprofit group working with the Guatemalan refugee community in the U.S., particularly Los Angeles.

Great Expeditions Magazine
4505 Falls of Neuse Road
Raleigh, NC 27609
Tel. (919) 872-6684
Excellent bimonthly oriented toward "adventure" travel and nature-based tourism.

Guatemala News
Guatemalan News and Information Bureau
P.O. Box 28594
Oakland, CA 94604
Tel. (415) 835-0810
Periodic reports on sociopolitical situation in Guatemala.

Katalysis
North/South Development Partners
1331 N. Commerce Street
Stockton, CA 95202
Information on rural economic and environmental development programs in western highlands.

NACLA Report on the Americas
National Congress on Latin America
475 Riverside Drive, Suite 454
New York, NY 10115
Tel. (212) 870-3146
Published 5 times a year, this publication provides a good update on human rights and politics south of the border.

Times of the Americas
1001 Connecticut Ave. NW
Washington, D.C. 20036
Biweekly newspaper concentrating exclusively on news of Latin America.

Transitions Abroad Magazine
18 Hulst Road
P.O. Box 344-6330
Amherst, MA 01004
Helps place volunteers with nonprofit organizations working for social change in Guatemala and other countries.

Voice of the Village
Honorary Village Citizens
206 Sixth Street West
Bonita Springs, FL 33923
(813) 992-3011
Sponsors reforestation, education, health care, and economic development programs in Indian villages of Guatemala's western highlands.

Witness for Peace
2201 P Street NW, Room 109
Washington, D.C. 20037
(202) 797-1160
Active in human rights and refugee resettlement programs. Produces books, videos, and other materials. Arranges volunteer work assignments in Guatemala.

Suggested Viewing and Listening

"Central America: The Burden of Time," 1-hour, fifth episode of the public television series "Legacy," hosted by Michael Wood and produced in 1991 by England's Central Independent Television in association with Maryland Public Television and NHK Enterprises of Japan. Available from Ambrose Video Publishing, 1290 Avenue of the Americas, Suite 2245, New York, NY 10104.

"Bill Moyers: God & Politics, A Kingdom Divided," 90-minute documentary produced by Public Affairs Television, Inc., in 1987 for broadcast on the Public Broadcasting Service. Available from PBS Home Video, 50 N. La Cienega Boulevard, Beverly Hills, CA 90211.

"*Ixcan*," documentary film on human rights abuses involving Mayan Indians in Guatemalan highlands. Contact producer Mike Sullivan in Santa Fe, NM, at (505) 983-6206.

"Keepers of the Forest," a documentary on the Lacandón Maya of Chiapas and the Petén. Available from cable TV network, The Discovery Channel, P.O. Box 1640, College Park, MD 20740.

"Guatemala: Rivers and Dreams," original video about whitewater rivers and remote archaeological sites. Contact Tammy Ridenour, Maya Expeditions, Guatemala City (See chapter 13).

"Guatemala" radio documentary, produced in 1980 for Options series and aired on National Public Radio network. Order program #800501 from NPR Audience Services, (800) 235-1282, ext. 2323.

Spanish / Mayan-English Glossary

Spanish/Mayan	English
aguada	ancient Maya reservoir
aguardiente	liquor made from sugarcane
aguas	nonalcoholic bottled drinks
alcalde	mayor
aldea	Indian village
altiplano	highlands
banano	banana (plátano is only used in cooking)
barranca/barranco	ravine
barrio	neighborhood
caballería	101.4 acres
cacique	boss

Appendix

Spanish/Mayan	English
camioneta corriente	a second-class bus
cargo	Mayan religious office or fraternity
efectivo	cash
cayuco	canoe carved out of single tree trunk
celaje	cloudscape
cenote	deep limestone sinkhole used for collecting water
chapín	Guatemalan
chicle	sap of sapodilla tree, used in chewing gum
chucho	meat wrapped in corn dough and husk
chupar	to drink liquor
cofradía	Mayan Indian civic-religious brotherhood
comedora	basic, inexpensive restaurant
corte	traditional Indian skirt
cusha	homemade liquor
en ocho días	in one week
evangélico	Protestant evangelist
fíjese	look!
finca	plantation-style farm, usually for coffee
glyph	figure in Maya writing and number system
gringo	any light-skinned foreigner
horita	right now, or right away
hospedaje, pensión	small, basic hotel
huipil, huipile	Mayan woman's embroidered blouse (also *güipil*)
indígena	preferred term for Indian (also *natural*)
invierno	winter, rainy season
jaspe	material woven from dyed thread
Ladino	a person of mixed ancestry or a Westernized Indian
legua	distance walked in an hour, 5.5 km
metate	flat stone used for grinding corn
milpa	field, usually used to grow corn, beans, or squash
monte	forest or jungle
mosh	oatmeal
nixtamal	ground corn or making tortillas
parque	park, usually a central city or town plaza
petate	woven mat
poncho	blanket, usually wool
principal	Mayan elder who has served in important posts
psst	an accepted attention-getting sound
pullman	first-class bus
rancho	small farm or rural building
refajo	skirt
regalarto	make a gift, polite form of "give me"
regatear	to bargain for (also *hacer trato*)
sencillo	change (i.e., coins), humble (origins)
sierra	mountain range
stela	free-standing carved stone monument
ticket	bus ticket
tienda	store
típico/a	typical, as in food or textiles
traje	traditional Indian clothing
tzut, tzute	headcloth or scarf worn by Indians
(el) verano	summer, the dry season
zaneudo	mosquito

Index

Other Books from John Muir Publications

Travel Books by Rick Steves
Asia Through the Back Door, 4th ed., 400 pp. $16.95
Europe 101: History and Art for the Traveler, 4th ed., 372 pp. $15.95
Europe Through the Back Door, 12th ed., 434 pp. $17.95
Europe Through the Back Door Phrase Book: French, 112 pp. $4.95
Europe Through the Back Door Phrase Book: German, 112 pp. $4.95
Europe Through the Back Door Phrase Book: Italian, 112 pp. $4.95
Europe Through the Back Door Phrase Book: Spanish & Portuguese, 288 pp. $4.95
Mona Winks: Self-Guided Tours of Europe's Top Museums, 2nd ed., 456 pp. $16.95

See the 2 to 22 Days series to follow for other Rick Steves titles.

A Natural Destination Series
Belize: A Natural Destination, 2nd ed., 304 pp. $16.95
Costa Rica: A Natural Destination, 3rd ed., 320 pp. $16.95 (available 8/94)
Guatemala: A Natural Destination, 336 pp. $16.95

Undiscovered Islands Series
Undiscovered Islands of the Caribbean, 3rd ed., 264 pp. $14.95
Undiscovered Islands of the Mediterranean, 2nd ed., 256 pp. $13.95
Undiscovered Islands of the U.S. and Canadian West Coast, 288 pp. $12.95

For Birding Enthusiasts
The Birder's Guide to Bed and Breakfasts, U.S. and Canada, 288 pp. $15.95
The Visitor's Guide to the Birds of the Central National Parks: U.S. and Canada, 400 pp. $15.95 (available 8/94)
The Visitor's Guide to the Birds of the Eastern National Parks: U.S. and Canada, 400 pp. $15.95
The Visitor's Guide to the Birds of the Rocky Mountain National Parks, U.S. and Canada, 432 pp. $15.95

Unique Travel Series
Each is 112 pages and $10.95 paper.
Unique Arizona (available 9/94)
Unique California (available 9/94)
Unique Colorado
Unique Florida
Unique New England
Unique New Mexico
Unique Texas

2 to 22 Days Series
Each title offers 22 flexible daily itineraries useful for planning vacations of any length. Included are "must see" attractions as well as hidden "jewels."
2 to 22 Days in the American Southwest, 1994 ed., 192 pp. $10.95
2 to 22 Days in Asia, 1994 ed., 176 pp. $10.95
2 to 22 Days in Australia, 1994 ed., 192 pp. $10.95
2 to 22 Days in California, 1994 ed., 192 pp. $10.95
2 to 22 Days in Eastern Canada, 1994 ed., 192 pp. $12.95
2 to 22 Days in Europe, 1994 ed., 304 pp. $14.95
2 to 22 Days in Florida, 1994 ed., 192 pp. $10.95
2 to 22 Days in France, 1994 ed., 192 pp. $10.95
2 to 22 Days in Germany, Austria, and Switzerland, 1994 ed., 240 pp. $12.95
2 to 22 Days in Great Britain, 1994 ed., 208 pp. $10.95
2 to 22 Days Around the Great Lakes, 1994 ed., 192 pp. $10.95
2 to 22 Days in Hawaii, 1994 ed., 192 pp. $10.95
2 to 22 Days in Italy, 1994 ed., 208 pp. $10.95
2 to 22 Days in New England, 1994 ed., 192 pp. $10.95
2 to 22 Days in New Zealand, 1994 ed., 192 pp. $10.95
2 to 22 Days in Norway, Sweden, and Denmark, 1994 ed., 192 pp. $10.95
2 to 22 Days in the Pacific Northwest, 1994 ed., 192 pp. $10.95
2 to 22 Days in the Rockies, 1994 ed., 192 pp. $10.95
2 to 22 Days in Spain and Portugal, 1994 ed., 208 pp. $10.95
2 to 22 Days in Texas, 1994 ed., 192 pp. $10.95
2 to 22 Days in Thailand, 1994 ed., 192 pp. $10.95

22 Days (or More) Around the World, 1994 ed., 264 pp. $13.95

Other Terrific Travel Titles
The 100 Best Small Art Towns in America, 256 pp. $12.95 (available 8/94)
Elderhostels: The Students' Choice, 2nd ed., 304 pp. $15.95
Environmental Vacations: Volunteer Projects to Save the Planet, 2nd ed., 248 pp. $16.95
A Foreign Visitor's Guide to America, 224 pp. $12.95
Great Cities of Eastern Europe, 256 pp. $16.95
Indian America: A Traveler's Companion, 3rd ed., 432 pp. $18.95
Interior Furnishings Southwest, 256 pp. $19.95
Opera! The Guide to Western Europe's Great Houses, 296 pp. $18.95
Paintbrushes and Pistols: How the Taos Artists Sold the West, 288 pp. $17.95
The People's Guide to Mexico, 9th ed., 608 pp. $18.95
Ranch Vacations: The Complete Guide to Guest and Resort, Fly-Fishing, and Cross-Country Skiing Ranches, 3rd ed., 512 pp. $19.95
The Shopper's Guide to Art and Crafts in the Hawaiian Islands, 272 pp. $13.95
The Shopper's Guide to Mexico, 224 pp. $9.95
Understanding Europeans, 272 pp. $14.95
A Viewer's Guide to Art: A Glossary of Gods, People, and Creatures, 144 pp. $10.95
Watch It Made in the U.S.A.: A Visitor's Guide to the Companies that Make Your Favorite Products, 272 pp. $16.95 (available 7/94)

Parenting Titles
Being a Father: Family, Work, and Self, 176 pp. $12.95
Preconception: A Woman's Guide to Preparing for Pregnancy and Parenthood, 232 pp. $14.95
Schooling at Home: Parents, Kids, and Learning, 264 pp., $14.95
Teens: A Fresh Look, 240 pp. $14.95

Automotive Titles
The Greaseless Guide to Car Care Confidence, 224 pp. $14.95
How to Keep Your Datsun/Nissan Alive, 544 pp. $21.95
How to Keep Your Subaru Alive, 480 pp. $21.95
How to Keep Your Toyota Pickup Alive, 392 pp. $21.95
How to Keep Your VW Alive, 15th ed., 464 pp. $21.95

TITLES FOR YOUNG READERS AGES 8 AND UP

American Origins Series
Each is 48 pages and $12.95 hardcover.
Tracing Our Chinese Roots
Tracing Our German Roots
Tracing Our Irish Roots
Tracing Our Italian Roots
Tracing Our Japanese Roots
Tracing Our Jewish Roots
Tracing Our Polish Roots

Bizarre & Beautiful Series
Each is 48 pages and $14.95 hardcover.
Bizarre & Beautiful Ears
Bizarre & Beautiful Eyes
Bizarre & Beautiful Feelers
Bizarre & Beautiful Noses
Bizarre & Beautiful Tongues

Environmental Titles
Habitats: Where the Wild Things Live, 48 pp. $9.95
The Indian Way: Learning to Communicate with Mother Earth, 114 pp. $9.95
Rads, Ergs, and Cheeseburgers: The Kids' Guide to Energy and the Environment, 108 pp. $13.95
The Kids' Environment Book: What's Awry and Why, 192 pp. $13.95

Extremely Weird Series
Each is 48 pages and $9.95 paper. $12.95 hardcover editions available 8/94.
Extremely Weird Bats
Extremely Weird Birds
Extremely Weird Endangered Species
Extremely Weird Fishes
Extremely Weird Frogs
Extremely Weird Insects
Extremely Weird Mammals
Extremely Weird Micro Monsters
Extremely Weird Primates
Extremely Weird Reptiles
Extremely Weird Sea Creatures
Extremely Weird Snakes
Extremely Weird Spiders

Kidding Around Travel Series
All are 64 pages and $9.95 paper, except for *Kidding Around Spain* and *Kidding Around the National Parks of the Southwest*, which are 108 pages and $12.95 paper.
Kidding Around Atlanta
Kidding Around Boston, 2nd ed.
Kidding Around Chicago, 2nd ed.
Kidding Around the Hawaiian Islands
Kidding Around London
Kidding Around Los Angeles
Kidding Around the National Parks of the Southwest
Kidding Around New York City, 2nd ed.
Kidding Around Paris
Kidding Around Philadelphia
Kidding Around San Diego
Kidding Around San Francisco
Kidding Around Santa Fe
Kidding Around Seattle
Kidding Around Spain
Kidding Around Washington, D.C., 2nd ed.

Kids Explore Series
Written by kids for kids, all are $9.95 paper.
Kids Explore America's African American Heritage, 128 pp.
Kids Explore the Gifts of Children with Special Needs, 128 pp.
Kids Explore America's Hispanic Heritage, 112 pp.
Kids Explore America's Japanese American Heritage, 144 pp.

Masters of Motion Series
Each is 48 pages and $9.95 paper.
How to Drive an Indy Race Car
How to Fly a 747
How to Fly the Space Shuttle

Rainbow Warrior Artists Series
Each is 48 pages and $14.95 hardcover.
Native Artists of Africa
Native Artists of Europe (available 8/94)
Native Artists of North America

Rough and Ready Series
Each is 48 pages and $12.95 hardcover.
Rough and Ready Cowboys
Rough and Ready Homesteaders
Rough and Ready Loggers (available 7/94)

Rough and Ready Outlaws and Lawmen (available 6/94)
Rough and Ready Prospectors
Rough and Ready Railroaders

X-ray Vision Series
Each is 48 pages and $9.95 paper.
Looking Inside the Brain
Looking Inside Cartoon Animation
Looking Inside Caves and Caverns
Looking Inside Sports Aerodynamics
Looking Inside Sunken Treasures
Looking Inside Telescopes and the Night Sky

Ordering Information
Please check your local bookstore for our books, or call 1-800-888-7504 to order direct. All orders are shipped via UPS; see chart below to calculate your shipping charge for U.S. destinations. **No post office boxes please; we must have a street address to ensure delivery.** If the book you request is not available, we will hold your check until we can ship it. Foreign orders will be shipped surface rate unless otherwise requested; please enclose $3 for the first item and $1 for each additional item.

For U.S. Orders

Totaling	Add
Up to $15.00	$4.25
$15.01 to $45.00	$5.25
$45.01 to $75.00	$6.25
$75.01 or more	$7.25

Methods of Payment
Check, money order, American Express, MasterCard, or Visa. We cannot be responsible for cash sent through the mail. For credit card orders, include your card number, expiration date, and your signature, or call 1-800-888-7504. American Express card orders can only be shipped to billing address of cardholder. Sorry, no C.O.D.'s. Residents of sunny New Mexico, add 6.2% tax to total.

Address all orders and inquiries to:
John Muir Publications
P.O. Box 613
Santa Fe, NM 87504
(505) 982-4078
(800) 888-7504